Martin Roll

Asian Brand Strategy

HOW ASIA BUILDS STRONG BRANDS

First published 2006 by
PALGRAVE MACMILLAN
Houndmills, Basingstoke, Hampshire RG21 6XS and
175 Fifth Avenue, New York, N.Y. 10010
Companies and representatives throughout the world

PALGRAVE MACMILLAN is the global academic imprint of the Palgrave Macmillan division of St. Martin's Press, LLC and of Palgrave Macmillan Ltd. Macmillan® is a registered trademark in the United States, United Kingdom and other countries. Palgrave is a registered trademark in the European Union and other countries.

ISBN-13: 978–1–4039–9279–6
ISBN-10: 1–4039–9279–7

This book is printed on paper suitable for recycling and made from fully managed and sustained forest sources.

A catalogue record for this book is available from the British Library.

A catalog record for this book is available from the Library of Congress.
Library of Congress catalog card number: 2005044658

10   9   8   7   6   5   4
15   14   13   12   11   10   09   08   07   06

Printed in China

CONTENTS

LIST OF FIGURES

LIST OF TABLES

LIST OF ILLUSTRATIONS

ABOUT THE AUTHOR

Martin Roll is founder and CEO of Venture-Republic, the leading strategic advisory firm on branding excellence to corporate boards and top-management in numerous industries.

He delivers the combined value of an experienced international branding strategist, a senior advisor to boards and management teams and an internationally renowned speaker and sought-after workshop host.

He brings more than 15 years' experience from the international advertising industry, and has served in various management positions, focusing particularly on global marketing and branding strategy, brand/product advertising and corporate communications.

Prior to establishing VentureRepublic, Martin was Vice President of Global Marketing and PR for a leading technology company. Based in Singapore, he led all corporate marketing, branding and PR projects worldwide as part of the global executive management team. Before this appointment, he served as Chief Marketing Officer with Europe's leading e-healthcare company.

Martin was also an account director for ten years with two global advertising agencies, Bates and DDB Needham Worldwide, where he directed many successful global marketing and branding programs. His clients included Ericsson Mobile Phones, McDonald's, Tele Denmark (TDC), Time Warner Music, SONY, Best Buy Toys and Scandinavian Seaways (DFDS).

Martin Roll lectures regularly at INSEAD, and is Visiting Professor in Strategic Brand Management at the China European International Business School (CEIBS) in Shanghai. He is dedicated to sharing his experience with the international audience, and regularly accepts invitations to chair and speak in prestigious events around the world. He also contributes leadership opinion articles on marketing and branding issues to several international publications.

Leading speaker bureaus in the world represent him as an international speaker and workshop host.

At industry level, he currently serves as the Copenhagen Goodwill Ambassador to Singapore for Wonderful Copenhagen and Copenhagen Capacity, two leading trade and business promotion associations in Denmark. He was chair of the Danish Marketing Management Board, and a board member of the Danish Business Association of Singapore.

Martin holds an MBA from INSEAD in France, a bachelor degree from the Copenhagen Business School and a diploma from the International Advertising Association (IAA). He is a Danish citizen, a Singapore permanent resident and divides his time between East and West.

Martin Roll can be contacted at: contact@asianbrandstrategy.com or via www.asianbrandstrategy.com

FOREWORD

A strong brand is able to help a company differentiate itself from its rivals, stand out from the competition, influence a consumer's purchase decision in the company's favor, build customer loyalty and boost the company's financial performance.

Asian Brand Strategy explores these issues focusing on the Asian market environment and on attempts to build Asian brands.

Brand management is essential if a firm wants to achieve sustained success, especially when competition is increasingly intense and product differentiation difficult. This situation is observed in many parts of Asia and in many product categories, and has led too often to the commoditization of markets, in which pricing is the only rule of the game.

Branding is one way out of commoditization and its consequent profit erosion. It is a process requiring long-term commitment, and profits need to be sacrificed in the short term in order to build a strong brand.

Unfortunately, many Asian companies traditionally favor investment in tangible assets such as manufacturing capacity and property. Intangible assets such as intellectual property, proprietary technologies and products, systems and brands have generally been given lower priority. This is reflected in the percentage of companies' market value accounted for by intangible assets – just under 50 per cent and as low as one-third, even in the case of large Asian companies recognized as brand leaders. On the other hand, it is more than 75 percent for Western branded consumer goods companies, which own the most prominent brands. In addition, Asian firms tend to use price to push sales, thereby undermining both the implicit guarantee of the consistency of the offer and the quality perception that are essential to brand building. As a result, few Asian brands are considered globally strong and those that are in the top league come mainly from Japan and more recently, in the case of Samsung, from Korea.

The overall weakness of Asian brands in international markets does not mean that local brands do not exist or are not preferred in some Asian countries. For instance in China, home-grown Haier Group, one of the biggest home appliances manufacturers in the world, claimed to hold a domestic market share of 30 percent for refrigerators, freezers, tumble dryers and washing machines. Similarly, the computer market is dominated by the

Chinese brand Lenovo, despite tough competition in the country from leading international brands such as Dell. In the Philippines, local brand Jollibee has a 65 percent share of the domestic fast-food market, beating established global brand McDonald's. Giordano, a Hong Kong Chinese firm, established itself well as a leading garment retailer in the territory while facing plenty of competition from Gap and Benetton.

The real challenge for many of these local brands comes when they try to sell to consumers outside their domestic shores. Very few have succeeded in doing so, and attempts to build regional brands in a global marketplace have proved difficult. However, the need to differentiate their products from low-priced products made in China gives suppliers from the emerging countries of Southeast Asia, Korea and Taiwan no choice other than to launch new brands or make refinements to existing brands in order to better appeal to consumers.

These companies are operating in an increasingly uncertain and competitive landscape. The dynamics of Asian countries are proving to be a double-edged sword. The immense population, increasing base of middle-class consumers and unexploited market territories make Asia a thriving marketplace. On the other hand, the diverse cultures, the disparity between rich and poor, the changes in infrastructure and evolving mindsets represent enormous challenges.

Branding in Asia is often wrongly referred to as an exercise in which the company logo, design style and color scheme are changed. It is often accompanied by a new corporate slogan, and everyone expects immediate results. Naturally, these are important elements to consider and potentially change once the strategy has been decided upon, but strategy development must come first. Branding is a serious, long-term undertaking and involves more skills and activities than the mere production of an updated glossy marketing facade with meaningless jargon.

In the Asian context, this is very evident. Branding is seen as a cost center for many companies and is driven tactically at a low level of the organization. More often than not, advertising and promotion are the core activities driving efforts to build brands. Branding, as Martin Roll discusses vividly in the book, is still not fully appreciated at boardroom and senior management level. Beyond that, the inherent characteristics of Asian companies, many of them family owned, have resulted in a short-term view on return on investment for branding. Such a view, while not entirely flawed, will not help companies build a profile that is strong enough to compete in the international arena.

Companies need to realize the strategic importance of branding. This calls for Asian boardrooms and management teams to take charge of the branding domain themselves. A strong brand strategy can add significant value in terms of helping the entire corporation as well as the management team to implement the long-term vision, create unique positions in the market and, not least, unlock leadership potential within the organization.

Successful brands are managed by the top level of management and implemented by the entire organization through multiple actions, behaviours and customer touch points. Few publications in the past have detailed the strategic aspects of branding in Asia. In *Asian Brand Strategy* Martin Roll has succeeded in tackling head-on many of the challenges illustrated. He has also included in the examination and application of branding many critical factors in the Asian environment such as culture and corporate structure. *Asian Brand Strategy* demonstrates how successful brands are helping top-tier Asian companies to penetrate the global stage and how some aspiring Asian companies are beginning to make their mark against larger Western players. These brands share the same common denominator– a strong commitment to branding by their boardrooms and senior management teams.

Asian Brand Strategy provides insights, tools and practical step-by-step guides that demystify the process and delivery of brand development and management. It demonstrates clearly why boardrooms and management teams in Asia must begin to improve the competitiveness of their companies through branding. Martin Roll provides a very compelling framework and a winning formula for this process. *Asian Brand Strategy* is solid proof that there is no longer any excuse for not building strong Asian brands and delivering better shareholder value across the region.

PROF. DR. HELLMUT SCHÜTTE
Dean of Asia Campus
INSEAD

PREFACE

My first encounter with Asia goes back to September 1992 when I flew into Tokyo Narita Airport in the early morning. The sun was shining brightly on Mount Fuji, a breathtaking scene for an Asian first timer. It was a classic and picturesque scene taken from a leisure travel guide. I was in Asia for the first time with an open mind and eager to learn about the region. What made a great impression on me that early morning in Japan was the start of a journey which has lasted since 1992. It became a journey deeper and deeper into the Asian region with a fascination for all her myths, ancient histories and blend of cultures, people and traditions. A region which combines low and high tech like no other place on earth, where the past is sometimes part of the present and the future, and where one has to expect the unexpected – all Asian style at a fast pace.

I have been intrigued since that defining moment in Japan. Having worked with branding for many years, I was familiar with many Japanese brands. But I found it hard to recognize any brands from other Asian countries. This observation has lasted, although admittedly more Asian brands have been developed throughout the 1990s. Yet Asia only represents a fraction of all the strong brands in the world, and today there is still a huge imbalance between East and West in terms of branding. This finally led me to write *Asian Brand Strategy*.

A large part of the findings and recommendations in this book has been drawn from my many years in international advertising and brand consulting. Through innumerable consulting projects with boardrooms and corporate management teams across the world, including several Fortune 500 companies, I have made observations and gained insights and knowledge which have helped to shape the arguments in the book. In addition, delivering keynote speeches, being a panelist at many international conferences and hosting many boardroom workshops globally every year have further distilled the ideas presented. The audiences attending these events have served as valuable sounding boards and discussion partners.

Asian Brand Strategy is written for boardrooms and corporate management teams. The book is aimed primarily at two groups of readers: Asian business leaders and Western observers.

Firstly, Asian boardrooms are facing defining moments for their corporations to enhance shareholder value. This is where comprehensive, consistent and truly committed brand building comes into place, with all its intricacies and challenges. Branding done right is not easy – yet it seems simple. Secondly, Western business leaders are looking toward Asia like never before. The region not only provides cheap manufacturing and new growth opportunities, but also represents potential threats from tough Asian competition; non-branded or branded. These are worth watching.

Asian Brand Strategy offers first-hand insights into Asian consumers, markets and companies' efforts to build strong brands. The book details the strategies and activities with which to build, manage and leverage stronger Asian brands in the future. I also hope the book will inspire researchers, students and anyone else interested in the world's most fascinating and fast-paced region.

I have been inspired by many friends and business associates throughout my career while living in Asia, and without these wonderful people this book could not have been written. One particular person has contributed significantly to my profound interest in Asia which later led me to live and work there: Professor Hellmut Schütte, Dean of Asia Campus, INSEAD. Hellmut introduced me to and inspired my interest in Asia with his brilliant classes at INSEAD. He remains an inspiring mentor and a good friend, for which I am grateful.

A book is a large project and a myriad of puzzles which need to find their right place. In this work, lecturer Julien Cayla from the Australian Graduate School of Management in Sydney has contributed many invaluable insights and helped to shape many of the ideas and arguments presented throughout the book. The discussions were numerous and I thank Julien for sharing his passion and contributing greatly to this project from the first day we started on it in September 2004.

Several other people have made great contributions and it would take too much space to mention them all. Special thanks to Pierre Chandon, Amitava Chattopadhyay, Jill Klein, Peter Williamson, Ziv Carmon, Mike Sherman, Lily Lou, Aaron Lau, Michael Backman, Mervin Wang, Susan Fournier, Anil Thadani, Maisy Koh, Lay Cheng Teo, Roshini Prakash, Kosuke Tomita, Mutsumi Takahashi, William Yue, Eric Booth, Abel Wu, Gaurang Shetty, Raymond Ng, Steve Lee, Gerry Oh, Michael J. N. Tan, Marcus John, Andre Tegner, Ji-Suk Kang, Jakob Hinrichsen, Melissa Kang Su Yi, Sarah Young, Ryoko Orihata, Erik van Vulpen, Renzo Scacco, Lydie Lamont, Ian McKee, Karen Low, Johann Tse, Ray Poletti, Andrea

Newman, Sarah-Anne Fong, Lars Wiskum, Myungwoo Nam, Midori Matsuoka, Alan Tan, Tyan Yee Ho and Jay Yaw.

I am grateful for the contributions made by my research associate Abhijith Holehonnur who has been a valuable discussion partner and a good colleague throughout the entire journey, upholding the spirit during many days and nights.

Finally, I would like to thank my editor Stephen Rutt and his team at Palgrave Macmillan in Basingstoke, Hong Kong and New York for believing in this project from the first minute we met in May 2004. They have supported me and helped to shape the book. I also thank Professor Christian Pinson from INSEAD who introduced me to Palgrave Macmillan after which this project accelerated quickly.

Designers Folkmar Roll and Anders Roll from Roll Design Group Ltd in Copenhagen have created a distinct identity and book jacket for *Asian Brand Strategy*. It encapsulates the soul of the book and I am very happy with it.

It should be noted that every effort has been made to trace all copyright holders, but if any have been inadvertently overlooked, the publisher will be pleased to make the necessary arrangements at the first opportunity.

MARTIN ROLL
Singapore 2005
www.asianbrandstrategy.com

CHAPTER 1

INTRODUCTION

A journey of a thousand miles begins with a single step.

Confucius

The face of business in Asia is changing faster than one can blink one's eyes. Asian companies that used to be back-end workhorses, manufacturing consumer goods cheaply for Western companies, are slowly realizing the benefits of branding. A case in point is Pantech, a South Korean firm which began by selling pagers in the early 1990s. By the end of the 1990s, Pantech was selling mobile phones as an original equipment manufacturer (OEM) to Western companies like Motorola and Audiovox. But Pantech's 42-year-old chairman Park Byong Yeop knew that in the face of cheaper competition, his business model had to change.

In the past few years, Pantech had heavily invested in developing its brand, allowing the company to more than double margins. In 2004, Pantech sponsored the hit TV series *Lovers in Paris* and used the South Korean pop star BoA to advertise its products. Soon after the release of the series, Koreans were buying 1,000 Pantech phones a day in just one electronics market alone.[1] Park aims to sell 80 percent of the mobile phones under Pantech's brand name in 2005, up from just 31 percent in 2004. The company spends 7 percent of sales on research and development (R&D) and has earmarked US$200 million to develop the brand's identity in 2005.[2]

Park is portrayed in local media as a successful entrepreneur rather than someone who inherited a conglomerate.[3] His vision is to become the world's number five mobile phone maker, and targets shipment of 28 million handset units and sales of US$3 billion in 2005.[4] Pantech has come a long way from its modest beginnings as an OEM only 15 years ago.

In a market where competition implies slashing prices on their unbranded products, Asian businesses are slowly becoming more attentive to the power of brand identity in capturing consumers and returning larger profits on their investments. Firms are realizing that whereas they were wearing themselves down on razor-thin margins to compete with the next supplier, they could increase returns by investing in their brands. This then is the shift in thinking that is pushing boardrooms in Asia toward creating strong brands to differentiate themselves and consequently realize greater profits.

Most Asian firms, however, still view branding as advertising or logo design. If firms are to benefit from branding, they must recognize that it impacts the entire business – the structure, goals, attitude and the very outlook of those in the boardroom. Managers will need to see branding not as an appendage to the ongoing business, but rather as an infusion which seeps through the very spirit of the organization, as a healthy return on investment (ROI). In fact, it will require a shift in focus and priority for every functional aspect of the organization aligned around multiple customer touch points.

Before branding can be taken on board, however, it is important to understand its implications, its various shades and hues, its forms and practices, its purpose and its advantage. It is no less than a paradigm shift that executives must undertake across Asian boardrooms. How this change in thinking can be analyzed, captured and managed by Asian boardrooms and corporate management teams is the core of this book.

Lack of value creation

A 2003 report by Goldman Sachs forecast that, by 2041, China will have overtaken the US economy in size and will become the world's largest economy. The Indian economy would be larger than Japan's by 2032.[5] China and India are indeed leading Asia's growth path, with implications for industries and companies all over the world. But as Rajat Gupta, a senior partner with McKinsey & Co (and former worldwide managing director), has said:

> Though Asia has been growing, the growth has not been enough to make it a superpower. For Asia to earn the right to be a superpower, we not only need to make a significant contribution to the world economy, but also and perhaps more importantly we need to see the emergence of several successful global companies out of Asia.[6]

The changes in the Asian competitive environment are driven by several factors: the rapid development of China and India; increasing deregulation and trade liberalization; and the implications of new demographic and social trends throughout the region. These changes involve entire value chains in manufacturing and services, issues related to efficiencies in operations and productivity gains, innovation and design, a reduced focus on broad diversification, which has been the prevalent structure of Asian businesses particularly within Asian family businesses, and distribution and collaboration within industries.

The eroding low-cost advantage

A large part of Asia's economic development until now can be attributed to low-cost advantages which enabled Asian companies to gain market share from other suppliers. In the past two decades, Asian countries have slowly but surely attracted many industries: light manufacturing in Guangdong, electrical equipment in Guangxi and software development in Bangalore. But Western companies, by buying some of these Asian firms or aggressively outsourcing some of their operations, are already streamlining their cost structures. Low cost alone no longer provides a significant advantage. The cut-throat competition in many industries, resulting in tremendous pressure on margins, has forced companies to look for additional measures to survive and grow their businesses. One example is mobile phones, where contract manufacturers are doing well if they reach 15 percent in gross margins while brand owners can reach margins double that.[7]

Asia is still one of the world's biggest providers of commodity products. At the same time, Asian manufacturers mostly produce for other companies and the majority of these products are therefore non-branded. In other words, these are volume products without strong brand identities. Instead, the largest part of the financial value is captured by the manufacturers' customers – the next player in the value chain – primarily driven by strong brand strategies and successfully planned and executed marketing programs.

The difference in the proportion of value captured as represented by the Asian manufacturing price and the Western retail price serves as a good example. A branded sports shoe is produced in Asia at an estimated US$5, sold to the sports shoe brand for US$10 and the consumer buys it in the retail store for US$100 – in other words, a twentyfold increase throughout the "product-to-brand" value chain. This leaves the Asian manufacturer with only a fraction of the substantial value that consumers are willing to pay for the brand in the end.

Figure 1.1 illustrates four scenarios of how a brand is integrated in the value chain. In certain cases, companies are vertically integrated and can own part of the channels, including retail outlets, the distributors and/or the production facilities. For example, Nike operates many of its own retail outlets.

In the last 10 years, the number of distributors in the sports goods industry has decreased more than 50 percent as many sports brands have become distributors themselves. This is particularly the trend among the largest brands. The sports shoe brand captures an estimated 40–95 percent of the entire financial value depending on its level of vertical integration.[8] In other words, brands capture a significant portion of the total value.

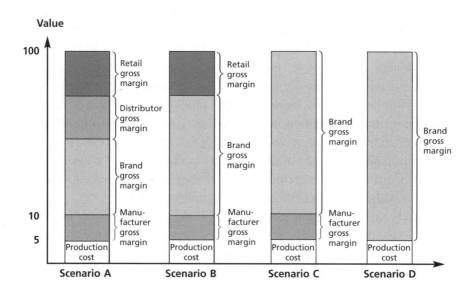

Figure 1.1 Four scenarios for value creation through branding
Source: VentureRepublic

Successful global companies share certain common characteristics, one of which is strong brand equity in the market. Despite Asia's size and economic growth, it has not seen the emergence of many strong and international brands.

Less than 10 global brands originating from Asia

In a study measuring the financial value of worldwide brands conducted by Interbrand and *Business Week* in 2004, one important finding was that only four of the top brands originate in Asia.[9] Three classic brands come from Japan and a fast-growing ambitious brand comes from South Korea: Sony, Honda, Toyota and Samsung.

A simple question then remains: What about the rest of Asia? Looking at the region as a whole, there are less than 10 powerful global brands originating from Asia. Brands like Singapore Airlines, Shangri-La Hotels, Banyan Tree, Acer, HSBC, Shiseido and a couple of others are powerful global brands with a strong Asian heritage.

But given the size and volume of Asian business today, it is evident that Asia could build many more prominent brands and capture more financial value from better price premiums and customer loyalty. Branding can become an important driver of shareholder value for Asian companies in the future, as this book will illustrate.

Reasons for the lack of strong Asian brands

There are many reasons why Asian companies have not fostered many global brands until now. The appreciation of branding as a strategic concept can be influenced by:

- The stage of economic development of societies

- Less focus on innovation

- Broad diversification of businesses

- The Asian business structure

- Implications of intellectual property (IP) protection.

These five factors are now discussed.

The stage of economic development of societies

The Asian countries are at different stages of development. At one end of the spectrum are developed countries like Japan, South Korea, Singapore, Taiwan and Hong Kong. At the other end are developing countries like Vietnam, Cambodia and Indonesia. In between are countries like Malaysia, Thailand, China and India which are moving through rapid transitions. The development stage of these countries can influence business priorities, the degree of business sophistication and where to fit into the value chain on the overall level.

When countries and industries move from low to high tech, they are generally more inclined to supplement their low-cost advantage with a holistic value perspective. Very often they are forced to move up the value chain while losing their low-cost advantage in manufacturing to competitors with lower labor costs. Although the value perspective does not exclude seeking to drive costs down constantly, it aims primarily at creating additional perceived value for products and services. This is where brands often start to play their role as drivers of shareholder value through better price premiums and enhanced customer loyalty.

It would not be entirely correct to assume that the economic stage of development and degree of branding are correlated. In general, any company, regardless of country origin, can decide to build brands. However, the economic development stage of a country and the level of sophistication of an industry can serve as important indicators to estimate whether branding gains wide appreciation and momentum.

Regional technology clusters are already emerging in Asia.[10] An example is India where low and high tech go hand in hand. Bangalore is a well-known cluster of strong technology firms like Wipro and Infosys. A service company, Jet Airways from Mumbai, is catching up quickly, based on excellent standards in all operations, and provides world-class service, as illustrated in Chapter 8. Therefore, Asia is a region where branding as a strategic discipline is work in progress.

Less focus on innovation

Although innovation is difficult to measure, R&D spending as a ratio of gross domestic product (GDP) can be an indication. On a national level, Asian economies lagged behind the rest of the world on R&D spending as a ratio of GDP from 1987 to 1997, with the exception of Japan and South Korea.[11] Japan and South Korea each currently spend 3 percent of GDP on R&D, compared to 2.7 percent in the US.

But indications show that the innovation deficit is likely to change. China is targeting to spend 1.5 percent of GDP on R&D in 2005, compared to 0.6 percent in 1996. Asian countries are also trying to take a lead in three areas likely to generate the next wave of innovation: biotechnology, nanotechnology and information technology (IT). As an example, Asia spends as much as the US and Europe combined on nanotechnology. In addition to this, China, India, South Korea and Taiwan are shifting from top-down, state-directed technology policies to more flexible, market-oriented approaches in order to foster innovation and entrepreneurship.[12]

As low cost is ceasing to provide a competitive edge for Asian companies, differentiation driven by enhanced innovation capabilities will be paramount for future success. Innovation needs to become a top priority for Asian companies aspiring to build strong brands.

Although design is only a tiny part of an entire brand strategy, it can help to create visible differentiation for products and shape customer perceptions. The internationally recognized designer Philip Starck gave his view on how Asia lacks its own design:

Today the designer in Hong Kong or Taipei opens the magazine and looks at the best-seller and copies that. But to be successful you have to find your own designs and energy.[13]

Broad diversification of businesses

Another impediment to building brands in Asia in the past was the diversification of businesses spanning many industries with limited overlap and synergies. The prevalent mindset in Asia is based on trading, rather than branding, and the generation of revenues, rather than profits. But it is hard to create a relevant, clear and differentiated brand strategy, and build a corporate brand which encompasses all areas, when a business has its hands dipped in every pie.

Thailand's Charoen Pokphand (CP) Group is an example of an Asian company moving against the common diversification trend. Traditionally, it had interests in telecommunications, satellite, cable television, motorcycle manufacturing, petrochemicals and brewing. Despite its diversified businesses, CP has continued to expand its integrated food business by controlling the entire supply chain. By transferring its agribusiness formula to other agricultural products and across countries, CP has also become one of the world's leading agribusiness groups. With higher demand for quality processed foods from US, Europe and Japan, CP has renewed its focus on increasing value-added in its agriculture business to become the "kitchen of the world".[14]

The Asian business structure

Another important reason for the lack of strong brands can be found in the prevalent business structure within Asia, which consists of many small and often family-owned businesses – with diversified business interests as illustrated before. It is much harder to overcome the barriers to brand building when resources are limited. In this case, the management perspective would favor short-term business wins against brand strategies which require more resources and long-term perspectives. Despite a younger generation taking over as leaders, it can still be a major barrier to convince the older generation about the need for investing in intangibles in the form of brands as it runs against the business heritage and prevalent internal wisdom.

But being family-owned and small does not necessarily leave branding out of the equation, as Singapore-based Banyan Tree Hotels and Resorts has proven very successfully in less than 10 years. It made the transition from a disused tin mine on a strip of land in Phuket, Thailand, in 1994 to an internationally recognized and highly awarded hospitality brand, with quality resorts throughout Thailand, Indonesia, China, India, and the Maldives and more destinations being planned.

As Ho Kwon Ping, chairman of Banyan Tree, reflected:

> I felt that Asian business would never get anywhere if it didn't own brands. Partly this reflected the earlier experience in our family business of putting in the energy to build a brand as agent for an overseas principal, only to lose it when they eventually took the brand in-house. I also knew the problems of competing in commodity markets where the business disappears as soon as a cheaper supplier comes onto the scene.[15]

Banyan Tree has achieved this position with limited spending on marketing and advertising and has instead relied on effective public relations and third-party endorsement programs to build the brand. Chapter 10 illustrates further how Banyan Tree is successfully managing the brand.

Implications of IP protection

The implications of IP protection in Asia have been a major barrier against building brands. In their own backyards, many Asian companies have faced rampant counterfeiting and infringement of IP rights. Until and unless legislation and law enforcement get better in the region, it may be a hurdle that prevents a deeper appreciation and respect for intangible asset management in the Asian boardroom.

The World Customs Organization estimates that 5–7 percent of global merchandise trade, amounting to US$450 billion, is due to counterfeits. China alone is estimated to be contributing to almost two-thirds of all the fake and pirated goods worldwide.[16] In 2004, for example, French luxury house LVMH spent more than US$16 million on investigations, busts and legal fees against counterfeiting.[17]

> One of the famous spots in Bejing used to be Xiushui or Silk Street. Ranking in the top three of Beijing's attractions, the narrow and crowded street would attract thousands of foreigners every year to buy cheap counterfeit versions of global luxury brand names like Ralph Lauren, Louis Vuitton, Prada and many others. It was recently closed down by the Chinese authorities for renovation. Instead, stall holders would have an option to take up a stall at the nearby Xiushui shopping center, where a trading corner of less than 5 square meters will auction for as much as US$400,000.

A new paradigm for the Asian boardroom

Many of the ideas and recommendations contained in this book are driven by the Asian brand leadership model, illustrated in Table 1.1. The model illustrates the paradigm shift that Asian brands need to undertake in order to unleash their potential.

First, mindsets and practices need to change in the Asian boardroom. This book invites a complete shift in the way that Asian boardrooms think of branding: from a tactical view to a long-term, strategic perspective; from fragmented marketing activities to totally aligned branding activities; from a vision of branding as the sole responsibility of marketing managers to branding as the DNA and most essential function of the firm led by the boardroom.

Second, this new perspective must be steeped in a more acute perspective on consumer behavior patterns. Asia is not a homogeneous entity. Even more importantly, Asian countries are more and more traversed by cultural flows permeating the region: cinema, music and fashion trends that at present extend beyond national borders to capture the imagination of millions. Moreover, branding and brands do not operate in a vacuum, but are closely linked to developments in society, to people and cultures.

Third, managers wanting to succeed in Asia need to abandon the idea of the oriental Asia of the past. Asian consumers are all vying for an Asian type of modernity that has nothing to do with colonial imagery.

TABLE 1.1 **Asian brand leadership model**		
	Old paradigm	**New paradigm**
Success factors for Asian boardrooms	Manufacturing-driven agenda	Branding-driven agenda
	Production	Design, innovation and production
	Tactical advertising	Strategic branding and marketing
	Low cost/low perceived value	Low cost/high perceived value
	Silos of activities	Collaboration
	Price as driver of sales	Value as driver of sales
	OEM	Trademarks and IP
	Short-term financial value	Long-term brand value
	Mid-level and separate marketing functions	Boardroom-driven marketing functions
	Fragmented marketing activities	Totally aligned marketing programs
	Disparate product lines	Synergies between brands (brand architecture)
	Marketing through promotion	Branding through people
	A function drives the brand	An organization drives the brand
	Company-centric value creation	Co-creation of value
Consumer behavior	Collectivist	In-group/out-group
	Regional homogeneous	Scapes/flows/hybrids
Symbols	Oriental	New Asia
	Products and services	People and places
	Western celebrities	Hybrid + Asian celebrities
Culture	Following trends	Creating trends
	Japanese and Korean icons	Fragmented icons, Pan-Asian icons
	Silos of activities	Collaboration
Strategy drivers and measures	Sales perspective	Branding perspective
	Market share	Brand equity
	Awareness	Brand audit
	Tangible financial value on balance sheets	Tangible + intangible value on balance sheets
	Marketing as cost	Branding as strategic investment

Source: VentureRepublic

Fourth, to create iconic brands, Asian managers will have to become trendsetters. The perspective developed in this book is that, in order to be successful, Asian brands need to capture the spirit of the region, but they also need to lead the way by creating that spirit.

Finally, this shift can be achieved only if everybody in the company is convinced of the power of branding. And, in turn, this can only happen through accountability and systematic monitoring of branding investments and performance. It is only then that Asian brands will become truly great.

The scope of the book

This chapter has discussed the implications for a new Asian business landscape, where Asian companies can step up and capture more financial value through brands.

Chapter 2 looks at branding and how the discipline relates closely to business strategy. Branding can drive shareholder value. There are many managerial challenges, processes and tasks needed to succeed with it, which are discussed further.

Chapter 3 is dedicated to Asian consumers and cultures and describes some of the transformations taking place in Asia. It provides a new way of looking at the region and covers issues like group versus individual orientation, roles, symbols and family. The chapter looks at the transformation from a purely collectivist perception toward an in/out-group perspective, which can help us to understand Asian consumers better. It also discusses scapes, flows and hybrids.

The quality perception of a brand can be derived from the perception of a given country. Chapter 4 discusses country branding and the country of origin effect, how it affects brands and which measures companies should take to benefit the most from a given country's image. This also includes examples of how some Asian countries have branded themselves.

Strong brands are often driven and influenced by popular culture and multiple activities and trends in society. Celebrities and other public figures can act as potential endorsers for products and services and be an instrumental part of a brand strategy. Chapter 5 discusses how to involve celebrities and other endorsers, and their ability to support Asian brand building.

Chapter 6 is dedicated to brand strategy. It provides frameworks for aligning the brand and an entire brand management model.

Chapters 7 and 8 illustrate case studies of successful as well as aspiring

Asian brands. The two chapters illustrate different angles of building and managing brands in an Asian context through a selected portfolio of Asian brands. The multiple and diverse brand stories can inspire the Asian boardroom and serve as discussion points when crafting future brand strategies.

Chapter 9 is a step-by-step guide to brand building for Asian boardrooms, and discusses the processes and systems needed to successfully manage brands.

Finally, Chapter 10 provides a discussion of the challenges in the years to come for Asian boardrooms, what the brand change agents will become and how Asian brands can potentially challenge their Western counterparts.

The appendix provides a useful guideline to brand valuation based on the method used by Interbrand.

Notes

1 http://joongangdaily.joins.com.html.
2 "Another Korean cell-phone power?", *Business Week*, 4 April 2005.
3 "Park loves the nightlife", *Institutional Investor*, International Edition, **28**(7), 2003.
4 "Pantech refocuses on North America, EU", *The Korea Herald*, 10 March, 2005.
5 "Dreaming with BRIC's: The path to 2050", Global Sachs Global Economics paper 99. See www.gs.com/insight/research/reports/99.pdf.
6 *The Hindu Business Line*, November 17, 2003.
7 "Brand and deliver", *CFO Asia*, 30 March, 2004.
8 Author's interview with Lars Wiskum, a leading international consultant in the sports goods industry.
9 See: http://www.businessweek.com.
10 Enright, Michael J. (1998), "Regional clusters and firm strategy." In Chandler, A. D., Hagstrom, P. and Solvell, Ö. (eds) *The Dynamic Firm*, pp. 315–42. Oxford: Oxford University Press.
11 *Winning in Asia*, Peter Williamson, Harvard Business Press, 2004, page 91, Figure 4.1.
12 "Is America losing its edge?", *Foreign Affairs*, November–December, 2004.
13 "A Starck vision of Asia's future as elite producer of brands", *Wall Street Journal*, 7 April, 2004.
14 "CP Group: From seeds to kitchen of the world", Case by Peter J. Williamson and Keeley Wilson, INSEAD Euro-Asia Centre, Singapore, 2003.
15 Chua Chei Hwee, "Banyan Tree Resorts and Hotels: Building an international brand from an Asian base", in Geertz, C. (ed.) (1983).
16 "New initiative to assist WCO members to respond to counterfeiting in the Asia/Pacific region", press release by the World Customs Organization, 6 February, 2004, www.wcoomd.ord/ie/En/en.html.
17 "Fakes! The global counterfeit business is out of control, targeting everything from computer chips to life-saving machines", Frederick Balfour and Carol Matlack in Paris, Amy Barrett in Philadelphia, Kerry Capell in London, *Business Week*, 7 February, 2005.

CHAPTER 2

BRANDING – THE DRIVER OF A SUCCESSFUL BUSINESS STRATEGY

The way we made money in the past was by saving money, by cutting costs. Now we have to make money by spending money, by investing in our brand.[1]

Eric Yu, CFO, BenQ

Today, businesses and consumers are placing increasing importance on brands. Brands give consumers a sense of identity, stimulate their senses and enrich their life experiences. People have a need to affiliate and surround themselves with things they know well, trust and aspire to be. From a customer viewpoint, a brand is a signal of quality and creates a bond of trust with the manufacturers behind them.

TABLE 2.1 **Nine characteristics of a strong brand**
1. A brand drives shareholder value
2. The brand is led by the boardroom and managed by brand marketers with an active buy-in from all stakeholders
3. The brand is a fully integrated part of the entire organization, aligned around multiple touch points
4. The brand can be valued in financial terms and must reside on the asset side of the balance sheet
5. The brand can used as collateral for financial loans and can be bought and sold as an asset
6. Customers are willing to pay a substantial and consistent price premium for the brand versus a competing product and service
7. Customers associate themselves strongly with the brand, its attributes, values and personality, and fully buy into the concept which is often characterized by an emotional and intangible relationship (higher customer loyalty)
8. Customers are loyal to the brand and would actively seek it and buy it despite several other reasonable and often cheaper options available (higher customer retention rate)
9. A brand is a trademark and marque (logo, shape, color and so on) which is fiercely and proactively protected by the company and its legal advisors

Source: VentureRepublic

There is a distinct difference between companies, products and services of which customers might be aware, and *real brands* with strong brand equity. Therefore, strong brands are more than trademarks and trade names (logos that identify the products and services). Before delving into an analysis of branding, it is important to get the branding terminology right. "Branding" is a widely misused and misunderstood term, around which clusters everything even vaguely related to strategy, marketing and communication. Branding is an investment that must be perceived as such and is required to deliver ROI and shareholder value like any other feasible business activity. It must appear on the left side of the balance sheet as an intangible asset and its value is subject to change upward and potentially downward. A strong brand is defined and characterized by the dimensions in Table 2.1.

Lifestyle over technology

Asian consumers are known for being very technologically savvy and early adopters of new gadgets. The mobile phone usage penetration and the number of SMS messages sent in Asia are just two examples. But consumers do not just buy technology. Instead, they buy lifestyle, design and tap into a "brand culture". This is indeed the case in the competitive MP3 player market. When Singapore-based Creative Technology launched its new Zen Micro MP3 player in November 2004, the company offered it free or heavily discounted for anyone surrendering their Apple iPods in Singapore. But Apple fans valued brand culture over technology and price promotion. Only 20 people gave up their iPods for a Zen.[2]

Psychological research demonstrates that brands are durable because people are cognitive misers. Modern society is overloaded with information, and the average person receives far more information than one can possibly digest properly. Therefore people seek to simplify the world by relying on a variety of heuristics to minimize the amount of searching and information processing needed to make reasonable decisions. Once people believe that a brand works for a certain purpose or reason, they are less likely to seek out new information that challenges that assumption. Sociological research also demonstrates why people are less likely to switch brands. Many elements – images, stories and associations – are attached to a brand. As these elements are shared collectively by groups and networks of people, they form generally accepted conventions about brands. It is therefore relatively difficult for individuals to switch brands and thereby abandon these shared conventions.[3]

As many cultures in Asia are collectivist in nature, the social context of brands plays an important role. Brands provide competitive advantages as they create strong bonds and loyalty with customers and create barriers for competition.

Even today a large part of Asia is still developing. As Professor Prahalad, University of Michigan, and Professor Lieberthal's research proves, a significant percentage of the population is at the bottom of the pyramid (BOP).[4] Although Asia's rapid economic development will result in an increase in people's disposable income, the divide between the "haves" and the "have-nots" is still significant. This segment (BOP) of the society has traditionally aspired to own brands of international repute as symbols of social class and prestige. In the future, many from the bottom of the pyramid will be able to afford internationally known brands. Given these facts and developments, Asian customers crave to get their hands on a Louis Vuitton bag, drive a Mercedes, run in their Nike shoes, wear their Giorgio Armani suit, and listen to music on their iPod from Apple.

Chinese luxury shoppers

A 2004 report from Goldman Sachs notes that the Chinese customer base represents the third largest for the luxury goods industry. The Chinese accounted for an estimated 12 percent of global luxury goods sales in 2004, with 2 percent derived from local spending in China and 10 percent from overseas Chinese travelers including Hong Kong. By 2010, Chinese luxury consumers could account for 23 percent of industry sales, and by 2015, with an estimated 29 percent of sales, they could become as important as their Japanese counterparts. The Japanese currently account for approximately 41 percent of global sales.[5] Many global luxury goods firms are attracted by the rapidly expanding Chinese customer base and are investing significantly in opening multiple stores and spending heavily on marketing in China. For example, Giorgio Armani plans to open 20–30 new stores in China by 2008.[6]

In business-to-business (B2B) environments, branding also plays an important role. Most decision makers would feel comfortable choosing IBM (known for quality), buying networks from Cisco (security), acquiring consulting from McKinsey & Co (credibility), ordering shipping services from Maersk (precision) or leasing aircraft engines from Rolls-Royce (reliability) and so on.

Perceived risk

One of the main underlying reasons for the above behavior pattern is the trust that customers develop in certain brands. This trust helps customers to reduce the inherent risks involved in any purchase. Researchers refer to this concept as "perceived risks" and define it as "the consumer's perception of the uncertainty and adverse consequences of buying a product and service".[7] Perceived risks have six dimensions: performance, financial, opportunity/time, safety, social and psychological risks.[8] Table 2.2 illustrates some of the different types of perceived risks that customers can face during the purchase phase.

Brands can help to reduce these perceived risks by authenticating the source of the goods and serving as a strong promise of the perceived value of the goods sold. By providing these promises of value through a brand, customers are assured in the purchase decision process that the risk-to-reward ratio of purchasing a strong brand is higher than that of purchasing a similar unbranded good.

TABLE 2.2 **Potential perceived risks involved in a purchase**[9]	
Performance	Will the product or service perform to expectations?
Financial	Is the product or service worth the price charged?
Opportunity/time	Will there be associated opportunity costs if the product or service fails?
Safety	Is the product or service safe to use? Does it pose a threat to the health or the environment?
Social	How will the product or service be perceived in a social context?
Psychological	Does it fit the personality and values of the customer?

Branding drives shareholder value

The primary objective of boardrooms is to build and sustain shareholder value, and deliver competitive returns to shareholders.[10] One of the ways to achieve this is to build a brand with strong brand equity. "Brand equity" is the reputational asset that any successful business builds in the minds of customers and other stakeholders.[11] Brand equity is also one of the main reasons why the market capitalization of a company often exceeds its book value. The strength of the brand equity can therefore be an indication of future financial performance. The concept of brand equity is discussed in more detail in Chapter 6.

The right pricing can be an effective way to increase profits. A strong brand allows for better premiums as illustrated in this example. For the average income statement of a Standard & Poors (S&P) 1500 company, a *price increase* of 1 percent, if volume remained stable, would generate an 8 percent increase in operating profits; an impact almost 50 percent greater than that of a 1 percent *decrease* in variable *costs* like materials and direct labor, and more than three times greater than the impact of a 1 percent *increase in volume.*[12]

Therefore, marketing strategies and activities must be equally aligned with business strategy to fulfill the corporate objectives. For modern companies, the creation of value increasingly depends on the control of intangible assets such as brands, intellectual property, systems and data, human capital and market relationships.[13]

Many Asian companies traditionally focused on asset-intensive industries. In a study by McKinsey in 2002, it was demonstrated that the most profitable Asian companies focus on intangibles such as human capital, exploiting network effects, and creating synergies based on brands or reputation, rather than investing in tangible assets.[14]

In other words, intangible assets like brands play a significant role in value creation and can become an important driver of shareholder value for many more Asian companies today. The following example will illustrate the impact of strong brands, how they contribute to drive shareholder value and outperform the market in respect of several indicators.

The brand consultancy Interbrand, part of Omnicom Group, is well known for its published tables of the world's most valued brands featured every year in *Business Week*.[15] The company uses a widely accepted method for brand valuation, recognized by auditors and tax authorities in many countries around the world. Despite several similar methods provided by competing providers, Interbrand's methodology of defining brand value as the net present value (NPV) of future profits attributable to the brand has been tested in empirical and academic studies. For example, a study published in *Review of Accounting Studies* found that the brand valuation estimates were relevant and sufficiently reliable for use in financial reporting statements.[16] Another study found a positive relationship between market-to-book ratios and brand values.[17] These and other studies provide strong evidence that brand equity greatly impacts brand valuation and hence the market valuation of companies.

Brands and market capitalization

For many Western companies, a large part of their intangible assets is related to the value of their brands. An examination of the market capitalization of companies on Western stock exchanges demonstrates that a large proportion of a company's value is derived from powerful brands and the profit streams they provide. On the New York Stock Exchange and NASDAQ, intangible assets are known to account for 50–75 percent of the market capitalization of the listed companies, where the majority is accounted for by their brands. The market-to-book ratio for Fortune 500 companies is approximately 3.5 which indicates that more than 70 percent of the market values of Fortune 500 companies are comprised of intangible assets.[18] Similarly, the market-to-book ratio for the UK's largest companies averages 3.0.[19] Compare that with companies on any Asian stock exchange where the intangible financial value derived from brands is insignificant or lacking.[20]

TABLE 2.3 **Contribution of brands to shareholder value**		
Company	2002 brand value ($billion)	Brand contribution to market capitalization % of the parent company
Coca-Cola	69.6	51
Microsoft	64.1	21
IBM	51.2	39
GE	41.3	14
Intel	30.9	22
Nokia	30	51
Disney	29.3	68
McDonald's	26.4	71
Marlboro	24.2	20
Mercedes-Benz	21	47

Source: Interbrand/*Business Week* 2002

Susan Fournier from Boston University and her colleagues found in a study that, on average, the brand values published by Interbrand constituted 37 percent of a company's market capitalization.[21] Table 2.3 shows the contribution of brands to shareholder value. For example, the Coca-Cola brand contributes 51 percent of the overall market capitalization of the company and McDonald's as much as 71 percent. In other words, these companies rely heavily on leveraging their intangible assets in the form of brands.

Brands' contribution to stock market performance

Fournier et al. also investigated the causal linkage between branding and shareholder value creation, using statistical tools and concepts from the finance discipline. They also examined whether the performance of companies with "strong" brands would outperform the overall market, and whether these returns remain after adjusting for risk.[22] The strong brand portfolio (a selection of 111 companies with strong brands) yielded an average monthly return of 1.98 percent against 1.34 percent for a benchmark portfolio (a large selection of companies from major US stock exchanges). The risk attached to a business is determined by the volatility and vulnerability of its cash flows compared to the market average.[23] The financial community uses beta as a measure of risk. The less volatile and vulnerable cash flows, the less risk leading to a lower beta measure. The risk was 0.85 for the strong brand portfolio against 1.07 for the benchmark portfolio – the average market risk is 1.0. In summary, the strong brand portfolio outperformed the market with less market risk.

Madden et al.'s study illustrated the findings with the following example. If US$1,000 was invested in August 1994 in the strong brand portfolio, the investment would have become US$4,525 by December 2000. The same US$1,000 investment in the overall stock market would have turned into US$3,195. In other words, the strong brand portfolio performed 42 percent better (US$1,330) than the market over the six years – a clear and tangible demonstration of shareholder value increasing because of branding.

The same study analyzed the performance on different financial ratios for the strong brand portfolio compared to the benchmark portfolio, as illustrated in Table 2.4. The strong brand portfolio outperformed on most financial ratios.

TABLE 2.4 **Impact of brand performance on financial ratios**			
Financial ratios[24]			**Results**
Liquidity ratios	Current ratio	Measure a firm's ability to meet cash needs as they arise	The strong brand portfolio outperformed both benchmark groups in liquidity
	Quick ratio		
Activity ratios		Measure the liquidity of specific assets and the efficiency of managing assets	The strong brand portfolio outperformed the benchmark groups on only one indicator: the average collection period where they collected funds from their customers in approximately half the time
Leverage ratios	Times interest earned	Measure the extent of a firm's financing with debt relative to equity and its ability to cover interest and other fixed charges	There was significant difference between strong brand portfolio and the benchmark portfolio on the times interest earned ratio
Profitability ratios	Gross profit margin	Measure the overall performance of a firm and its efficiency in managing assets, liabilities and equity	The strong brand portfolio outperformed on all aspects. It also demonstrated greater return on equity
	Operating profit margin		
	Net profit margin		
	Return on equity		

Source: Adapted from Madden et al., 2002[25]

Growing significance of intangible assets

Today, corporations are not only trading factories, retail outlets, aircrafts and other types of tangible assets; increasingly they are trading intangibles, of which most are related to brands, brand equity and the financial value of those brands.

A recent example is the Chinese computer manufacturer Lenovo's acquisition of IBM's PC division, announced in December 2004, for US$1.25 billion.[26] Lenovo obviously bought tangible assets, high-quality product know-how, distribution networks and a strong customer base. But a significant part of the deal is unquestionably related to the brand value. The brand value of the deal itself is undisclosed. Table 2.3 illustrated that the IBM brand contributes 39 percent of the overall market capitalization of IBM. A fair estimate is that Lenovo paid US$488 million, or approximately 39 percent of the acquisition price, for the right to use the globally recognized IBM Think brand on laptops for the next five years.

It is therefore important to understand what drives the valuation of brands and how brands can be managed throughout organizations as Asia enters a new era of consolidations, alliances, joint ventures, and mergers and acquisitions. Organizations and brands will change owners, and it will be imperative to understand the strengths and values of brands in order to make fair value assessments of the intangible assets. Chapter 6 discusses an approach to brand strategy, brand metrics and brand valuation in further detail.

The market capitalization of corporations with strong brands demonstrates clearly that the market is putting a premium on them. Their market capitalization is larger than the book value. Corporations are seeking to build an individual brand or a portfolio of strong brands in order to capitalize on growth opportunities, capture a better price premium, create and maintain better customer loyalty, manage better control and power over distribution channels and many other related issues leading to enhanced competitiveness and profitability.[27]

The need for brand-driven organizations in Asia

Branding and brands might appear more or less by good luck and happy incidents, when a great advertising campaign combines with hitting a fast-moving fashion trend that suddenly creates a short-term sales success. But long-term branding success will only occur through a planned and well-managed exercise where the corporate management team knows exactly what the complex drivers behind the brand are. They need to know how the drivers interoperate, how to achieve and leverage all elements of the brand equity, and how to evaluate the performance of the brand portfolio. In other words, corporate managements need to know how their brand contributes to enhance shareholder value. Only then can branding become a relevant and trusted strategic discipline in the Asian boardroom along with other well-recognized functions like operations, logistics, finance and human resources (HR).

A strong brand is characterized by a unique brand promise (the customer focus) and an outstanding brand delivery (the organizational system and performance behind the promise). The brand promise and the brand delivery must be consistently balanced to achieve branding excellence (Table 2.5).

TABLE 2.5 **Branding excellence model**		
STRONG BRANDS HAVE TWO BASIC COMPONENTS		
A. Brand promise ⟷		**B. Brand delivery**
▪ Brand essence		▪ Attributes, benefits and values
▪ Brand identity		▪ Organization and distribution
▪ Brand position		▪ Brand image
Characteristics		
1. Brand promise and brand delivery are equally balanced and leveraged		
2. Uniqueness and differentiation are key drivers		
3. Consistency across products, markets, organizations and cultures		
4. Strong brand management systems and processes in place		
5. Board and corporate management are deeply engaged and committed		

Source: VentureRepublic

Singapore Airlines is an example where the brand promise and brand delivery are well balanced. The brand promise of "A Great Way to Fly", with its emphasis on service and technology excellence, has long served the airline well and been consistently communicated since the airline was founded in 1972. Other airlines could easily promise something similar. So what sets Singapore Airlines apart from competitors is the dedication of the corporate management to ensure delivery of the promise throughout the entire organization. The airline runs a highly structured and comprehensive training scheme, standard operating procedures (SOPs), and has numerous guidelines, benchmarking schemes and detailed performance evaluations on every thinkable function and aspect of the organization.

The former deputy chairman, Dr Cheong Choong Kong, has described it:

So much has been written about SIA's in-flight service that one might be forgiven for thinking that customer focus begins with the Singapore Girl. Nothing could be further from the truth, for practically every aspect of airline management focuses on customer service. The most caring attention from our wonderful Singapore Girl would be insufficient if we do not provide engineering reliability, ease of reservations, efficient ground handling and all the rest of it par excellence.[28]

The Singapore Airlines example illustrates how branding is not just the communication of a distinct promise, but drives the promise throughout the entire delivery. Branding has to be built around something real and must be infused throughout the business – not just in marketing or advertising. Although advertising is often one of the most visible parts of an organization and its offerings, it plays a relatively small part in the entire brand building process. The methods and processes to build and manage the brand promise and brand delivery are covered in Chapter 6.

The modern brand-driven organization is characterized by three distinct characteristics which set it apart from less brand-focused organizations:

- the right boardroom *mindset* toward and *beliefs* about branding

- the right *skill sets* to build and manage brands

- the allocation of the right *organizational and financial resources* to achieve the various business objectives and build sustainable brand equity.

At first glance, these three elements seem obvious and fairly easy to achieve in any organization, but in real business life, it is more complicated to get them right. It requires orchestrated and detailed efforts in all parts of the organization and a long-term perspective, which can also survive short-term downturns in the overall economy, in the industry and among customer segments. The following examines the three characteristics.

Boardroom mindset and beliefs

Many Asian business leaders still have strong reservations about investing in intangible assets like brands as opposed to their Western counterparts. It is not uncommon that branding is perceived as and referred to as "marketing communication (advertising)", a "cost on the marketing budget" on the profit and loss statement, and as a "discipline residing in and managed by the often lower level marketing department" in the corporate structure. These perceptions are barriers for building more successful and international Asian brands.

It has been clearly demonstrated in this chapter that a significant amount of shareholder value is created by and tied up in brands. Therefore, as Asian boardrooms are primarily responsible for driving shareholder value and earning positive returns to investors, they must be equally involved in measuring, managing and directing brands and their strategies.

Branding is a comprehensive process

As will be illustrated throughout the book, successful branding must encapsulate the entire company and its multiple and cross-functional actions and activities. When everyone in the organization serves the customers and creates customer value, then everyone is doing marketing, regardless of function or department.[29] This comprehensive task of aligning and managing customer touch points cannot be left to or even controlled successfully by marketing departments alone. All customer touch points have to be aligned and optimized around the brand. This calls for a more cross-functional orientation of marketing in the Asian organization as well as dedicated boardroom attention to ensure that it happens. Hence branding is not a one-off session run by a separate marketing function by mid-level marketing managers but a truly integrated part of the boardroom strategy along the lines of finance, operations, HR and legal issues. This will require a major shift in how the Asian boardroom and corporate management team are structured and operated.

Singapore Airlines is a brilliant example of a dedicated, professional brand strategy throughout a diversified, global organization. The Singapore Airlines brand has been instrumental for the airline from the early start. It serves as one of the leading brand cases from Asia for other established brands as well as any aspiring brands. The Singapore Airlines brand is unique in the sense that the boardroom and corporate management take dedicated leadership of the brand strategy.

Take the examples of companies like Sony, Starbucks, Microsoft, Apple, Giorgio Armani, L'Oreal and Nike. They are all strong and highly aspirational brands where the boardroom and corporate management play a major role in all activities related to building and managing their brands, being involved from high-level brand strategy decisions to monitoring the representation of the brand in local markets.

CEOs as main brand ambassadors

Asian business leaders can benefit tremendously by representing and leading their brands by example, both internally and externally. This does not imply being overly exposed in public and becoming personal media stories themselves. However, most Asian business leaders prefer to stay private and rarely appear in public media unless absolutely necessary. Asian business leaders can help to build their brand portfolios by appearing more outside the boardroom, and acting as the primary spokesperson of the brand vision and identity, internally and externally. This can add tremendously to the success of the brand and also be cost-effective in many instances.

The success of UK-based Virgin Group, led by its legendary founder and CEO Sir Richard Branson, is indisputable. Branson has been successful mostly because of his ability to attract media attention for the company's widespread activities and worldwide marketing launches. This strategy, along with his charisma and talent for being in the limelight at the right time, have helped to build the Virgin brand into a global success, comprising music, airlines, mobile communications and many other businesses. At the same time, the strategy has been cost-effective as it required less spending on marketing communications.[30]

Zhang Ruimin, founder and CEO of the Chinese company Haier, is an example of an Asian business leader following the same media strategy. He is regularly featured in the international business press, which has contributed tremendously to the growth and recognition of the Haier brand outside China. One benefit of the publicity has been the fraction of the costs compared to a strategy using mass communication channels like advertising alone.

A mindset change is inevitably needed in the Asian boardroom mindset if more companies wish to succeed in building strong brands. Branding is not a luxury. It is a necessity for those Asian companies which aspire to compete successfully in the future, capturing better gross margins and enhancing customer loyalty. The journey starts with the right mindset and beliefs about branding.

Skill sets

It is important to note that the marketing function and discipline have come under increasing pressure to demonstrate financial results.[31] Marketers have traditionally been perceived as implementers of tactics, linked strongly to the classic four P's (product, place, price and promotion). This has helped to cement the internal perception of marketing as an expense rather than an investment that drives shareholder value. At the same time, with increasing market fragmentation, product commoditization, strong competition, shorter product life cycles and powerful distribution channels among other factors, the role of marketing has never been more important than it is today.[32] To solve this paradox, the role and scope of marketing has to change within the Asian organization. Two important changes need to take place.

The first change is related to the *role* of marketing. As marketing is increasingly taking place along the entire value chain, marketing is not the responsibility of the marketing function alone. Instead, everyone in the organization is involved. An example is the hotel industry, where many functions within the organization deliver customer value, from doormen, front staff, and check-in personnel to back-end functions like accounting, purchasing and training. This requires a more cross-functional orientation of marketing, with a solid understanding of all the elements in the value chain including skills within engineering, purchasing, manufacturing, logistics, finance and accounting. This requires the Asian marketer to focus heavily on multifunctional teamwork throughout the organization and a strong focus on the integration of marketing in all processes. This might require an upgrade of skill sets and ongoing training of the marketing personnel.[33] The marketing function must be seen as an important driver of strategy and what has been described as a "transformational marketing effort" throughout the entire organization.[34]

The second change required is related to the *outcome* of marketing. Traditionally, marketers have focused on measures tailored to activities in the marketing function, for example advertising and promotions. For the marketing function to become an integrated part of the boardroom agenda, the key issue for the future is to focus on demonstrating the financial consequences of marketing expenditures. Many academic marketing interest groups are investing large resources in this important area. For example, the Marketing Science Institute (MSI) has had marketing metrics and marketing productivity as two of its main research priorities since 1998.[35] The ordinary language in companies is based on accounting and finance, so the challenge is to provide the translations of marketing outcomes into financial measures.[36]

Apart from the cross-functional team and financial orientation described above, the key skill set required is a brand toolbox. It comprises three components: brand audit, brand strategy and brand marketing plan. Furthermore, it requires insights and knowledge about the society and cultures the brand will be part of as it heavily influences the many decisions around the brand. A strong brand arises from the synergy between what the corporation aspires to become (the brand vision) and how well the brand and its aspirations (the actions taken by the company) resonate with target customers who are strongly influenced by the surrounding society and its norms, beliefs, cultures and many other intricacies. Brand building is therefore strongly related to how well the corporation understands consumers, markets and upcoming trends, and how effectively it responds to them.

The success of these efforts can be measured and managed through brand metrics and brand equity which are key performance indicators for the boardroom and corporate management team. A framework for brand management and metrics is presented in Chapter 6.

Resources

A carefully planned brand strategy driven by the Asian boardroom will only be successful if the entire organization is empowered around the brand vision and the brand strategy, and adequate financial resources are allocated. Therefore, the last cornerstone of successful Asian branding refers to organizational and financial resources, their allocation and management.

The human resource aspect is an often overlooked issue at the boardroom level when it comes to branding. Most often, branding is an isolated activity in a mid-management level marketing department vaguely related to other aspects throughout the organization. The entire organization is crucial in bringing the brand to life and the marketing function cannot carry this out alone. It requires the boardroom and all functions to be directly involved. The entire organization must be fully aware of the brand objectives, the brand marketing plan and all activities involved and how to execute them properly.

Watson Wyatt, a global consulting firm specializing in human capital, has been conducting studies in the US, Europe and the Asia Pacific region to establish the link between human capital and shareholder value since 1999. The 2001 US study showed that the better an organization does in managing its human capital, the better its returns for shareholders. The companies were broken into three groups depending on their human capital index scores computed on multiple dimensions. Those in the low group averaged a 21 percent five-year (1996–2001) total shareholder return and the medium group averaged 39 percent. Those with high human capital index scores returned 64 percent.[37]

The above point once again proves the correlation between employees and brands. The more everyone throughout an organization can be trained and involved in delivering on the brand promise, the more efficient and competitive the brand strategy will become. The boardroom must make sure that everyone throughout the organization delivers on the brand and stays true to it.

Brand management is a dynamic, continuous process that needs a consistent investment of time and money. The boardroom must ensure that brand management is allocated a specific budget, as it is much more than mere marketing communications. Due to the intangible nature of branding, the results may not accrue in a short period of time, as it takes time and reinforcement to build customer loyalty.

Many companies increasingly complain that financial markets focus on short-term results and give little credit for long-term value creation strategies. These claims are contradicted by empirical evidence.

A McKinsey study has shown that expectations of future performance are the main driver of shareholder returns. Across industries and stock exchanges, up to 80 percent of a company's market value can be explained only by cash flow expectations beyond the next three years.[38] These expectations are driven by growth judgments and long-term profitability. An examination of the stock prices of leading consumer product companies illustrated that future growth accounts for 54 percent of the stocks' total value.[39]

TABLE 2.6 **Asian boardroom audit**
Mindsets and beliefs
Does the boardroom believe in branding? Why? Why not?
Does the boardroom believe that branding drives ROI?
What are the opportunities and challenges moving forward with a brand strategy?
Does the boardroom have a shared brand vision for the entire corporation? Will the overall brand management be led by the boardroom?
Skill sets
Has the boardroom conducted a strategic brand audit comprising the relevant brand portfolio (including the corporate brand) to assess strengths and weaknesses?
Has the boardroom decided on a comprehensive, long-term brand strategy linked closely to the overall business strategy?
Has the boardroom developed a company-wide brand marketing plan?
Resources
Has the boardroom ensured a strong company culture around the brand?
Has the entire organization been given training and guidelines on how to live the brand?
Will the brand strategy and its implementation be supported with adequate financial resources?
Does the company have a human capital strategy and the necessary recruiting procedures to ensure recruitment of competent talent?

Source: VentureRepublic

Another study by McKinsey of S&P 500 companies from 1984 to 2004 illustrated that the average total returns to shareholders were 9.4 percentage points better among the companies that balanced short- and long-term performance compared to less balanced peers.[40] The best performers also survived longer in the market, the CEOs of these companies generally remained in office three years longer, and their stock prices were significantly less volatile.

Therefore, corporate management must align short- and long-term objectives and expected outcomes of branding, and be committed to support them accordingly with well-balanced strategies and time horizons.

Table 2.6 illustrates how the boardroom can carry out an internal audit of the level of the three crucial cornerstones of branding and the implications for the corporation.

Notes

1 "Brand and deliver", *CFO Asia*, 30 March, 2004.
2 "Zen versus iPod", Jeremy Au Yong, *The Straits Times*, 28 November, 2004.
3 For a more elaborate explanation of brands and brand cultures, see "Brands and branding", Douglas Holt, Class discussion note, Harvard Business School, 2003.
4 "The end of corporate imperialism", C.K. Prahalad and Kenneth Lieberthal, *Harvard Business Review*, August 2003.
5 "Luxury goods Europe, analysis of Chinese demand potential", Goldman Sachs, 20 December, 2004.
6 "Business: luxury's new empire; conspicuous consumption in China", *The Economist*, **371**(19), 2004.
7 Dowling, Grahame R. and Richard Staelin (1994), "A model of perceived risk and intended risk-handling activity," *Journal of Consumer Research*, (21) 119–34.
8 Cunningham, Scott M. (1967), "The major dimensions of perceived risk," in Donald F. Cox (ed), *Risk Taking and Information Handling in Consumer Behavior*, Boston, MA: Harvard University Press, pp. 82–108.
9 Figure inspired by the six perceived risks dimensions developed by Cunningham, 1967, ibid.
10 "Value-based marketing", Peter Doyle, *Journal of Strategic Marketing*, **8**, 2000.
11 "Market metrics: What should we tell the shareholders?", Tim Ambler, *Balance Sheet*, Bradford, 2002, **10**(1), 47.
12 "The power of pricing", Michael V. Marn, Eric V. Roegner and Craig C. Zawada, *McKinsey Quarterly*, (1), 2003.
13 Tim Ambler, 2002, op. cit.
14 "Winning Asian strategies", *McKinsey Quarterly*, (1), 2002.
15 "The 100 Top Brands", *Business Week*, 2 August, 2004.
16 "Brand values and capital market valuations", Mary E. Barth, Michael B. Clement, George Foster and Ron Kaszkik, *Review of Accounting Studies*, **3**, 1998.

17 "Exploring the brand value – shareholder value nexus for consumer goods companies", Roger A. Kerin and R. Sethuraman, *Journal of Academy of Marketing Sciences*, **26**, 1998.
18 "Market-based assets and shareholder value: a framework for analysis", Rajendra K. Srivastava, Tasadduq A. Shervani and Liam Fahey, *Journal of Marketing*, January 1998.
19 Peter Doyle, 2000, op. cit.
20 See for example: *Winning in Asia*, Peter J. Williamson, Harvard Business School Press, 2004, page 129, table 5–2.
21 "Brands matter: an empirical demonstration of the creation of shareholder value through branding", Thomas J. Madden, Frank Fehle and Susan Fournier, *Journal of the Academy of Marketing Science*, 2005, forthcoming.
22 Madden et al. 2005, forthcoming, op. cit.
23 "Principles of corporate finance", Richard A. Brealey and Stewart C. Meyers, 5th edn, McGraw-Hill, 1996.
24 *Understanding Financial Statements*, Lyn Fraser and Aileen Ormiston, 7th edn, Upper Saddle River, NJ, Prentice Hall, 2004.
25 "Brands matter: An empirical investigation of brand-building activities and the creation of shareholder value", Thomas J. Madden, Frank Fehle and Susan Fournier, Working Paper, 02-098, 2 May, 2002.
26 "Lenovo completes acquisition of IBM's personal computing division", press release, www.ibm.com, 1 May, 2005.
27 *Strategic Brand Management*, Kevin Lane Keller, 2nd edn, Prentice Hall, 2003.
28 "High in the sky", *Straits Times*, Singapore, November 20, 2003.
29 *Marketing as Strategy*, Nirmalya Kumar, Harvard Business School Press, 2004, page 5.
30 "The business life, perfected", *Fortune* magazine, No. 19, October 2003.
31 For a more elaborate discussion, see *Marketing and the Bottom-line*, Tim Ambler, 2nd edn, FT/Prentice Hall, 2003.
32 Kumar, 2004, op. cit.
33 "A credibility gap for marketers", *McKinsey Quarterly*, (2), 2005.
34 Kumar, 2004, op. cit.
35 Marketing Science Institute, research priorities, www.msi.org.
36 "Metrics for linking marketing to financial performance", Raj Srivastava and David J. Reibstein, Working paper, 19 October, 2004.
37 "US Human Capital Index Study", 2001, Watson Wyatt Worldwide.
38 "How to escape the short-term trap", Ian Davis, *McKinsey Quarterly*, web exclusive, April 2005.
39 "Bringing customers into the boardroom", Gail J. McGovern, David Court, John Quelch and Blair Crawford, *Harvard Business Review*, November 2004.
40 "Balancing short- and long-term performance", Janamitra Devan, Anna Kristina Millan and Pranav Shirke, *McKinsey Quarterly*, (1), 2005.

CHAPTER 3

TRANSFORMING HOW WE UNDERSTAND ASIAN CULTURES AND CONSUMERS

*Asia is not going to be civilized after the methods of the West.
There is too much Asia, and she is too old.*   Rudyard Kipling, 1891

Introduction

As Asian brands strive to become global, they will increasingly need to look at what happens in neighboring countries and how that experience impacts the way people think and feel about themselves and their neighbors.

This chapter looks at these connections between countries and people across Asia, as a way to understand the region and the way it is building a new form of modernity. Companies interested in building successful brands should be particularly interested in understanding these crucial dynamics of Asia. As explained in Chapter 2, Asian brands will increasingly have to move beyond functional benefits to appeal to Asian consumers emotionally. They can only do so by understanding the culture of these consumers. It is especially important for companies to shift their thinking to realize that Asia is (see Table 3.1):

- A mosaic of cultures rather than a homogeneous region

- An urban form of modernity rather than an exotic continent

- A region of countries connected by history, cultural heritage, religious affiliations, migration and the pattern of rural vs. urban divide

- A region where Asian music and images are gaining prominence every day, rather than being invaded by American imperialism.

Finally, developing brands that are successful in the Asian market also requires that companies understand the psychology of the Asian consumer by:

- Nuancing the view that all Asian cultures are collectivist by looking at the different forms of in-group affiliations in Asia

- Looking at the specific form of conformity existing in Asia where consumers try to be different but in the same way as other people around them, using an individualist type of conformity.

TABLE 3.1 **Blueprint to change the way we think of Asia**	
Transforming the way we view Asian culture	
From	**To**
Homogeneous region	Mosaic of cultures
Exotic Asia	Modern urban Asia
Separate countries	Connected countries
Invaded by American images	Prominence of Asian images and music
Transforming the way we view Asian psychology	
Collectivist cultures	Different types of in-group affiliations
Conformist cultures	Being different but in the same way

Source: VentureRepublic

From a homogeneous region to a mosaic of cultures

Any marketer with considerable knowledge of Asia would agree that Asia is far from being a homogeneous entity. The company De Beers quickly realized this when they researched the Asian market for diamonds. In South Korea, jewelry purchases are centered around weddings. In Southeast Asian countries like Thailand, on the other hand, it is the desire for adornment that motivates jewelry purchases. Finally, in China, De Beers' usual positioning of diamonds as a symbol of everlasting love did not resonate with young Chinese couples' desire for success and their belief that marriage was "the graveyard of love".[1] Shying away from a purely romantic proposition, De Beers eventually decided to position diamonds as symbols of a harmonious and successful future for couples.

McDonald's, while often used as a symbol of American imperialism, is also the most striking illustration of cultural differences across the region and the power of local forces in indigenizing global brands. To show how local McDonald's has become in Japan, Den Fujita recounted how a Japanese boy scout, while traveling in the US, was pleasantly surprised to find his favorite restaurant there. "Once a group of Japanese Boy Scouts visited the

United States and were asked by a local television station what their impression of America was. One boy replied, 'I didn't know that they had McDonald's in the United States, too'".[2]

A myriad of local adaptations and perceptions of McDonald's can be found in Asia. In Japan, McDonald's caters to high school and middle school students as well as mothers with small children. To fit with Japanese perceptions of what a meal should be, McDonald's Japan created rice-based dishes and teriyaki burgers. In Korea, McDonald's caters to women who chat over coffee, hold reading club meetings and study groups. In Taiwan, McDonald's is a hangout where good students do their homework. In Hong Kong, McDonald's is the place where kids have lavish birthday parties with trendy fruit cakes that establish their status. It is also a youth haven where teenagers hang out until late in the evening to avoid the tensions of cramped households. Finally, in China, McDonald's has been able to establish a sense of *renqing* (goodwill, concern) with customers by building good personal feelings between staff and customers. For example, McDonald's staff regularly asks children to record their names, addresses and birthdates on a list called the Book of Little Honorary Guests. The restaurants capitalize on the attention that Chinese families devote to their children, what some social commentators have called the Little Emperors.

From exotic Asia to modern urban Asia

Geishas, samurais, jonques, pagodas and lush jungles: these are the images of Asia that still resonate with many Westerners. These exotic images still imbue many of the advertising campaigns striving to sell Asia in the West. For many Westerners, Asia is still a mystery to be solved. But as a researcher recently pointed out: "We have to be careful not to stereotype what is meant by 'Asian' – that it has to be traditional or that it has to be filled with history."[3] Seeing only the exotic and the traditional side of Asia would be misleading. Of course, many Asian brands have actively reinforced traditional Asian values: hotel brands such as Banyan Tree and Shangri-La have all emphasized hospitality, airlines such as Thai Airways and Singapore Airlines have also stressed Asian hospitality. BritishIndia's clothes evoke images of colonial times in India, while Shanghai Tang surfs on the pre-Communist era of the 1920s, when Shanghai was one of the most cosmopolitan cities in the world.

Images of an exotic Asia, such as the ones published in an advertisement for Tiger Beer in the UK, would probably not appeal to most Asians.[4] Shanghai Tang, while popular with a portion of the Hong Kong middle class, does not fare so well with a majority of Chinese, to whom the idea of buying a watch with Mao pictured on it would probably seem absurd. Similarly, BritishIndia would probably not appeal to Indians. Both brands are unsurprisingly much more popular with Westerners.

Focusing on a traditional or exotic Asia is missing half the picture. There is a new form of Asian modernity emerging, one that is true to its Asian roots, but is imbued with the images of a new Asia that is looking at its future with hope and optimism. A perfect illustration of this is the case of Chang Beer, one of the most successful beer brands in the Asian market. Before 1997, the Thai beer market was dominated by Singha beer. Singha strived to represent all things that were stereotypically viewed as "Thai" – traditional Thai dancers, temples and pagodas. Its positioning was that of the son of the soil. Singha's managers tried to portray the heritage that had built Thailand as a country.

In 1997, Thailand suffered one of its most severe economic crises, along with other countries in the region. After decades of keeping its currency fixed to the dollar, in July 1997 the Thai government announced that it was letting the baht float. The currency quickly reached an all-time low and was devalued by 50 percent, causing surging inflation. The Thai middle classes and their high expectations were suddenly wiped out by the recession.

Times had changed and Chang Beer saw an opportunity to attack the positioning of Singha as the true Thai beer, because the symbols, the imagery and the tone of Singha's communication were not relevant any more in the new economic context in which Thais found themselves. Singha represented the past of Thailand. The past, as Thais saw it in 1997, was synonymous with disappointment. Chang positioned itself as the true son of the soil that did not play on an exotic image of Thailand but expressed Thai traditional values in a modern way. The pagodas and temples were replaced by a popular singer used to singing tunes of hope and renewal. In a television ad, the singer At Karabao sings about the beer "the Thais make themselves". The advertising campaign was a resounding success and Chang has not looked back since then. Chang leveraged its symbol and name (Chang means elephant in Thai) to become *the* Thai beer. It is now the main sponsor of the English soccer team Everton, it has a dominant market share in the Thai beer market and is well poised to become part of the star Asian brands.[5]

The Chang Beer example illustrates the importance for Asian brands to stay tuned to the rapid developments in Asian societies; the need for Asian brands to capture what it means for consumers to be modern and Asian. This recommendation can even be extended to include a regional outlook.

SK-II – premium Asian appeal

Many people across Asia believe that SK-II is a Japanese beauty brand while in fact it is owned by Procter & Gamble (P&G). It was developed in 1980 by a Japanese unit of US-based Max Factor which was acquired by P&G in 1991. The SK-II brand was not introduced into the US market until 2004 when 11 Saks Fifth Avenue department stores started to sell the products.[6]

SK-II is widely popular in Asia and regarded as a premium brand. The product has the "Japanese myth" around it, and the color scheme is deep maroon – seen as more sedate than a typical American cosmetics brand. In addition, SK-II hits the spot of whitening the skin which is the Asian concept of beauty: white and flawless.

When SK-II was launched, whitening skin care was nothing new, as Japanese brands Shiseido, Kanebo and Kose had similar products already. But P&G was the first to use popular Asian movie stars, models and singers with white and flawless skin to promote the brand, such as the singer and actress Sammi Cheng from Hong Kong, model Qi Qi from China and singer Sandy Lam from Singapore.[7]

SK-II became popular in South Korea when word of mouth spread common perceptions about the brand – the quality was high, it made a difference and prices were higher than other products. It quickly became a status symbol. South Koreans are very status-driven compared to other Asian cultures, and they regard only French and Japanese cosmetics brands as high quality and must-haves. Interestingly, there are many South Korean mid-market cosmetics brands which are popular in Southeast Asia, but not at home.

Adding to the brand experience, SK-II products have no usage instructions in South Korean or English – only in Japanese. This leaves no option for the customers but to go to upscale department stores, where highly trained sales assistants will demonstrate the products and answer questions. Freebies and testers are restricted to maintain the value of the brand.

From separate countries to connected ones

It is important to see the increasing number of interconnections between countries in Asia. The proliferation of images, music and the movement of people across the region create all sorts of connections between Asians that did not necessarily exist before. It creates opportunities for marketers who want to take advantage of these connections to launch pan-Asian initiatives for their products and services.

Globalization theorists have emphasized these interconnections. Arjun Appadurai,[8] a well-known commentator on globalization, argues that nation-states are becoming more and more irrelevant in an era of flowing images, people and finances. What is important in this new era, according to Appadurai, is what people imagine. It is not so much the physical geography of their current location that is important, but the geography that they construct and hold onto in their minds. The country and culture they left when they migrated, the images, sounds, practices and languages that connect people living in different parts of the world create a much stronger impact than mere physical geography. Indians accessing live online video feeds of their favorite deities in India, Pakistanis listening to prayers recorded in mosques in Pakistan or Iran as they drive their cars to work in Sydney, and the Chinese carrying their rice cookers and food when traveling all testify to this point. People move around and carry their homes with them in their hearts and minds, accessing them more easily now than ever before through various forms of media – email, satellite television, digital down-loadable music and DVDs of ethnic movies – the list is endless. As people move around more and more, the relevance of the nation as a definer of iden-tity is slowly fading away. With the help of this burst of media, it is through our imagination that we construct our versions of home, culture and, there-fore, the identities that define us. Brands too can play the same role.

To make sense of globalization, Appadurai has structured his theory of globalization and modernization on "scapes". These are the imaginary landscapes that we create in our minds and around which we build our identities. These are shifting sands, nebulous worlds that change into and take on new shapes and forms, new accents and colors as the imaginers move around, and are subject to influence from various sources and, in turn, are agents of influence on other people. A good example is the grow-ing popularity of Bollywood. A commercial for Motorola in India, made by Ogilvy & Mather India, featured a teenager on a local train who, when he plugs his headphones into his new Motorola MP3 mobile phone, is trans-ported atop a rural train in a Bollywoodesque singing and dancing extrava-ganza. The ad was recreating a famous scene from a Bollywood song

("Chamma Chamma" from Raj Kumar Santoshi's *China Gate*) which was a hit several years ago, and which was picked up by Baz Luhrmann for the soundtrack of his film *Moulin Rouge*. Motorola remixed the original song into a clubby version for the ad, which was a big hit. So Motorola released it as a single which got plenty of airtime in nightclubs in India and it cut a longer version of the ad and released it as a music video. Motorola executives liked the ad so much that they also released it throughout Southeast Asia. What was originally made in India went around the globe, back to India, and then spread through Southeast Asia.[9] What goes around comes around, but with a new accent, a new shape and a new color. There is no longer a definable center which pulls people toward it and orders their world, even as they move around. What is important in this theory is its dynamism, the idea that cultural influence does not necessarily come from the US or Europe. What Appadurai suggests is a decentralization of the world: the world not according to America, but according to wherever people choose to imagine themselves. This is of particular interest to understanding and creating brands in Asia.

Given the global availability of local TV channels via satellite, countries in Asia are now more connected to each other than ever before. This is the Asian mediascape. Koreans, Japanese or Taiwanese are often watching the same TV soap operas, such as the hit *Tokyo Love Story*, or listening to the same music. Cultural similarities between the different East Asian countries have boosted sales of TV programs, CDs and movies. Most TV shows are conservative and steeped in Confucian values, revolving around the issues arising in extended families and love stories. The Japanese drama *Oshin* was particularly popular in Asia, having tremendous success in Singapore, and amazing audience ratings of 89.9 percent in Bejing. When the Taiwanese government lifted the ban on Japanese imports in 1994, *Oshin* became an instant hit there.[10] *Oshin* follows the story of a Japanese woman, from her birth in a poor family to her struggles living in Tokyo, the suicide of her husband and, finally, her success as a founder and owner of a supermarket chain. *Oshin* was popular in Asia because of the values it espouses – perseverance, hard work, diligence, patriotism – values which resonated with Asian audiences. Importantly, Asian audiences enjoy these dramas because they are so familiar, culturally close, yet not quite.[11]

The Korean wave

South Korean pop culture *"hallyu"* – embracing fashion, music and film – is rapidly becoming an export success for South Korea. The rise in popularity of Korean pop culture led the Chinese media to call it the "Korean wave" in 2001.[12] The wave or *hallyu* has spread to Southeast Asia and lately to Japan where it has had a strong impact. In 2000, a 50-year ban on the exchange of popular culture between Korea and Japan was partly lifted, which has helped the surge of Korean popular culture among the Japanese.[13] South Korea's broadcast authorities planned to send a delegation to promote their TV programs in India, Indonesia and Thailand in May and June 2005. By 2008, the Kyonggi provincial government is planning to open a US$1.95 billion entertainment hub, "Hallyuwood", north of Seoul. Hallyuwood is a compound word of *hallyu* and Hollywood.[14]

Hallyu boosted South Korea's income from merchandise, film and television programs exports and tourism by US$1.87 billion in 2004 or 0.2% of national GDP according to the Korean International Trade Association.[15] The number of foreign tourists to South Korea increased to 968,000 in 2004 from the previous year, of which 67 percent, or 647,000 tourists, visited the country due to *hallyu*.[16]

This is the phenomenon that some anthropologists have called "close distance".[17] Close distance is a type of relationship with films or other cultural products where audiences are both drawn to the unfamiliar and comforted by the familiar, close but at a distance. The producers of Channel V, one of the pan-Asian TV channels based in Hong Kong, have perfectly understood the phenomenon of close distance: "producers knew that an all English veejay [video jockey] [brought] abysmal ratings while an all-vernacular veejay [was] not hip enough for a country that generally worshipped English-Hinglish, Gujlish, Tamlish, Anthinglish."[18] These hybrid forms of entertainment have become increasingly popular, not entirely foreign while not entirely domestic or vernacular. This is evident from the popularity of hybrid singers, actors and models. For example, Tata Young is one of Thailand's most famous singers. The daughter of an American father and a Thai mother, she has already sold more than 12 million albums and she is only 23. On Asian silver screens, one of the rising stars is Takeshi Kaneshiro. Half-Taiwanese and half-Japanese, he is a big star in both countries and easily crosses the border between Chinese and Japanese movies. Hybrid models and hybrid actors are the perfect illustration of close distance, people who look familiar but alien enough to become aspirational. This logic also applies to music in Asia, with a mix of Asian and outside influences.

There is an Asian musicscape. Bands like Japanese Dreams Come True or Taiwanese 5566 are gaining pan-regional popularity. In April 1999, six of the top ten music singles were by Japanese artists and bands. Korean bands are also gaining prominence in the region. Bands like Seo Taiji, The Boys or UpTown sing pop and rap lyrics that are, interestingly, devoid of violence and sex, the themes usually explored by American rappers. The issues that resonate with young Asians are tense relations with conservative parents, rebellion against strict teachers and feelings of alienation. Asian teenagers feel rebellious but not to the extent of identifying with American gangsta rap. Korean hip hop transforms the genre into a form that is accessible to Asians.

From American images to prominence of Asian images and music

These trends are likely to become even more important in the next few years. Asian countries are increasingly recognizing the importance of cultural industries. For example in 1999 South Korea's government decided that cultural industries could boost the economy, and moved to deregulate them.[19] It has invested heavily in broadband technology and considers the game industry as a national economic priority. That industry is already a huge business in South Korea, representing revenues of US$11 billion dollars, surpassing box office receipts of a couple of years ago.

As reported in the *Wall Street Journal*, the Yankee Group predicts that advertising within video games, will increase from US$79 million in 2003 to US$260 million by 2008. Asian countries are likely to follow this trend. For many East Asians, the anonymity of the virtual gaming world allows them to express their individuality in ways they can't in the relatively formal and rigid Asian societies.[20] The South Korean movie industry is also growing, with film exports increasing more than fivefold in the past ten years. Japan is the biggest foreign market, accounting for 44 percent of movie export revenue in 2002,[21] and Hong Kong has 9.9 percent of exports and Thailand 5.5 percent. Since 1995, the movie industry's revenue has more than doubled, playing a significant role in the country's GDP growth.

Asian managers can draw three lessons from looking at the music and media landscape. First, rather than seeing the region as a homogenized product of American imperialism, it is important to think of Asia as increasingly traversed by diverse flows of culture coming from different cultural centers: Tokyo, Taipei, Hong Kong, Seoul and so on. For Cambodians, Bangkok's trends may be as important as New York's. For young Japanese, Shanghai is the most happening city in the world. For the Taiwanese, Tokyo is the place to emulate, to the extent that a Taiwanese magazine wrote an article on Japanese popular culture titled "Watch out! Your children are becoming Japanese".[22] In Singapore, Japanese brands and products are extremely popular. In a recent survey, researchers found that 44 percent of Singaporean teenagers either always or often watch Japanese television programs, 30 percent regularly listen to Japanese music and 42 percent regularly eat Japanese food. They look upon Japan as an elite model and desire to emulate Japanese youth by adopting similar icons, listening to similar music and watching similar programs.[23]

Second, the type of modernity Asians have created for themselves is different from that found in the West. This alternative form of modernity is showcased in the toned-down lyrics of Korean pop songs or in the themes of popular TV shows across Asia where stories of family tensions are still the most popular. Most countries in Asia are adopting new technologies but retaining their identity at the same time. There has been a resurgence of nationalism in Asia in the past ten years, which suggests that, rather than becoming like the West, Asian countries are developing their own forms of modernity. Consequently, Asian managers should be careful when analyzing the future of Asian consumers. Extrapolating from the experience of consumers in Europe and North America to predict how Asian consumers will be is dangerous. The failure of many multinationals in Asia shows how models developed in the West are not easily adaptable to the Asian context.

The third lesson is that Asians need to think beyond Asia as a collection of states. Because of globalization, people moving and migrating, financial resources moving rapidly across the globe, it is important to recognize the new forms of connection between people. The British sociologist Anthony Giddens defines globalization as "the intensification of worldwide social relations which link distant localities in such a way that local happenings are shaped by events occurring many miles away and vice versa".[24] Despite the heterogeneity in religious and ethnic affiliations within countries in Asia, people are connected across countries in ways that have powerful economic implications, as discussed below.

Opportunities in subcultures

The Chinese diaspora in Asia

Ethnic commonality is clearly facilitating the growth of economic relations between the People's Republic of China and Hong Kong, Taiwan, Singapore and the overseas Chinese communities in other countries. In his influential book on China, Murray Weidenbaum[25] predicts that the Chinese-based portion of the Asian economy will rapidly gain importance:

> This strategic area contains substantial amounts of technology and manufacturing capability (Taiwan), outstanding entrepreneurial, marketing and services acumen (Hong Kong), a fine communications network (Singapore), a tremendous pool of financial capital (all three), and very large endowments of land, resources and labor (mainland China) … From Guangzhou to Singapore, from Kuala Lumpur to Manila, this influential network – often based on extensions of the traditional clans – has been described as the backbone of the East Asian economy.

The Chinese diaspora has tremendous economic weight in the Southeast Asian region.[26] To give an idea of this importance, look at Malaysia, Singapore and Indonesia: in Malaysia[27] the Chinese minority generates some US$40 billion, representing more than 40 percent of the country's GNP. In Singapore, the Chinese produce 81 percent of the GNP. In Indonesia, Chinese businesses and interests still represent approximately 10 percent of the economy, even after an ethnic backlash occurred against them.[28]

The cultural similarities amongst ethnic Chinese, such as their adherence to Confucian values and their common cultural heritage, provide avenues for Asian brand managers wanting to develop products or services targeting this population. Brands that can leverage a Chinese heritage, or even better, a platform of Chinese cosmopolitanism in this situation, are at an advantage. The image of the cosmopolitan Chinese who has succeeded abroad has a lot of currency in the Chinese diaspora. Brands that take advantage of that cosmopolitan platform are likely to appeal to the Chinese community.

The Muslim scape in Asia

Approximately two-thirds of Muslims live in Asia. While the common perception is that most Muslims come from the Arabic-speaking world, the vast majority of Muslims actually live in Asia. Less than 20 percent live in Arabic-speaking countries. The four largest Muslim countries are Indonesia, with 194 million Muslims, India with 149 million, Pakistan with 144 and Bangladesh with 71 million Muslims. This significant chunk of the world population, it can be argued, has a distinct set of beliefs and needs that have largely been ignored by mass-marketing efforts.

The first area to consider is banking and financial services. Consider the dilemma that Muslim consumers face: the teachings of the Koran prevent Muslims from any dealings involving the payment of interest. Consequently, instead of the usual types of loans, Islamic banks structure profit-sharing agreements for their loans and other products which usually generate interest. Deposit accounts operate like trusts, with funds invested on the depositor's behalf and a share of the profits replacing interest payments.

Understanding the intricacies of Islamic banking is especially important for Asian managers interested in the financial services sector. Islamic banking is a promising avenue to research and do business in. As of 2004, the assets of Islamic financial institutions approximate $230 billion worldwide. There are now Islamic products available in about 75 countries, including non-banking products, such as insurance, micro-lending and Islamic mutual funds.[29] It is becoming increasingly common for Islamic and Western financial institutions to form joint ventures to provide services which meet the needs of Islamic investors. Foreign banks such as HSBC and Citibank are aggressively pursuing Muslim consumers in different Asian markets such as Malaysia and Indonesia. Big local banks are also targeting this emerging segment. Almost all financial institutions in Malaysia have opened separate Islamic departments.

After banking, the second business sector where Muslim beliefs have a large impact is food. Beliefs in the Koran have an important impact on food marketing, with all food products having to be halal. Muslims use two main terms to describe food: haram and halal. In Arabic, *halāl* means permitted or lawful, while haram means forbidden or unlawful. Halal is an important part of Islamic life. The restrictions of halal are similar to kosher requirements: no pork, no blood, the name of Allah must be pronounced at the moment of slaughter and intoxicants of any kind are forbidden.

The success of soft drinks targeting the Muslim population in Europe, such as Mecca Cola,[30] show that there are interesting opportunities ahead for companies wanting to target Muslim populations in different parts of the world. In Asia, astute companies have already launched technological products targeting Muslim populations. At the end of 2004, the Korean company LG Electronics launched a cell phone featuring a compass which allows consumers to find the direction in which to pray.[31] Malaysia-based website www.travellingmuslim.com offers a watch which gives prayer times and another gadget giving the direction of Mecca to traveling Muslims.

Paying attention to the distinctiveness of Muslim consumer behavior is likely to become even more important in the years to come. According to projections by the United Nations (UN), Pakistan's population will be about 434 million by 2050, making it the third largest country in the world after China and India.[32] The immense majority of this population will undoubtedly be Muslim. Understanding the needs and preferences of Muslims in Pakistan, but also other countries in Asia, remains essential.

Rural and low-income consumers in Asia

An important segment that marketers cannot ignore in Asia is the bottom of the pyramid and those Asian consumers living in rural areas. The challenges that marketers face in trying to address these consumers are high because of the fragmented nature of the rural market and the low margins of this trade. There is no denying though that rural consumers want to access brands, if only because they are a promise of quality. For Asian marketers interested in tapping the huge rural markets in China and India, there are important issues to consider.

First, rural consumers have less purchasing power. In China, the income gap between urban and rural residents, which is around 5 to 1, greatly restricts rural people's consumption of products. There is also a significant difference in the way wages are earned, with a majority of the working population in rural markets being paid daily instead of weekly or monthly wages. This means that consumers in rural markets will generally spend their daily wage on necessities such as food, and have little left to spend on personal care items and other relatively luxurious items. This has driven companies like Unilever to sell sachets in rural China and India, instead of the normal sizes of detergent and shampoo. One-third of India's shampoo sales in 2000 came from sachets in rural India, with Unilever, the British-Dutch company, accounting for 70 percent of those sales of sachets. The company is increasingly relying on Asian rural markets to drive its sustained growth. Hindustan Lever, Unilever's Indian subsidiary, is now a major force in the Unilever network of subsidiaries, with many strategies emerging from India. For example, the company used the expertise of its Indian managers in rural markets to help to develop the Chinese market for shampoos and soaps. Another example is Coca-Cola which began to sell 200-milliliter bottles of Coke in India in 2003 to increase demand among consumers who cannot afford bigger portions.[33]

The income disparity between rural and urban consumers can drive companies to innovate to address these differences. A case in point is Baron International, an Indian company which distributed the Japanese Akai's audio and video products in India in the 1990s. Kabir Mulchandani, Baron's flamboyant manager, recognized that there was a great potential to sell television sets to Indian consumers in urban areas. Since the economic liberalization of the 1990s, India has seen a dramatic increase in the middle-class family's purchasing power. However, inherent in the Indian consumer psyche is the reluctance to part with goods that are in working condition. Influenced by Gandhi's ideals of frugality, Indians do not like to waste, and would not be convinced to throw away their old television sets.

Baron's managers saw a great opportunity in the rural market. They realized that here was a huge market for used television sets, so they quickly created a trade-in scheme that linked urban and rural retailers, whereby urban dealers sold their used sets to rural retailers. Urban consumers were able to part with their old TV sets without feeling guilty about it and the dealers were able to fund the scheme by selling them the latest, more expensive TV models. In the process, rural consumers could buy affordable television sets. Until Akai took away its license in the late 1990s, Baron was the most profitable firm in the television business, making a 46 percent return on capital employed – three or four times that of local rivals.[34]

A second element of difference between rural and urban consumers is density. The number of villages in China and India is extremely high, pushing companies like Unilever and Coca-Cola to develop extensive distribution networks.

Companies that know how to address the needs of rural and low-income customers are well set to compete in Asia. In the Chinese market, SAB (South African Breweries) is a rare example of a successful foreign brewery. The company adopted a different strategy from its competitors

Heineken and Budweiser. It started its expansion in China with the northern hinterland, gradually expanding into other markets. This allowed the company to build its capacity slowly, without having to face the tough competition of the foreign breweries ready to slash prices in Shanghai or Beijing. As in other markets, SAB started its Chinese expansion by establishing a beachhead, then slowly increasing its presence in ever-expanding circles until it had the region firmly under its control. In 2004, SAB was the second largest beer maker in China. This is no small achievement in what is already the largest market for beer in the world: demand for beer in China increased by more than 40 percent between 1997 and 2002, compared to just 4 percent in the US during the same period.[35]

In the Indian market, the detergent maker Nirma adopted a similar strategy of developing a base in the hinterland and the rural areas before attacking the big metropolises. Karsanbhai Patel, Nirma's founder, knew chemicals well enough to develop an effective, low-priced detergent of good quality but did so starting in his home state of Gujarat before launching in other regions.[36] He called the yellow powder detergent "Nirma" after his daughter. He started by selling to his neighbors for a small profit and built his consumer base slowly. Because a strong distribution network is so important in emerging markets like India, he concentrated on widening his distribution network. Nirma began surfacing all over Gujarat, in small shops in the remotest villages. Today Nirma owns a 34 percent market share in the detergent market, competing head to head with Unilever.[37]

Another great example of a company with rural expertise is the Indian company Asian Paints. The company has almost 50 percent of the market for house paints in India, despite the presence of major foreign multinationals. The company has succeeded by developing an extensive distribution network in the rural market. Its products are priced low and so have been successful in other developing countries, such as Nepal and Fiji. Asian Paints has developed an expertise in dealing with low-income, often illiterate consumers who only buy small quantities of paint that they later dilute to save money. The company has developed two brands, Utsav and Tractor, that are tailored specifically to the needs of this market.[38]

Companies like Asian Paints, Nirma and SAB have understood that the key to succeeding in markets like China and India is a good understanding of the rural consumer and a vast distribution network.

Overall, while Asian countries are diverse and need to be understood in their own context, there are similarities and threads that cut across the region. Companies like Unilever, Asian Paints and HSBC have captured some of these similarities in the development of brands that address segments with similar needs in different countries. As Asian companies venture into new markets and try to appeal to consumers from other Asian countries, an understanding of these similarities as well as the specificities of Asian consumer psychology remains essential.

Transforming how we view Asian consumer psychology

The Western conception of a person as a bounded, unique, more or less integrated, motivational and cognitive universe, a dynamic center of awareness, emotions, judgment and action, organized in a distinctive whole is, however incorrigible it may seem, a rather peculiar idea, within the context of world's cultures. Clifford Geertz[39]

Most of the consumer behavior models that are used in Asian boardrooms today were developed in a handful of Western countries. Marketers still do not know very well how marketing techniques and theories can be applied to non-Western contexts. Many models that are used by companies today are based on the assumption that, as the well-known anthropologist Clifford Geertz puts it, the person is "a bounded, unique, more or less integrated, motivational and cognitive universe". Most marketing and management theories rely on what we can call a Western perspective of the individual as an independent, autonomous identity, free to make decisions based on purely personal desires and affiliations, living life in accordance with Maslow's hierarchy: food, shelter and clothing are the most basic needs, after which might come haute cuisine, decoration and fashion. Mankind universally, it would seem, operates just as rationally.

Marketing textbooks still use this model to show how consumers move from the satisfaction of basic needs to higher order goals such as self-actualization. This model, however, fails to consider cultural differences. The widespread practice of dowry in India, although illegal, highlights the plight of parents who are forced to save money and forego its benefits to buy enough jewelry for their daughters' weddings. In some emerging countries, people may deprive themselves of food to buy a refrigerator to enhance their social class.[40] Clearly, the hierarchy of priorities is different in an Asian context, where interpersonal relationships and social interactions are more valued, on average, than self-actualization needs. As is evident in Figure 3.1, the Western need for self-actualization is replaced in the Asian context by social needs of status, admiration and affiliation. Autonomy and independence are not as important or at least do not have the same connotations as in the West.

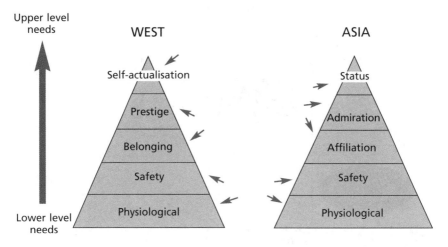

Figure 3.1 Maslow's hierarchy of needs and the Asian equivalent
Source: Schütte with Ciarlante 1998[41]

Hofstede's well-known model of national cultural difference is more culturally attuned than Maslow's hierarchy of needs. The four dimensions of cultural difference – the level of power distance within the country, the extent of masculinity, the predominance of individualism or collectivism and the level of uncertainty avoidance that societies engage in – have shaped marketers' thinking for many decades.[42] Figure 3.2 illustrates the conceptual differences between Asia and Western countries on two of Hofstede's dimensions.

These dimensions make up the social psyche of the individual. So a country that seeks to avoid uncertainty will have rules of behavior and strict structures for thought that ensure that individuals do not face uncertainty. A country that is highly masculine will be one where men's and women's roles will be divided distinctly by gender, the masculine side being more assertive, and the feminine side being more caring and modest. In feminine countries, on the other hand, both men and women will share the same values of modesty and caring. A culture that is individualistic expects individuals to be independent and look after only their own immediate family.

The ties between individuals are looser, compared to a collectivist culture where individuals are part of a group from birth, which protects them in return for unquestioning loyalty. There is greater conformity to the needs and goals of the group. Social psychologists label this as in-group vs out-group. Those who form part of this in-group are viewed favorably; those who do not form part of it are regarded as outsiders.

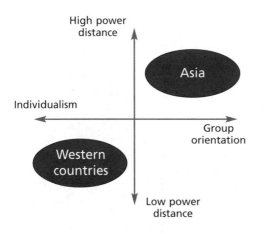

Figure 3.2 Power distance versus individualism/group orientation[43]

Although the concept of in-groups and out-groups exists universally, when combined with collectivist cultures, the in-group becomes exceptionally strong. Group membership is salient and individuals belong to a number of in-groups, usually family, school, company and country.

The importance of in-groups in Asian cultures

Asian cultures have a different conception of individuality, placing more emphasis on the way individuals are connected to the people around them: attending to others, fitting in and living in harmony. Many non-Western cultures do not value a strict separation of the self from the family unit and the community, while in the West, individuals generally define themselves through certain individual talents, abilities and personality traits.

In many Asian cultures, people believe in the fundamental connectedness or interdependence of individuals within the same in-group. These differences are captured in Figure 3.3. In most Western cultures, people will have an independent self where the individual is the primary locus of consciousness. In contrast, in cultures where the interdependent self dominates, it is better to think of the self as connected to others, as always within the context of others.

This concept of interdependent self is evident in Japan with the importance of *Ie*, which is often translated as family or household. *Ie*, researchers have argued, is seen to be fundamental to understanding various social organizations in Japanese society, from kinship to the company. *Ie* refers to a family institution, a recruitment strategy for household succession, and a group enterprise.[44]

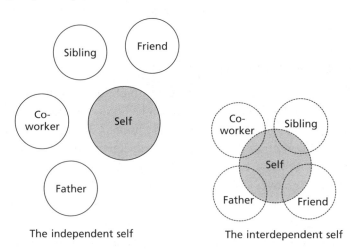

The independent self   The interdependent self

Figure 3.3 Independent versus interdependent self
Source: Markus and Kitayama 1998[45]

The differences between Western and Asian cultures are not black and white, though. It would be too simplistic to label all Asian cultures collectivist and Western cultures individualist. After all, the number of associations, church groups and other types of social engagement is extremely high in the US. On the other hand, with the recent advent of economic liberalization, many Asians have embraced individualist pursuits. Despite these, it can still be argued that the Western concept of the self is different from that in most Asian cultures: an independent versus an interdependent self.

Within Asia, there are vast differences in the way the interdependent self is expressed. There is a tendency across the region to engage in socially engaging behavior but the form of this behavior varies greatly. For example, the Japanese view of the self is evident in everyday episodes where Japanese emphasize the notion of "losing face", acting on the basis of others' expectations and needs, blurring the distinction between self and others.

In contrast, Indians' in-group is limited to their family and their ethnic community. With 18 official languages, regional differences, religious feuds and extreme social class disparities, the ability of Indians to empathize with others becomes limited at best. Instead, in India the interdependent self means enduring loyalty and a sense of belonging to a community defined by caste, language, geographic origin and social class. What constitutes the Indian in-group is different from the Japanese or Chinese in-group. Overall, though, it is important for marketers to realize the importance of the in-group for consumers who will seek advice, think of products and evaluate products within an in-group.

Being different like everybody else

The importance of the in-group does not mean total social conformity though. L'Oreal's high sales of hair dyes in Japan testify to the importance of being different.[46] The importance of luxury brands in Asia shows consumers trying to differentiate themselves from other members of society through iconic brands such as Chanel, Louis Vuitton and Gucci.[47] In 2004, 29 percent of the total turnover of French luxury giant LVMH was concentrated in Asia[48] and 58 percent of cognac producer Remy Martin's turnover is generated in the region.[49]

The popularity of luxury brands depends largely upon the perceived scarcity of these goods. According to that principle, people assign more value to options, including products, when they are less available. Marketers have long used some of these scarcity tactics such as advertising "limited number available" or "deadline". This principle works because we typically value things that are difficult to obtain and also because we can't stand to lose any freedoms. According to psychological reactance theory, the more we lose freedoms (such as the opportunity or the ability to buy a luxury item), the more we want to retain these freedoms.[50]

The scarcity principle can also explain the Asian madness for collectable items. Consider the case of limited editions of toys: in Taiwan, after McDonald's started selling Hello Kitty dolls, customers, having stood in lines for hours, started to get into fights. A McDonald's restaurant was ordered to close because of the chaos. Another toy fanatic threatened McDonald's staff at knife-point when they ran out of Hello Kitty toys.[51] Some disappointed customers suffered nervous breakdowns after failing to obtain the prized dolls. A Hong Kong security guard was arrested by police after stealing 21

McDonald's Snoopy collectable figurines from office desks.[52] The scarcity principle holds even more for these items not only because they are newly scarce but there is also a sociological component to the principle: we desire scarce products more when we compete with others for them.

But the scarcity principle, while it helps to explain the type of behavior mentioned above, does not, on its own, explain the manic fascination for luxury brands in Asia. Japanese teenagers, for example, could hardly see Louis Vuitton bags or Gucci sunglasses as scarce items. In some categories of the Japanese population, the penetration of such items reaches more than 90 percent.[53] There are distinct forces in Asian societies that lead Asians to adopt icons projecting their social status. One of these forces is the concept of "face". The amount of *mien tsu* or face stands for the kind of prestige and is a function of social status. Thus, an individual is forced to consume commodities that measure up to his social class, as not doing so would mean a loss of face. Even though the traditional Chinese values have changed rapidly over the past 20 years in the process of the country's modernization, many studies show that some of the traditional values, such as face, still exist and influence social orientations. Researchers have also shown evidence that the Chinese conform to strong pressures to behave like members of their social class.[54]

Another force leading to the purchase of status symbols is the level of what Hofstede has called "power distance". Hofstede defines power distance as the extent to which less powerful members of society accept power to be distributed unequally. In other words, cultures with high power distance believe that the more powerful people must be deferred to and not argued with, especially in public. In contrast, low power distance cultures believe in more equality. China, for example, has a significantly higher power distance level of 80 compared to 60 for the other Southeast Asian countries, and a world average of 55. This illustrates a high level of inequality of power and wealth within the society. It is not necessarily forced upon people, but rather accepted by the society as their cultural heritage. Luxury brands are purchased to show dominant status and distance to other consumers. As Worm argues: "In China, personalized relationships combined with greater power distance tend to result in greater emphasis on status and status symbols than in Scandinavian countries where status symbols are viewed as suspicious and negative by other employees."[55] Some of the key differences between low and high power distance countries appear in Table 3.2.

TABLE 3.2 **Differences between low and high power distance countries**[56]	
Low power distance	High power distance
Privileges and status symbols frowned upon	Privileges and status symbols expected
Teachers expect initiatives from students in class	Teachers are expected to take all initiatives in class
Inequalities between people should be minimized	Inequalities between people are expected and desired
Parents and children treat each other as equals	Children respect parents and parents expect obedience
Ireland, Scandinavia, Austria, Israel	Malaysia, China, India, The Philippines

Conclusion

This chapter has mapped some of the most important forces, flows and dimensions of Asian culture that can influence how Asian consumers think and behave. There is an important caveat to this analysis though and it has to do with the dynamism of the region. Societies in Asia are moving fast and the dimensions described above are not set in stone. Asian countries are increasingly connected to other countries within and beyond Asia. These connections only enhance and increase the rapidity of the Asian evolution. What remains, though, are these connections between these different countries. Contrary to popular thinking, the biggest Asian companies do most of their business in Asia.[57] The examples discussed in this section testify to the rich cultural exchanges between Asian countries. To become astute marketers and understand Asian consumers, the corporate management of companies will first have to look within Asia.

Companies striving to build successful brands in Asia should understand this unique mosaic of cultures that is Asia. As discussed, Asia represents a blend of modernity and traditionalism. This is a doubled-edged sword for companies seeking to develop brands in Asia. On the one hand, this presents a huge set of opportunities with diverse customer segments, latent rural demand, and an immense potential to weave exciting new stories. But on the other, it also compels companies to find a balance between the different perspectives to become local and regional at the same time. Fine-tuning products and services to satisfy local tastes and preferences while also appealing to a pan-Asian identity by leveraging the common underlying cultural underpinnings will be one of the possible ways ahead for companies in Asia.

Notes

1 Probert, Jocelyn and Hellmut Schütte (1999), *De Beers: Diamonds are for Asia*, INSEAD Euro-Asia Centre, Case 599-011-1, p. 12.

2 "Talk with Den Fujita," *Twenty Year History of McDonald's Japan*, Tokyo: McDonald's, 1991, 82.

3 See Wee, C.J. W.-L. (2004), "Staging the Asian modern: Cultural fragments, the Singaporean eunuch, and the Asian Lear," *Critical Inquiry*, **30**(4), 781.

4 *How Asia Advertises: The Most Successful Campaigns in Asia-Pacific and the Marketing Strategies Behind Them*, Jim Aitchison, John Wiley & Sons Asia, 2002.

5 http://www.asiamarketresearch.com (accessed 17 April 2005).

6 "Woman sues SK-II over skin damage", *Straits Times*, 9 March, 2005.

7 http://www.sk2.com.

8 See Appadurai, Arjun (1996), *Modernity at Large: Cultural Dimensions of Modernity*. London and Minneapolis: University of Minnesota Press.

9 "Saris and bhangra rhythms: ads in Asia go Bollywood", *Asian Wall Street Journal*, December 17–19 2004, A5–A7.

10 Iwabuchi, Koichi (2002), *Recentering Globalization: Popular Culture and Japanese Transnationalism*. Durham, NC: Duke University Press.

11 See Iwabuchi, Koichi (1992), *Feeling Asian Modernities: Transnational Consumption of Japanese TV Dramas*, Hong Kong: Hong Kong University Press.

12 "Korean wave to be promoted in new regions", *Korea Times*, 17 March, 2005.

13 "How Korea became cool", Victoria James, *New Statesman*, 7 March, 2005.

14 "Korean wave to be promoted in new regions", *Korea Times*, 17 March, 2005.

15 "Hallyu boosts Korea's GDP by 0.2%", www.korea.net, 4 May, 2005.

16 "Hallyu boosts Korea's GDP by 0.2%", Kim Sung-jin, *Korea Times*, 3 May, 2005.

17 See Mazzarella W. (2003), *Shoveling Smoke: Advertising and Globalization in Contemporary India*. Durham, NC: Duke University Press.

18 In Parks L. and Kumar S. (eds) (2003), *Planet TV: A Global Television Reader*. New York: NYU Press, pp. 341–59.

19 Park, Seah (2003), "Coming to a theater near you?; South Korean movie exports mark shift away from manufacturing", *Wall Street Journal* (Eastern edn). October 3, p. A.10.

20 Fong Mei, (2004), "The little people: personal avatars are big business in Korea; Can they make it big in other countries?", *Wall Street Journal* (Eastern edn). March 22, p. R.4.

21 Korean Film Commission.

22 In Iwabuchi, Koichi (2002), *Recentering Globalization*, Duke University Press, p. 124.

23 See Xiaoming, Hao and Teh Leng Leng (2004), "The impact of Japanese popular culture on the Singaporean youth", *Keio Communication Review*, (26), 17–36.

24 Anthony Giddens (1991) *The Consequences of Modernity*. Stanford, CA: Stanford University Press, p. 54.

25 Murray Weidenbaum, *Greater China: The Next Economic Superpower?*, St. Louis: Washington University Center for the Study of American Business, (1993), pp. 2–3.

26 Wang Gungwu, *China And The Chineseeng* (2004); "The Impact of Japanese Popular Culture on the Singaporean Youth", *Keio Communication Review*, (26), 17–36; in *The Consequences of Modernity Overseas*, Singapore Times, Academic Press, 1993.

27 Lee Kam Hing and Lee Poh Ping, "Malaysian Chinese business: who survived the crisis?", *Kyoto Review Of Southeast Asia*, Review Essay, October 2003, p. 7.

28 In her book *World on Fire*, Amy Chua describes the backlash against the Chinese minority in Indonesia. During the elections, many politicians called for the confiscation of Chinese assets. Consequently, many Chinese left the country, taking their capital with them, thereby throwing Indonesia into an economic crisis.

29 Middle East Banker, "Drawing the roadmap for Islamic banking", http://www. Bankerme.Com.

30 See www.mecca-cola.com.

31 LG press release, 15 September, 2003 http://www.lge.com.

32 United Nations Population Division (1999), *The World at Six Billion*. See also: http://www.un.org.

33 "Innovation blowback: disruptive management practices from Asia", John Seely and John Hagel III, *McKinsey Quarterly*, (1), 2005.

34 See *The Economist*, "Mumbai's marketer: Kabir Mulchandani makes televisions. He also thinks he knows how to sell them to India's elusive middle class," **347**(8074), 66 (1) 1998.

35 *Euromonitor*, "China usurps USA as world's largest beer market", 12 November 2002.

36 "Karsanbhai Patel – a clean sweep", June 2002, seen at http://www. indiaprofile.com.

37 "Hindustan Lever Limited: levers for change", Sumantra Ghoshal and Charlotte Butler, INSEAD case study, 2001.

38 "Competing with giants: survival strategies for emerging market companies", Niraj Dawar and Tony Frost, *Harvard Business Review*, March–April 1999, 119–29.

39 *Local Knowledge: Further Essays in Interpretive Anthropology*. New York: Basic Books, 1983, p. 59.

40 Belk, Russell W., "Third world consumer culture", in E. Kumçu and A. Fuat Firat (eds), *Research in Marketing*, supplement 4, JAI Press, Greenwich, CT, 1988.

41 *Consumer Behaviour in Asia*, Hellmut Schütte with Deanna Ciarlante, Macmillan Business – now Palgrave Macmillan, 1998, p. 93, Figure 4.2.

42 *Culture's Consequences: International Differences in Work-related Values*, Hofstede, G., Beverly Hills: Sage, 1980.

43 Adapted from *Culture's Consequences: International Differences in Work-related Values*, Hofstede, G., Beverly Hills: Sage, 1980.

44 Murakami, Yasuske (1984), "Ie society as a pattern of civilization: an introduction by Kozo Yamamura," *Journal of Japanese Studies*, **10**(2), 281–363.

45 Adapted from H. Markus and S. Kitayama (1991), "Culture and the self: implications for cognition, emotion and motivation", *Psycological Review*, 1998, pp. 224–53.

46 "Japan's gross national cool", Douglas McGray, *Foreign Policy*, May–June 2002, pp. 45–54.

47 *Consumption and Material Culture in Contemporary Japan*, Michael Ashekenazi and John Clammer (eds), 1999, New York: Columbia University Press.

48 www.lvmh.com.
49 *The Regional Multinationals: MNEs and Global Strategic Management*, Alan Rugman, 2005, Cambridge University Press.
50 Cialdini, Robert B. (2001), *Influence: Science and Practice*. Allyn & Bacon. 4th edn.
51 http://www.ieatpe.org.tw/tit/tit2_16.htm, accessed 23 January 2005.
52 "I'll Have that Snoopy Please," Jessica Tan, *The Straits Times* Monday, October 4, 1999, p. 5.
53 Chadha, Radha (forthcoming), *Luxury Brands in Asia*, Columbia University Press.
54 Tse, D. (1996) "Understanding Chinese People as Consumers: past findings and future propositions." In M.H.Bond (ed.) *The Handbook of Chinese Psychology*, Hong Kong: Oxford University Press. See also Leung, K. (1996) "The role of beliefs in Chinese culture." In M. H. Bond (ed.) *The Handbook of Chinese Psychology* (p. 249). Hong Kong: Oxford University Press.
55 Worm, V. (1997), *Vikings and Mandarins*. Copenhagen: Munksgaard International Publishers, pp. 116–17.
56 Adapted from Hofstede, Geert. 1991. *Cultures and Organizations: Software of the Mind*. Maidenhead: McGraw-Hill.
57 Rugman, Alan and Alain Verbeke (2004), "A perspective on regional and global strategies of multinational enterprises", *Journal of International Business Studies*, **35**(1), 3–18, 2004.

CHAPTER 4

ASIAN COUNTRY BRANDING

If you do things well, do them better. Be daring, be first, be different, be just.　　　　Anita Roddick, Founder, The Body Shop

The past few decades have seen many Asian countries embrace market capitalism and open their economies to foreign participation and influence. There has been a considerable increase in the number of global companies setting up shops in Asia. With exotic locales, unique cultures and sun-kissed beaches, tourism has become one of the booming industries in Asia. Recently, the active promotion of high-quality, affordable healthcare and a renewed focus on developing a world-class education system has developed health and edu-tourism.

As many Asian countries are able to boast one or more of the above attractions, the need to differentiate and brand themselves to attract capital and people is rapidly gaining importance.

Countries create distinct identities in the minds of potential tourists, business travelers, traders, importers and consumers. As the number of tourist arrivals and business travelers continues to increase in the world,[1] countries must increase their share of the pie by building strong top-of-mind awareness. Recall of the destination should be instant when they try to plan a holiday or the venue for the next company-wide conference. Branding is the answer.

Although one of the obvious reasons that countries brand themselves is to persuade tourists (and their dollars) away from other, often neighboring, countries, the more important reason is to create a positive image and gain instant cachet for local products, when exported. Selling Italian shoes and German engineering is much easier than selling Australian shoes and Czech engineering. Branding can also serve a purpose in the global marketplace through attracting investments and skilled workers.

Internally, governments can use their new brand identity to channel development and boost public morale. For many decades, due to Asia's relatively lower level of social and economic development, the products and services emerging from the Asian region did not enjoy a positive country-of-origin effect. Studies done in the 1970s portrayed a dire picture for Asian companies. But now, with new branded identities to rely on, they can fight entrenched beliefs not only in their home countries but outside as well.

Overall, country branding can be divided into three main categories by the purpose they serve:

■ Export branding

■ Generic country branding

■ Internal country branding.

The benefits of each branding activity are listed in Table 4.1. But while branding is beneficial, it also offers different types of challenges. Some of these challenges are analyzed later in the chapter by looking at country branding campaigns that have been developed in Asia.

TABLE 4.1 **Benefits of branding places**	
Country branding activities	**Benefits**
Export branding	Positive halo effect on products
	Increased ability to export
Generic country branding	Ability to attract tourists and skilled workers
	Increased ability to attract investments
	Ability to reduce incentives for investors
	Increased cost pressure on competition
	Resilience to financial crisis
	Ability to sustain higher prices
Internal country branding	Ability to retain skilled workers
	Increased productivity from better morale

Source: VentureRepublic

Export branding

International marketers have long realized that stressing the origin of their country can help their sales: German cars, French wines or Asian hotels all stress their country of origin to leverage the positive associations with these places. "Made in" Germany, France or Japan helps to increase a brand's equity, especially for companies that do not have a high-profile name. In these cases, a product's country of origin acts as a proxy for judging the quality of the product. A country's intangible assets are associations on quality dimensions that a country has gradually acquired through the export of goods and services.

A product's country of origin acts like a heuristic or rule of thumb for consumers. Psychologists emphasize that most people are "cognitive misers", relying on mental shortcuts to make decisions. Princeton researcher Daniel Kahneman's research on these shortcuts won him the Nobel prize in 1996. In several studies carried out with the late Amos Tversky, he showed that the framing of information greatly influences how we perceive it. In one study, they asked people to decide hypothetically what procedure to take to cure a disease. Unsurprisingly, most preferred a procedure that "saved" 80 percent of people to one that "killed" 20 percent.[2]

Consumers will rely on the origin of a product when they are unable to detect the true quality of the product before purchase. For example, consumers typically infer the quality of a Japanese car from the "halo effect"[3] of Japan's association with high-quality, reliable products. Country image, in this case, is used as what researchers call an "extrinsic cue", a piece of information that is distinct from the product characteristics but tells the consumer something about the product.

Paying attention to country-of-origin labels is particularly important for brand managers whose brands are in the initial stages of development. For relatively unknown brands, consumers are more likely to rely on the country of origin. In contrast, for brands with more awareness and loyalty, the country of origin is likely to play a minor role. In a 2003 study conducted by ad agency Leo Burnett, 65 percent of Asian consumers surveyed claimed to "buy the brands I like regardless of where they come from".[4]

In another survey on global brands done at Harvard Business School,[5] researchers found that most people actually dissociated American brands from the actions of the American government. About 88 percent of people selected well-known global brands rather than local alternatives when asked which products they would like to buy. For these consumers, buying global brands showed that they were connected to a global society. They did not regard big US brands as being identified with America itself. Only 12 percent did not want to buy such brands – a small number.

Asian managers should pay particular attention to the country associations for their products. In an academic study, researchers examined people living in a collectivist country (Japan) compared to those living in an individualistic country (US), and found that collectivists will favor products from their home country more so than individualists, because their group affiliations are stronger.[6]

One of the challenges of this kind of branding is to keep in mind historical and cultural sensitivity. It is crucial to remember the history of relations between different Asian countries when planning a branding campaign. In a study about Chinese perceptions of Japanese products, Jill Klein and her colleagues from INSEAD business school found strong animosity toward Japanese brands.[7] The authors developed a model called the "foreign animosity model" to capture how likely consumers are to boycott products from different countries. As Japanese brands try to expand in their former colonies such as Taiwan, South Korea and China, sentiments of animosity are likely to be rampant, especially among the older generations. In fact, until recently, Japanese television programs were banned in South Korea.[8] And in China, memories of the war still resonate strongly and impact the way that Japanese managers manage their brands.

The Toyota campaign in China serves as a good example of a campaign that went wrong because managers did not pay enough attention to this history. In 2003, Chinese consumers complained en masse about a series of magazine ads released by Japanese car maker Toyota, saying that Toyota had insulted their country. One of the ads featured a Toyota vehicle towing a truck, which looked like a Chinese military vehicle, through a Tibetan landscape. The other ad showed two stone lions, traditional Chinese symbols of authority, bowing in front of a Toyota truck. The copy read: "You cannot but respect the Prado." Chinese journalists commented that the pictures implied the superiority of Japanese products over Chinese ones. Confronted by these attacks, Toyota had to recall the ads. While Toyota remains a popular brand in Japan because of its products' quality, the company will inevitably have to be more sensitive to the history of relations between the two countries.[9]

Government's role in country branding

As discussed earlier, branding a country is far more complex than branding a product or a service. A strong country brand creates a strong channel for countries to attract foreign investment. Malaysia and Singapore serve as two examples where the governments have envisioned branding as one of the crucial factors to drive the country ahead.

The Malaysian government's commitment to branding the country on an ongoing basis has the support of Prime Minister Badawi himself. This was evident in his speech at the Invest Malaysia 2005 Conference, where he said:

> In branding Malaysia, let us be known as a nation that emphasizes quality, security, service and efficiency. In branding corporate Malaysia, let us be bold in reinforcing that we have large and well-managed companies ... and that Malaysian companies are able to compete with the best that the global business community has to offer.[10]

Similarly, in Singapore, International Enterprise (IE) Singapore (a government institution tasked with internationalizing domestic businesses) has taken the initiative to educate and encourage Singaporean companies to build successful brands. In 2002, IE Singapore launched the Singapore Brand Awards which recognized 14 Singapore-listed companies with a combined brand value of US$4.62 billion.[11]

Given the tremendous advantages that countries and their businesses can derive by creating a positive brand image, countries in Asia that have traditionally borne the brunt of a low-cost, low-quality image can benefit from building strong country brands.

Generic country branding

With generic country branding, an important challenge is to find a single, all-encompassing message that also differentiates the country from its competitors. Many countries have tried this in the past ten years, with different levels of success. Figure 4.1 documents the different initiatives of country branding in Asia. "Inclusiveness" refers to the ability of country branding campaigns to be comprehensive – whether these campaigns are able to capture the diversity of the country within their scope. "Differentiation" refers to the ability of country branding campaigns to project a unique positioning and value proposition to stand apart from other campaigns.

What makes it difficult to find one unifying message is that countries are, by their nature, diverse, with activities that are far more difficult to summarize than those of a company. Countries have diverse populations which are simultaneously audiences and stakeholders for the generic country branding campaigns. For Malaysia, this could have been a big challenge, given its ethnic diversity. But the country turned an apparent difficulty into a strength, developing one of the more successful branding campaigns for an Asian country. Malaysia, Thailand, Singapore and India are now discussed in more detail.

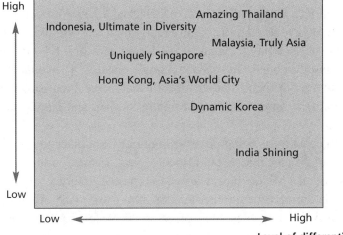

Figure 4.1 Country branding initiatives
Source: VentureRepublic

Malaysia, Truly Asia

In 1997, the Malaysian government launched the Malaysia, Truly Asia campaign to counter the crippling effects that the Asian financial crisis had had on its economy. It was time to build Brand Malaysia to attract the tourists and their dollars.

Although a former British colony, Malaysia was not as big a tourist destination for the British as other neighboring countries such as Thailand and Singapore. The Malaysian government was faced with the challenge of establishing a position in the minds of tourists who knew nothing about the country.

The brand team found a unique and differentiated positioning by projecting the country as a place to sample the diverse cultures of Asia – Chinese, Indian, Malay and those of other nationalities – in a safe, modern environment where customers could find great value for money. It also offered multiculturalism with cosmopolitanism, concentrating on the diversity of the region in terms of food and culture. It projected Malaysia as a safe destination for those tourists who feared the vastness and incomprehensibility of Asia – its cultural practices, its cuisines, and its languages. Malaysia could become a great destination for those who wanted a safe taste of Asia.

The campaign was a resounding success. Backed by vast amounts of money spent on tourism development, the country now sees approximately 13 million tourists annually.[12] January 2004 saw a record 1.4 million tourists, the largest the country has seen in a single month.[13] The country is also equipped to provide niche tourism – health and medical tourism, eco-tourism, edu-tourism, sport tourism, adventure tourism and culture and lifestyle tourism.

With time, the country is being promoted not only as a place to sample the melting pot of Asian cultures, but also as a great destination for shopping. Tourists from the Middle East, wary of Europe and America, are traveling to Malaysia during their summer months – May to August. Although hot itself, Malaysia is cooler than many places in the Middle East. Besides, the Middle Eastern tourists enjoy the water theme parks, love to shop and enjoy the diverse Malaysian cuisine because, having such a large Muslim population, halal food is freely available.

With the growing success of Brand Malaysia, there has been the launch of the Malaysia: My Second Home campaign. Aimed at wealthy retirees, it is popular with the British, Singaporeans and Chinese.[14]

With the maturity of Brand Malaysia, there has been a focus on the quality of goods and services being provided to the tourists. Tourists are no longer coming to Malaysia simply because it is cheap, but rather because it has some of the finest resorts, luxury getaways and secluded retreats to offer. Divers and golfers are heading to Malaysia from other parts of Asia because of the good quality that the country can offer in those fields.

Although the campaign has been a success so far, it is easy to foresee the difficulties it might have with time. Because of its heavy association with "Asia", the brand will take a beating if ever world events cause "Asia" to take on a negative connotation. Another challenge may be to stress qualities other than its diversity, because if ever ethnic tensions were to arise in Malaysia, its positioning of "Truly Asia" could risk becoming a grotesque joke. These are some of the challenges it faces as the brand moves forward.

Amazing Thailand

Another successful generic country branding campaign, "Amazing Thailand" was also created just after the economic crisis of 1997. It was able to cleverly bring together diverse aspects of a country under the umbrella of one word: amazing.

The Thai government launched the campaign in 1998. Together with ad agency Leo Burnett, hotel, tour guide, restaurant and souvenir associations, after two months of brainstorming they came up with the Amazing Thailand idea, cashing in on all the things that Thailand had to offer – historic and cultural sites, fabulous cuisine, beautiful beaches, and very friendly people.

The Thai government allocated US$37.9 million in 1998–99 for the promotion of Brand Thailand. Although this caused an uproar at the time because the country was facing an economic downturn due to the Asian financial crisis, the effects were extraordinary – tourist arrivals went up from US$7 million to US$10 million in the five years from the launch of the campaign. Amazing Thailand's focus was on increasing the tourist influx by promoting shopping, food, beaches and traditional massages.

The tagline for the campaign was successful because of its blanket nature – it was able to capture all aspects of Thailand that were amazing. If the royal palaces and beaches were amazing, so were the traffic and the spicy food. If Thai hospitality was amazing, so were the shockingly low prices. The slogan was able to create a discrete identity for Thailand by infusing every part of it with amazement for tourists. It was broad enough to capture the many aspects of life, be it leisure, culinary indulgence or historical sites, yet memorable enough to stand out for what it was selling: amazement.

With time, the tourism board has changed its positioning of Thailand, as the brand has established itself in the minds of people worldwide. Once it had carved a market for itself and made its presence felt in the minds of tourists, the government went on to develop a more mature brand. In 2003, the government launched the Unseen Thailand campaign which was expanded to cover not only culture, food, world heritage sites and boutique hotels, but golfing, adventure, diving and wedding packages as well. Thailand was also being promoted as the ideal destination to shoot films. The brand was reaching maturity. In an analogy with human maturity, one could say it went from a gawping backpacking tourist to a young urban professional looking for "something different".

The Thai positioning of 2004 was Happiness on Earth. Wanting to shed the earlier ambiguous connotation of amazing, the government wants to equate holidays, which people associate with happiness, with Thailand. The new stress is on the outstanding spa facilities, golf courses and river cruises that the country has to offer. These new offers position Thailand as a luxury brand, aimed at the rich professional looking for an indulgent holiday. Thailand has come a long way from the gawping backpacker it once was.

Uniquely Singapore

When Uniquely Singapore was launched in March 2004, there was a variety of reactions. The locals asked what exactly was unique about Singapore. The marketing world thought it was devoid of meaning because everything is unique and it was not a word that could be "owned"[15] and come to be associated with any brand, and members of the government were concerned that the advertisements were eroding the moral standards of the populace and projecting a sullied image of Singapore by promoting night clubs and bar-top dancing. They would prefer it to be a family destination.[16]

While it is true that the claim of uniqueness is too vacuous to create a powerful and evocative brand, it is also true that the advertisements have worked well for Singapore. For the first eight months of 2004, Indonesian and Thai visitors grew 28 and 24 percent respectively.[17]

A description of some advertisements might better explain why. The Uniquely Spiky advertisement shows a pair of tango dancers in Buenos Aires who are so inspired by Singapore's new twin buildings (Esplanade – Theatres on the Bay) that the woman has incorporated the metallic spikes in her costume. This is followed by a medley of images of the Esplanade, a mythical Chinese dragon, a spiky durian fruit and a Singapore girl with a hip, spiky hairdo. The Uniquely Poured advertisement shows a demure Japanese geisha serving tea to two businessmen. After delicately laying out everything, she pours the tea in "Teh Tarik" style (from a great height into the glass) with a lot of gusto. This is followed by some uniquely Singapore experiences – the "Teh Tarik" experience, the Singapore sling, the waterfall at Jurong Bird Park and a spa treatment.

Because Singapore is already a well-known Asian stopover and business destination, it was not necessary for the advertisements to educate the viewers about Singapore, unlike countries like Malaysia and Thailand. The ad creators stayed away from lilting images of beautiful countryside and exotic massages. Instead, what they created was an image of fun, and

Singapore as Destination Fun. It is in keeping with the government's aims to make Singapore a great weekend hotspot for people in Asia and Australia. They want to provide enough cultural and sporting activities, besides shopping, for the tourist to hop on a flight to Singapore for the weekend without having to consult any guide, secure in the knowledge that something or other would be on to entice and entertain them.[18]

The tourism board has already poured a lot of energy into changing the image of Singapore for the tourist. Extreme sports events are being held with regularity – bungee jumping off the Stamford Raffles building, Action Asia Challenge where participants have to get through a 50-kilometer race by completing gruelling tasks, and so on.[19] Singapore is trying to shift its image from a staid, clean, safe and chewing gum-banning country to one where the cultural and sporting events' calendar is so alive that people from all over Asia will want to stop by and partake of the year-round festivities in a uniquely Singaporean style.

The nature of the campaign works well in differentiating it from its neighboring countries' campaigns, like those for Thailand and Malaysia. While the latter seek to establish images of lilting peace and security in the minds of tourists, Singapore's ads deliberately go the other way – invoking images of energy and equating them with fun. This enables Singapore to strongly differentiate itself in the region.

India Shining

Over December 2003 and January 2004, Indians were bombarded with the government's advertising campaign called India Shining. It aired 9472 times on all the leading television channels, with print ads appearing 392 times during the first two weeks of January. The reason for this massive media attack was quite simple – the party in power had had a great run during its four-year term, and it was getting ready for early elections. Its win was never more assured. It was at the very height of its popularity.[20]

In October 2003, the government briefed several advertising firms on what it wanted to project through the ads. Of all the slogans created, one in particular seemed to hit the mark: India Shining. It was time to remind the people what a fabulous four years it had been of economic growth, prosperity and stability for everyone: urban and rural, old and young. The campaign was unique – it was the first time a political party in India had used corporate branding strategies to project itself to the people.

But the ads would not work if they were seen to be an overt political campaign. Therefore there was never any mention of the party. They were "government" advertisements.[21] The campaign was followed up with almost half a million phone calls made every day to the Indian public with a prerecorded message by the prime minister, leader of the ruling party, highlighting the achievements of his party. There was no escaping the campaign – there was also discussion and debate in all the leading media about the content.

The content of the advertisements tried to create a "feel-good" factor for the viewer. One example showed a young girl getting dressed for school, in front of the mirror. The punch line said: "I am going to study further. Lower interest rates on education loans." The message was that young children could continue their education because interest rates on education had been reduced significantly. Similarly, other ads sent messages like: despite low interest rates in the country, senior citizens were benefiting from higher interest rates on their investments through the "Dada Dadi" bonds; people were able to start their own businesses because of a US$2.3 billion fund created to promote small-scale industries; the state of the Indian economy was improving because of increasing foreign exchange reserves due to increased exports. The mood all around was soaring. India was truly shining.

All indicators pointed to a win for the party in power, the NDA (National Democratic Alliance) in the May 2004 elections. But to the surprise of all, the media and the NDA, it lost to the opposition, the Congress Party. Media watchers could not fathom how their opinion and exit polls could have been so wrong. But while the NDA was getting the viewers to Feel Good, the Congress Party had launched its own ad campaign. The advertising was in black and white only, in Hindi, and targeted the lower middle class and the rural market. It used the claims made by the NDA, reversed the imagery and used the slogan *Aam admi ko kya mila?* – What did the common man gain? The Congress Party focused on all the things the common man hadn't been a part of in the new, rising and shining India. There were still problems of infrastructure, water, electricity and unemployment. The chasm between the rich and the poor had never looked wider. The NDA government's policies had benefited the rich and had allowed the middle class to rise. Meanwhile, the rural citizens and those from the lower middle classes struggled harder to bridge the gap.[22]

There were many reasons for the failure of the NDA brand, but mainly it was the gap between promise and delivery. Some media pundits said that there was nothing wrong with the campaign; it was the core product that was not strong. Others said that the brand was not forward-looking, it did not promise anything to the viewer. What were the viewers going to get in exchange for their votes? Another important point was that the campaign was created in English, a language foreign to the masses of India. The slogan India Shining and the byline Feel Good have no straightforward equivalents in the regional languages,[23] hence alienating the largest voter bank. There was also the problem of the use of technology in connecting with the public. It was damaging to the prime minister's image to be perceived as the equivalent of a telemarketer.[24] The most important reason, however, was that the critical mass of people did not connect with the advertisement because it didn't portray their experience of the past few years.[25] To see the people who had benefited and compare their situation with that shown in the ad, people perceived the advertising as arrogant and callous.

So although the NDA had tried to take advantage of slick, emotional advertising techniques, one could say that the brand failed to take off because the difference between their projection and reality was visible to everyone. Also, to brand a country means having a unified communication – projecting the values of the brand in a cohesive message. But this is difficult to do when branding a country because there are a number of realities that need to be merged and streamlined. Inevitably, some will be skipped over. It was the NDA's downfall to have picked the smallest group – the urban middle class – as the key audience. It ignored the realities of those who had fallen by the wayside, something that the Congress Party was quick to pick up on in its reply.

Future opportunities

As the brand image for Asian countries is refined for tourism, other economic agendas need to be branded as well. After selling the beaches, cuisine and ancient temples, it is time to stress other financially advantageous qualities that can be developed into long-term, stable brand attributes. There are two areas of opportunity that seem especially promising and critical for Asia: education and healthcare.

Branding places for education

The market for education in Asia is booming and, given the population growth estimates, the market is likely to be even more pronounced in the next few years, especially in the postgraduate sector where institutes are competing for large cohorts of Asian MBAs. Between 1998 and 2003, the number of applicants to the GMAT, the qualifying entrance test for MBA schools, almost tripled in India and China.[26] This trend is likely to continue and even intensify. In the next five years, India will add 16 million people to the 25–34 age cohort, reaching almost 200 million.[27] Not surprisingly, many American and European schools are already seeing Asia as the only area of real potential growth. In contrast to the booming Asian market, the market for MBA students in the US is pretty sluggish, with an overall decrease of applicants in the past few years.

Many business schools in Europe, North America and Australia are already benefiting from this boom in the Asian education market. SUNY Buffalo offered the first MBA degree program in Dailian, China in 1984. Since then, many universities have followed in its footsteps, with similar programs throughout China. In India, many business schools are preparing to enter the market. There are, however, wide differences between India and China in the education market. In China, only 56 universities were given permission by the Ministry of Education to offer the MBA degree, with each school allowed to accept 200 MBA students annually. In India, the number of MBA programs offered in the past 10 years has skyrocketed. All over the country, institutes have been set up.

There are also wide differences in how managers from different Asian countries perceive MBA graduates. Managers in Hong Kong, Taiwan, Japan, and Australia hold MBA degrees in low esteem, but managers in India, the Philippines, and Thailand consider them important.[28] Attracting students from these three countries will consequently be easier.

For Asian countries to compete for this educational market there needs to be a concerted effort from governments, businesses and universities to brand countries as places for education. One of the pitfalls of country branding in Asia is that it focuses on the exotic, at the expense of other brand dimensions such as excellence, especially as it relates to knowledge development. Many countries in Asia have a strong tradition of promoting knowledge. Sima Qian, grand historian of the emperor and author of the first full history of China, emphasized the importance of knowledge in Chinese society:

A gentleman is eager and tireless in learning and makes unremitting efforts to improve himself. He always tries to extend the knowledge he has earned further, to expand it greater, to exalt it higher, and to explore it deeper.[29]

Countries such as India and China are rarely associated with great education though. For a long time, they were associated with low literacy levels. In the past five years, however, Asian engineering and business schools have gained credibility. Indian institutes of management and technology have been shown to be the most selective in the world, accepting only a small proportion of the thousands of applicants. They also have the highest test level scores, although this must be seen in the context of the high number of applications received by these institutions every year.

INSEAD – the global learning network

INSEAD is one of the world's largest top-tier graduate business schools, with two comprehensive and fully connected campuses in Asia (Singapore) and Europe (France). The business school provides a unique learning experience. Participants interact with faculty and fellow students in an unparalleled multicultural environment, gaining essential insights into international business practice. INSEAD's growing community of over 30,000 alumni worldwide creates lifelong opportunities for professional development and networking. This global and multicultural perspective sets INSEAD apart in the field of international management education and research.[30]

But Indian and Chinese schools have not gained the global reputation of institutions like INSEAD because they have failed to attract high-quality faculty or students from other countries. As trade between countries within Asia intensifies, more cultural and educational exchanges will be necessary to boost a better understanding of cultural and trade practices. In addition, attracting students from other parts of the world will increase the reputation of these institutions, by building a global image. The global orientation of a brand has already been shown to increase product evaluations.[31] There is no reason why this halo effect should not hold true for educational institutions. This is where INSEAD has found a unique differentiation against the competition, as INSEAD has always embraced cultural diversity and global perspectives in all matters.

Branding places for medical tourism

Another great opportunity for country branding is health tourism and medical treatment. Medical tourism is defined as a country's efforts to brand itself as a destination for healthcare services and facilities. With the European and North American population aging, the rise of medical treatment in these countries and the decrease of social security reimbursements, more and more people are looking at Asia for medical services. Add to that a lack of top-notch hospitals in the Middle East and Africa, and Asia is well poised to become a center for medical treatment and health tourism. Currently, Africans of Asian origin (such as the large Indian diaspora in East Africa) spend as much as US$20 billion a year on healthcare outside their countries – Nigerians alone spend an amazing US$1 billion a year.[32] While for a long time this market has been dominated by European and North American facilities, Asian countries are now quickly catching up.

An Asian country that is moving aggressively in this area is Thailand. In 2002, the number of foreign patients seeking treatment in Thailand grew by 13 percent[33] compared to the previous year, totaling more than 600,000 foreigners visiting private hospitals. Of this total, 60,000 individuals who specifically traveled to Thailand for medical treatment or health services accounted for another 10 percent. In 2003, rough estimates suggested that the number of foreign patients had grown to 1 million.[34] As news gets around that Thailand provides superior healthcare and medical services at very affordable rates, the destination is attracting an ever-increasing number of visiting patients.

Another rising star in that sector is India. India has already attracted many software companies looking for low-cost development and staying for quality. The same phenomenon is happening in the healthcare industry despite the fact that the country only has 51 doctors for every 100,000 people, compared with 279 per 100,000 in America.[35] India is increasingly taking advantage of a lower cost structure and excellent doctors to treat foreign patients. Strategy consulting firm McKinsey recently predicted that medical tourism could earn India more than US$2 billion a year by 2012.[36] The country attracted 150,000 foreign patients in 2003, and the large overseas population of Indian origin, nearly 1.5 million in UK alone, who may combine treatment with family visits.[37]

This is not surprising given the difference in costs with other countries. At Aravind Eye Hospital,[38] a leading facility specializing in the treatment of cataracts, the cost per operation is less than US$50, compared to around US$3,000 in the US. Aravind performs 200,000 cataract operations in the world. Open-heart surgery could cost up to US$70,000 in the UK and up to US$150,000 in the US; in India's private hospitals, it could cost between US$3,000 and US$10,000, depending on how complicated the case is. Knee surgery (for both knees) costs US$7,700 in India compared to double that amount in Britain. Cosmetic surgery costs three to four times less in India than in the West. Quality is ensured because of the high-level training that Indian doctors receive, as well as the number of operations they perform. As a result, some European health administrations are already considering sending cardiac patients to India to ease the burden of their congested hospitals. While the business of healthcare services has long remained essentially domestic, this is rapidly changing and becoming more global.

Conclusion

Countries, like brands, exert a considerable influence on the products or services that originate from them. Not only does a strong country brand attract tourists, but it also enhances a country's attractiveness to foreign investment. Most importantly, the strong brand equity of a country extends to the product and services emerging from that country. Given Asia's historic perception around low cost and thus its effect on the country of origin, this assumes special significance. Asian countries and their governments need to realize the criticality of branding their countries and must extend full involvement and support for branding initiatives. Moreover, understanding the complexity of the whole process, governments should take the initiative to ensure the buy-in of all internal and external stakeholders.

Notes

1   Between 1995 and 2000, the number of tourist arrivals in the world increased from 457 to 700 million arrivals. See http://www.world-tourism.org for the latest figures on world tourism.
2   See Tversky, A. and Kahneman (1974), "Judgment under certainty: heuristics and biases", *Science*, (211), 1124–30; Tversky, A. and Kahneman (1973), "Availability: A heuristic for judging frequency and probability", *Cognitive Psychology*, (5), 207–32.
3   Han, C. Min (1989), "Country image: halo or summary construct?" *Journal of Marketing Research*, (26), 222–9.

4 The survey was done in China, South Korea, India, Indonesia and the Philippines with 1,000 people. See Madden, Normandy (2003), "Brand origin not major factor for most Asians", *Advertising Age*, **74**(14), 33.

5 Holt, Doug, Quelch, John, and Taylor E. (2004), "How global brands compete", *Harvard Business Review*, **82**(9), 68–75.

6 Gurhan-Canli, Zeynep and Durairaj Maheswaran (2000), "Cultural variations in country of origin effects," *Journal of Marketing Research*, **37**(3), 309–17.

7 Klein, Jill G., Richard Ettenson and Marlene D. Morris (1998), "The animosity model of foreign product purchase: An empirical test in the People's Republic of China," *Journal of Marketing*, **62**(1), 89–100.

8 Iwabuchi Koichi (2004), *Recentering Globalization*, Durham, NC, Duke University Press.

9 "Toyota recalls 'offensive' sports vehicle ads in China", *Straits Times*, Friday, December 5, 2003.

10 Speech by Yab Dato Seri Abdullah Ahmad Badawi, prime minister and minster of finance of Malaysia at the Invest Malaysia 2005 Conference, 22 March, 2005.

11 Opening address by Lee Yi Shyan, CEO, International Enterprise Singapore, CEO Brand Forum, 15 November 2002, Singapore.

12 Nicole Yeong, "Investing in Malaysia: boost for tourism", *Asia Inc.*, 1 August, 2004.

13 Nicole Yeong, 2004, ibid.

14 Nicole Yeong, 2004, ibid.

15 "Anything but unique", *South China Morning Post*, 24 August, 2004.

16 "MPs want Singapore to be promoted as a family destination for tourists", Channel News Asia, 13 March, 2004.

17 Glenys Sim, "STB woos weekend visitors for fun breaks", *Straits Times*, 21 October, 2004.

18 Glenys Sim, 2004, ibid.

19 Tanya Fong, "S'pore on world map of extreme sports", *Straits Times*, 27 August, 2004.

20 *Political Advertising: The India Shining Campaign*, A. Suman, ICFAI Center for Management Research, 2004.

21 Branding the government of India, Harish Bijoor, http://www.indiainfoline. com/nevi/bran.html.

22 "Rural India humbles Vajpayee", Edward Luce, *Financial Times* (UK) 14 May, 2004.

23 *Taking the Shine off India* by Suhel Seth www.india-seminar.com, accessed 17 February, 2005.

24 *The Big Idea: Hubris at the Hustings* by Vir Sanghvi http://www.freeindiamedia. com, accessed 18 February, 2005.

25 *Japan Times*, Editorial. http://202.221.217.59/print/opinion/ed2004/ ed20040518a1.htm, accessed 18 February, 2005.

26 All figures on GMAT applications from www.gmac.com.

27 World Bank, World Development Indicators, United Nations.

28 "Seeking an MBA in Asia", *Far Eastern Economic Review*, March 16, 1995, **158**(11), 45–7.

29 In Ging D. and Y. Feng (eds) (1994), *Chinese: Golden Sayings of Chinese Thinkers over 5,000 Years*. Beijing: Sinolingua, p. 55.

30 http://www.insead.edu.

31 Steenkamp, Jan-Benedict E., Batra, Rajeev, V. Ramaswamy, Dana Alden (2003), "How perceived brand globalness creates brand value", *Journal of International Business Studies*, **34**(1), 53–65.

32 "India's global ambitions", *Far Eastern Economic Review*, November 6, 2003.

33 Department of Export Promotion, Ministry of Commerce; The Thailand Authority of Thailand.

34 "Get well away", *The Economist*, 10 September, 2004.

35 *The Economist*, 10 September, 2004, ibid.

36 *Far Eastern Economic Review*, November 6, 2003.

37 *The Economist*, 10 September, 2004, op. cit.

38 Prahalad, C. K. and Hammond, A. (2002), "Serving the world's poor, profitably", *Harvard Business Review*, **80**(9), 48–58; Prahalad, C. K. (2004), T*he Fortune at the Bottom of the Pyramid*. Wharton School Publishing.

CHAPTER 5

CELEBRITY BRANDING IN ASIA

It is only shallow people who do not judge by appearances.

Oscar Wilde

Michael Jordan vouching for Nike's shoes, Michael Schumacher endorsing Ferrari and Tiger Woods endorsing Accenture have been some of the more popular brand–celebrity collaborations in the Western world. Lately, we have seen the emergence of brand–celebrity collaborations within Asia with the Chinese basketball star Yao Ming endorsing a range of products from consumer electronics and clothing to fast-food chains in China, Bollywood superstar Shah Rukh Khan endorsing an ever-increasing portfolio of brands in India, and Jackie Chan speaking for many brands.

For a long time, companies have used well-known public figures, movie stars and sports personalities to endorse their brands, as it is widely believed that these celebrities help to build or reposition brands by extending their personality, character and popularity to the brands they endorse. This chapter looks into this brand building tool that is fast gaining currency with leading corporations in Asia.

Brand endorsement has been covered widely in the branding literature. Brand endorsement can be simply defined as a persuasive communications strategy used by companies to have their products and services represented by a spokesperson. This can be a paid, a value in kind or an unpaid activity. The main aim of product endorsement is to persuade consumers to buy a particular product/service, to shape their perceptions toward it and position it more as a lifestyle product or service rather than solely on its application merits. It is also intended to shape or change perceptions of a particular brand, increase brand popularity and consumer mind share of the brand, strengthen brand recall, and highlight differentiation and its uniqueness.

Asian brand endorsers

When China qualified for the World Cup in 2002, Adidas celebrated it by launching a campaign featuring one of China's leading football stars, Fan Zhiyi. It was the first time that Adidas had created a tailor-made TV commercial for the Chinese market.[1] In July 2004, the new Disneyland in Hong Kong named Jacky Cheung as the official spokesperson.[2]

Hong Kong pop star and actress Kelly Chen has appeared in commercials for Shiseido, Pepsi, De Beers, Epson, Samsung and many others. Kelly Chen is said to be one of the most sought-after female celebrities for commercials, so the media has dubbed her the "Queen of commercials". She was the first Asian celebrity to endorse Christian Dior's advertisements when she became the face of the brand's Capture 60/80 range of anti-aging products in 2004.[3] Kelly Chen also does charity work as Hong Kong's UNICEF ambassador along with her own Kelly Chen Children Education Fund.

Comprehensive research conducted in this field of marketing communications suggests that celebrity testimonials do increase advertisement readership. Through their extensive work in this area, many researchers have concluded that endorsement by celebrities has a positive effect on the overall branding communication and perception. Although no study has proved, in quantitative terms, any direct relationship between celebrity endorsement and an increase in sales, corporations worldwide resort to celebrity endorsements to create a positive effect for their brands.[4]

An Asian example is Jun Ji Hyun, the young South Korean actress and poster girl, who became famous after she appeared in the 2001 blockbuster movie *My Sassy Girl*. She has been used for magazine and TV commercials throughout Asia, and her TV campaign for Olympus digital cameras reportedly helped to increase the brand recognition by more than 15 percent, according to advertising company LG Ad.[5] Similarly, SK-II had a reported 50 percent sales increase in South Korea when P&G switched endorser from Shim Hae Jin to the famous movie actress Chang Jin Young in 2004.[6]

A case in point is Nike using endorsements by Tiger Woods and Cristiano Ronaldo to enter into the golf and football categories. Traditionally Nike has not been known for its products in either golf or football. Had Nike chosen the conventional marketing way of entering these segments, it would have taken some considerable time. Instead, by signing on the most famous golfer in the world, and the leading sports personality, who plays for one of the most famous football teams in the world, Nike has been able to shorten the time needed to make an impact. With Ronaldo endorsing Nike, the brand has almost established itself as an equal to Adidas, which has been the dominating brand in football for almost 50 years.

The concept of celebrity endorsements and their effect on brand building is derived from seminal research conducted in the areas of psychology and sociology. The basic premise is quite simple. With so many products in the marketplace, it is almost impossible for any consumer to absorb all the information and process it, and then decipher the information and evaluate its credibility. In such a scenario, customers seek to simplify things by depending on cues or easy rules of thumb. These cues can be either intrinsic or extrinsic and can be communicated through any medium. These simple rules of thumb help customers to sift through the massive amount of information to make an informed judgment or develop perceptions about products in the market.

With ever-increasing numbers of advertisements and newer ways of communications being devised, even these cues have become abundant. Thus, a brand endorsed by a celebrity seems to establish a connection with customers, as many relate to or aspire to emulate their personalities. As will be explained in Chapter 6, a strong brand will not only provide the basic functional benefits, but also provides its customers with an identity, a personality to whom they can relate and who expresses their own beliefs and attitudes. Using a celebrity to endorse a brand provides one such channel for the brand to associate itself with the unique identity and personality of the celebrity. At another level, a celebrity endorsement also helps the brand to achieve wider awareness and better recall. But having said that, to maximize the return on brand endorsement, companies must strive to arrive at a good match between the brand being endorsed and the endorser.

Many companies have long practiced this brand–celebrity matching. Nike, for example, uses the talent, attitude and charisma of Michael Jordan to endorse its line of shoes. Many toothbrush brands have used endorsements from dentists and dental associations to build credibility. Consumer electronics like digital cameras, laptops and so on are reviewed by the leading technology magazines and websites to drive home their value proposition. Household items like washing powder and washing-up liquid have actual users vouching for their quality and credibility. As can be seen from these examples, endorsements can be of different types, based on the product type, the value proposition, the complexity of the product offering and so on.

One of the classic examples of a successful and an effective celebrity endorsement is that of Michael Jordan endorsing Nike. Jordan, with his immense popularity, served as a role model for millions of kids around the world who aspired to become successful basketball stars. Thus, when Michael Jordan went on court wearing Nike shoes, and sporting the slogan "Just Do It", it sent a clear signal to millions of his fans and aspiring basketball players about the importance of wearing Nike if they wanted to emulate him.

Companies can use celebrities in four different roles, namely as a testimonial, an endorser, an actor or a spokesperson. In a testimonial, the celebrity endorses the brand based on his/her personal experience with the brand. As an endorser, the celebrity vouches for the brand by explicitly associating with the brand. As an actor, the celebrity becomes part of the brand story with an implicit endorsement. As a spokesperson, the celebrity is the official spokesperson for the brand, whereby he/she is explicitly identified with the brand and is authorized to express the position of the sponsor.[7]

Endorsements

Based on these many factors, endorsements can broadly be classified into four categories:

- Endorsements by ordinary people
- Endorsements by experts in their respective fields
- Endorsements by celebrities
- Mixed endorsements.

In discussing the product type as the basis for deciding the type of endorsement, the focus is usually on how motivated or involved consumers are in processing or searching for information about the product. Even though high or low involvement is relative, products can be classified into these two categories. For example, a less expensive consumer good like shampoo or soap could be categorized as a low involvement product, whereas an expensive digital camera, which requires an in-depth purchase evaluation, could be categorized as a high involvement product.

In discussing the product benefits as the basis for deciding the type of endorsement, these can be separated into two types, namely functional benefits/values and social benefits/values.

Functional benefits/values relate to consumers at a cognitive or logical level, where the product's functionality and features help consumers to perform a certain function in life. A simple example would be of a shampoo that cleanses hair.

An example of a systematic approach to celebrity endorsers is that of the French cosmetics and luxury brand company, L'Oreal. It has appointed several beauty ambassadors, among them Milla Jovovich, Laetitia Castia, Beyoncé Knowles, Andie MacDowell and Natalie Imbruglia.[8] Additionally, L'Oreal has always used famous models and actresses, like Indian actress Aishwarya Rai,[9] as endorsers for many products in its comprehensive brand portfolio.

Social benefits/values involve consumers at an emotional level. Not only do they provide consumers with a stronger bond toward the product/brand, but they also help them to project an image, or strengthen self-esteem. Today, although marketers for products like shampoo try hard to differentiate their value proposition, they are hardly about cleansing hair (a functional benefit). Whether it is to make hair silkier and smoother or give more volume, the basic premise is all about making consumers feel good about their hair and therefore about themselves and improving self-esteem. One of the key reasons in promoting the criticality of branding is that it allows firms to capture additional values through differentiation, which can no longer be achieved through mere promotion of product quality and functionality in today's competitive landscape.

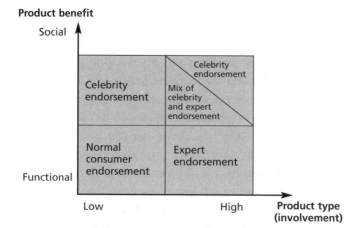

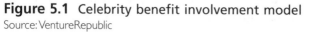

Figure 5.1 Celebrity benefit involvement model
Source: VentureRepublic

By diligently analyzing the needs of the product benefit and consumer involvement, companies can better decide on a particular endorsement type. The celebrity benefit involvement model in Figure 5.1 combines these two dimensions and provides useful guidelines for Asian companies in using endorsements as a viable channel for brand communications. This model provides useful guidelines to help companies to decide on the nature of endorsements that they may want to employ. Depending on the quadrants in which the products lie, companies can make an informed judgment for their celebrity communication strategy. The four categories are now discussed.

Endorsement by ordinary people

The bottom left quadrant consists of products which provide functional benefits, with low involvement. For these products, normal consumers can be used as product endorsers. The many advertisements for shampoos, detergents and so on, where it is common to see actual users being interviewed to gauge their opinion and experience of using that particular product, fall into this quadrant. Research shows that using an ordinary consumer as a product endorser for low involvement products has two main advantages.[10] The first is that, as the endorsing consumer belongs to the same community as other consumers, he/she is presumed to possess a similar lifestyle and product usage and is therefore in a better position to comment on the suitability of the product for that community of users. The second advantage is that the endorsing consumer is perceived to speak the truth as he/she belongs to the user community and is therefore perceived to be more believable than other paid endorsers. Despite this, there have been many instances where companies have used celebrity endorsements in low involvement categories to increase awareness levels and persuade customers to buy certain brands over others.

Endorsement by an expert

The bottom right quadrant represents products that provide functional benefits, with high involvement. For such products, endorsement by an expert would be a fitting match. An expert is someone who is seen to possess expertise related to the product class marketed and is able to give expert advice. Few people would probably argue about the effectiveness of the endorsement by the Indian dental association for Oral B's claims. The reason is simple. Customers tend to believe in the knowledge of the dental association. By the same token, a well-known appliance expert can be effective in endorsing refrigeration equipment, as would be a well-respected health practitioner for health-related products. Expert endorsement is more feasible for products with high functional and physical values. Products with such characteristics are most likely to be of high involvement, where the diligent consideration of information and evaluation of the true merit of the product are essential.[11]

Celebrity endorsement

The top left quadrant represents products which provide social benefits without high involvement. As social benefits include emotional and self-esteem benefits, consumers would like to see and emulate some well-known personalities who use those products that they want to purchase. By having a celebrity endorse these categories of products, consumers are provided with a strong personality and a persona to emulate. A celebrity can be defined as an individual who is well known by others and for whom most people have well-developed, trait-based impressions.[12]

> The South Korean cosmetics brand ETUDE used to be perceived as a brand at the lower end of the spectrum. Then actress Song Hye Gyo, who is famous across Asia because of the popular TV series *Endless Love* started to endorse it, and the brand achieved greater recognition, enabling the company to charge better price premiums.[13]

A celebrity can also be a person who is widely known to the public for his/her accomplishments in his/her respective field, be it the movies, sport, music or politics. Sometimes, however, the celebrity endorses a product or product class that has no match with his/her accomplishments or achievements. Some of the better known examples are Tiger Woods endorsing Accenture and Tag Heuer, the Bollywood star Amitabh Bachan endorsing Cadbury chocolates in India and Yao Ming endorsing McDonald's globally.

Despite this mismatch between the celebrity and the product class, companies still continue with such endorsements as these celebrities help to pass on their charisma and personality to the products they endorse.

Mixed endorsement

The top right quadrant represents products that provide social benefits, with high involvement. High end products like a premium luxury car, the latest mobile phone, or a high end consumer electronic item serve as suitable examples for this quadrant. This category of goods not only involves a lot of customer deliberation with regard to its functionality, its technology and design but also gives immense opportunity for customers to flaunt their personality and convey their beliefs. The nature of these products necessitates combining different types of endorsers for this category. Celebrities are used to bolster the self-esteem and image needs of customers and experts are used to covey the functional credibility of the products. But in certain categories like sports goods, the celebrity sports stars themselves double up as experts as they use the products on a regular basis.

Western celebrities in Japan

Japan has had a long affair with Hollywood celebrities who have endorsed many Japanese products and services. The Hollywood celebrities are often hidden from their international playgrounds where their fans cannot see their encounters with Japan. To avoid embarrassment outside Japan, the commercials they shoot often have clauses prohibiting them for export. There seems to be no limit to the fees charged by film stars and other foreign celebrities for work in Japan. However, sports stars are catching up enormously in Japan and attracting more and more attention as endorsers of brands. Football player David Beckham and his wife reportedly earned a fee of US$3.6 million from the cosmetics chain Tokyo Beauty Center on a three-day stopover in Japan – the highest fee ever paid to a foreign celebrity in Japan. David Beckham earned between US$43 million and US$50 million in 2003 on advertising alone, substantially more than his US$17 million football salary.[14]

The Japanese tend to idolize and depend on Western figures when it comes to improving their brand images. These Western celebrities have to be A list as illustrated with David Beckham. Otherwise, Japanese companies will tend to use national figures who customers can easily identify with, rather than Western figures of less than A-list status.

Numerous celebrities have appeared in countless commercials. These celebrities have been from various fields – sports stars, world famous athletes, prominent musicians, singers and popular Hollywood stars. Singapore Airlines, which has built its brand based on excellent service, has been successful in developing and managing the Singapore Girl as the iconic symbol of the brand. Using celebrity endorsement as a communication strategy has on many occasions been an effective way to influence consumer attitudes and generate positive purchase behavior for products with high social and emotional values, involving elements such as good taste, self-image, and the opinions of others.

Celebrity endorsements have been gaining higher levels of acceptance as an important tool to build brands by creating positive associations and building unique personalities.[15] Effective celebrity branding efforts focus on utilizing celebrity figures who can help to communicate a brand's unique value proposition, strengthen its identity and provide it with a desirable personality.[16]

Celebrity endorsers in Asia

When the Asian branding and endorsement landscape is analyzed, it usually excludes Japan and increasingly South Korea. They are ahead of all other Asian countries with regards to branding and have developed primarily by aligning their corporate strategies with their branding strategies. The same holds true for Japan's branding and marketing practices. Japanese companies have been known for using Western models and celebrities for their endorsements, unlike many other Asian countries, where companies predominantly use Asian celebrities. Further, these foreign brands all try to snap up popular Asian celebrities as ambassadors for their brands when trying to enter Asian markets. India's Bajaj Auto recently appointed Jackie Chan, the Hong Kong movie star, as the promoter of its latest offering, the 125-cc motorcycle, Discover. According to the company, Jackie Chan is a preferred endorser over foreign stars Tom Cruise and Pierce Brosnan in India.[17]

OSIM is another relatively new Asian brand. At the beginning of 2002, OSIM, a Singapore-based brand for healthy lifestyle products, announced the appointment of Chinese actress Gong Li as its brand ambassador in promoting the OSIM brand globally. It has always been the aim of OSIM to become a global leader in healthy lifestyle products. Incorporated in 1980 by Ron Sim, who is also the CEO and chairman of the company, OSIM offers various categories of home products with a focus on health, hygiene, nutrition, and fitness. The firm owns the largest healthcare equipment retail chain in Malaysia and, according to AC Nielsen and Gallup, is also the number one brand in the healthy lifestyle category in Singapore, Hong

Kong, Malaysia and Taiwan.[18] The appointment of Gong Li as the brand ambassador further signaled to the rest of the world the company's aggressive growth plan.[19]

Since her debut in 1992 in the movie *Red Sorghum*, an international award-winning performance, Gong Li has subsequently starred in over 20 films, including *Farewell My Concubine*, *Ju Dou* and so on. Gong Li possesses the healthy image of a modern Chinese woman – beautiful, strong, independent, and with a touch of elegance. More importantly to OSIM, Gong Li shares the company's philosophy of "Health is an attitude to life", and believes in the importance of maintaining a healthy lifestyle. While keeping a busy filming schedule, Gong Li values the time required to relax and re-energize between filming.

This made Gong Li an effective brand spokesperson because what she values in life is a good reflection of what OSIM stands for as a brand. In addition, Gong Li's fame in Asia and her recognition in the rest of the world gave her a unique advantage in helping OSIM to strengthen its brand awareness globally.[20]

Popularity is a key reason to use Asian celebrities, not only because they are well known by Asian countries and communities, but also because they are similar to the target audience. In general, it has been found that customers show a higher level of understanding and trust with things that they are familiar with and to which they can easily relate. Therefore, such things as similarity in ethnic background and cultural closeness can be important. The Chinese cosmetic brand Yue Sai Kan serves as a typical example of celebrity branding from Asia (see box).

Yue Sai Kan: the Chinese cosmetic brand

Yue Sai Kan, probably the most well-known woman in China, with the magazines *People*, *Time*, *Money*, and even the Chinese Women's Federation magazine, naming her the most renowned woman in China, is one of the earliest and best-known cosmetic brands to originate in China. Combining her command over the local practices, preferences and mindsets with her Western education and grooming, Yue Sai Kan has been successful in creating a line of cosmetics specifically for Chinese women and their skin type.[21] This is also a classic case that illustrates the fighting spirit of a Chinese woman that evolved into a very successful entrepreneur. Through her determination and business acumen, Yue Sai Kan steered her cosmetics company into the number one position in 1996 in the Chinese market. Later, by joining hands with the

American cosmetics company, Coty, she was able to expand the company's production into Shanghai, the cosmopolitan capital of China. The brand has been so successful that L'Oreal purchased the brand for an undisclosed sum of money.[22]

Using her personal charisma built over her years as a television anchor person, she also ventured into creating China's very own Barbie doll, by bringing out the Yue Sai Wa Wa (little one) doll. By creating a cartoon strip in a children's newspaper throughout China, she gave Chinese children their own girl hero.

Yue Sai Kan is an example of how Asian companies can build strong brands using their understanding of local knowledge, heritage and culture. Preserving local culture and taste, and blending it with modern management techniques instead of trying to simply copy Western brands, can be a successful way for Asian brands to move forward.

Celebrity endorsement is not an alien concept to the Asian business landscape. Many companies have already made use of this concept by hiring the services of celebrities like movie stars and pop singers to promote the company's offerings.

Compared to Western companies, however, Asian companies have not yet reaped the full benefits of celebrity endorsements. Few cases can match the phenomenal success that Nike has achieved with Michael Jordan. Two main reasons can be attributed to the lack of such successful celebrity endorsement stories from Asia. Primarily, the Asian trading mindset and way of doing business have prevented businesses from investing in building brands. Brand management as a corporate mantra is still catching up. Secondly, the number of A-list celebrities who command a wide popularity and fan base is smaller in Asia than in the Western world. This in turn has slowed the adoption of this channel of brand communications in Asia. But, as discussed in Chapter 3, the flows of pop culture across Asia will probably facilitate a generation of future Asian celebrities.

South Korean pop culture in Japan

There has been a movement in Japan over the past few years to look toward Asian celebrity figures. An example is the South Korean TV star Bae Yong Joon, star of the immensely popular South Korean television drama *Winter Sonata*, who became an A-list celebrity in Japan – much to the surprise of South Koreans. A South Korean celebrity in Japan would have been impossible to imagine just a few years ago. When Bae, nicknamed Yonsama, arrived in Tokyo to open an exhibition in April 2005, he was met by 3,500 screaming Japanese female fans at the airport.[23]

The drama *Winter Sonata* is shot at Nami Island in South Korea where almost 800 fans turn up every day. Korean Air has seen a passenger increase of 20–30 percent between Japan and South Korea, and the frenzy around the drama has contributed an estimated US$1 billion to the South Korean economy.[24] Bae has contributed significantly to the burgeoning popularity of South Korean pop culture across Asia and especially in Japan, where he was featured in a Sony digital camera campaign in 2004.[25] Prime Minister Junichiro Koizumi of Japan even referred to Bae at an international conference on The Future of Asia in June 2004, noting the increased sense of unity in the entire Asian region.[26]

Celebrity endorsement models

For any kind of celebrity endorsement to be effective, it has to fulfill certain basic prerequisites. When a company hires a spokesperson, be it a common consumer, an expert or a celebrity, in order for the endorsement to be effective, the endorser has to be attractive, should have a positive image in the society, and should be perceived as someone having the necessary knowledge. Based on these three basic requirements, researchers in this field have developed three main endorsement models. The descriptions of these three models provide companies with a strong basis for formulating and implementing celebrity endorsements strategies.

Source attractiveness model

This model states that an attractive endorser will have a positive impact on the endorsement. The endorser should be attractive to the target audience in certain aspects like physique, intellectual skills, athletic capabilities, and lifestyle. Research has proven that an attractive endorser can enhance memory to a brand.[27] However, it should be noted that the success of a celebrity campaign will depend on the "core capabilities" of the celebrity. If the celebrity is not successful in his/her respective field, the campaign may not be successful, despite the celebrity's attractiveness. But companies need to be diligent when they apply this principle in practice. Although the attractiveness of the endorser could be a major factor for enhancing brand awareness, this is truer in low involvement product classes. The reason is simple. As the product or the features themselves are not powerful enough to capture consumers' attention, the attractive celebrities would do that. Moreover, these products do not demand long deliberation on the part of the customer. Therefore the external cue of a celebrity can enhance customer perceptions. But for higher involvement products, consumers would usually be more concerned about the authentication of the claims presented in the advertisements and endorsements rather than the attractiveness of the endorser.

A case in point is the Cadbury brand in India, which suffered a major setback when worms were found in Cadbury's chocolates.[28] To counter this negative impact on the brand, the company hired Amitabh Bachan, who is considered a demigod in India, to advertise the chocolates. The charisma and stature of Bachan in the Indian mindset was so powerful that the endorsement not only turned around the perceptions about the brand, but also helped the brand to sell more than it had previously. As chocolate is a low involvement product, the attractiveness of Bachan worked extremely well with the masses.

Source credibility model

This model emphasizes that the effectiveness of an advertisement's intended message to its target audience is also based on the level of perceived expertise and trustworthiness of the deliverer or the endorser. A trustworthy celebrity is perceived to be honest and believable. On many occasions, the credibility factor can to a great extent be influenced by the likeability and ethnic origin of the endorser. This theory helps to explain the special appreciation of Asian celebrities for endorsing Asian brands, as mentioned earlier in the chapter.

The Chinese, for example, prefer A-list celebrities from the West, and after that, they prefer local celebrities to B-list Western celebrities. An example is the popularity of Cantonese pop artists from Hong Kong, despite their local origins.

Meaning transfer model

This model states that for the endorsement to be effective, a celebrity endorser should also possess a set of traits that are compatible with those of the brand which he/she endorses. This helps customers to build a positive association toward the product being endorsed.[29]

Bausch & Lamb uses the Chinese gold medal diver Tian Liang to endorse its contact lens cleaning solutions by using the match between the product and the background of the endorser.[30]

As a marketing communication tool, the celebrity endorsement enhances this process by using an endorser who has acquired a set of attributes after years of being in the public eye who speaks for the brand and transfers some of his/her attributes to the brand. These attributes can be status, class, gender, age, personality, or lifestyle. At the same time, the celebrity plays the role of a "super consumer", who has been to the place where the target audience is going. By borrowing some symbolic meanings from its endorser, the brand will be able to create strong positive images in the minds of its target audience.

In 2002, 12-year-old Scotch whiskey brand Dewar attempted to revitalize its "grandfather's drink" image. The brand used a campaign with the slogan, "Some age, others mature," to target countries across Asia and southern Europe. The company selected the movie star Sean Connery as the brand spokesperson and was able to successfully create a significant level of attitude change toward the brand, thus boosting sales. Sean Connery was an excellent choice for the job, being of mature years while retaining his rugged good looks and bags of charm.[31]

As companies fight it out to sign deals with the biggest and most popular movie stars, sports icons, pop singers and so on, it is evident that celebrity endorsement comes at a huge price. As there are not many Yao Mings or Shah Rukh Khans, it is important that companies use a systematic methodology to hire celebrities for endorsements. Although some celebrities can easily pull off endorsing literally anything from soap to a luxury car because of their immense popularity, it is important that companies examine the suitability and credibility of celebrities to their company's offerings.

Celebrity brand impact model

Based on the three main endorsement models discussed previously, the celebrity brand impact model in Figure 5.2 is a framework to measure the level of awareness and impact on the brand based on the celebrity endorsements.

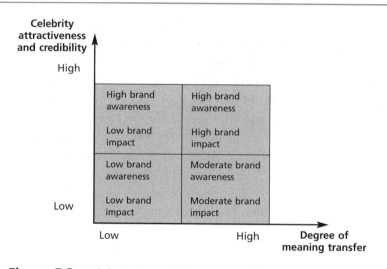

Figure 5.2 Celebrity brand impact model
Source: VentureRepublic

This model measures the degree of meaning transfer between the brand and the celebrity on the one hand, and the attractiveness (and credibility) of the celebrity on the other. The result of the framework is evaluated under two parameters: brand awareness and brand impact. Brand awareness refers to knowledge about the brand. It is customers' knowledge about the brand as a result of many past actions, interactions and experiences with the brand. Brand impact is the level of positive spillover of endorser equity onto the brand being endorsed.

Figure 5.2 provides guidelines for companies to decide on celebrity endorsements.

Challenges in celebrity branding

Despite the advantages of using a celebrity for brand endorsements, companies do face certain challenges. The four main challenges are discussed below.

Cost of celebrity endorsement

Celebrity endorsements can be extremely expensive. Companies can seek to use their resources judiciously by adopting innovative ways of using celebrities. Timing can also be crucial and signing an emerging star could prove prudent.

A case in point is Yanjing beer's deal with the Houston Rockets (an NBA team) and its access to Yao Ming. Yanjing beer is the second largest beer producer in China, following Qingtao. The beer is produced in China and distributed in the US through Harbrew Imports, which is the exclusive distributor. In 2002, Harbrew Imports signed a US$6 million deal with the Houston Rockets for their endorsement of Yanjing beer for six years. This was before the Houston Rockets selected Yao Ming, who has recently become one of the biggest Asian sports stars in the world.

Had the deal been signed after Yao Ming's inclusion in the team, the endorsement would have been more expensive or even unaffordable. Even though Yanjing beer did not sign any deal specifically with Yao Ming, the brand can still leverage Yao as he is one of the players in the Houston Rockets team (see below).

Another example is Chang Beer, the biggest Thailand brewer. Even though no Chang Beer is sold in the UK, it is the shirt sponsor for the Everton football team in the English Premier League. This sponsorship is used to Chang's advantage when it uses it for rebroadcast into Thailand.[32]

Risks involved with negative publicity

Managers should also be aware of and be prepared to deal with the risks involved in using celebrities for endorsements. Celebrities can deliver a low return on their endorsements because of low compatibility with the brand or a low level of meaning transfer. Their image can be tarnished due to unforeseeable negative events. Finally, their symbolic meaning may be weakened because of overexposure or poor management of images through multiple product endorsements.

Founder's dilemma

Certain brands bear the name of their founders and the identities of the brand and its founder become entrenched in one other. In such a scenario, the brand could suffer from the demise of the founder or any negative publicity that the founder attracts. One example is the world famous luxury brand Chanel. The company experienced a long period of inability to revive its brand in the 1970s, because the brand has always been hidden behind Coco Chanel, its founder, who passed away in 1971.[33] Today the Chanel brand is a well-recognized brand, with a lot of vintage value and a strong heritage.

Overexposure of the celebrity

Studies have also shown that the number of endorsements a celebrity engages in and the frequency of celebrity exposure are negatively associated with celebrity credibility. This can extend to the forming of unfavorable brand attitudes and a reduction in purchase intention.[34] In addition, celebrity endorsement is used intensively in today's marketplace: thus the market has become crowded and consumers are increasingly exposed to such promotional strategies. Celebrity endorsement might lose its advantage if companies are not careful about the relative match between the brand and the celebrity. Marketers will therefore have a tougher job to overcome the increasing skepticism toward celebrity branding in consumers' minds.

Yao Ming: the Chinese basketball star

Yao Ming, the three-time NBA all-star and Houston Rockets center, has been an unstoppable force wherever he appears; whether it is on court where he helps to improve the Rockets' game rating dramatically or in the business world where he is spokesman for the global brands Pepsi, McDonald's and Walt Disney.[35]

Yao Ming recently signed an endorsement deal with GARMIN, a GPS (global positioning system) manufacturer in the US.[36] Traditionally, GPS has been used by specialists in yachting, aviation, trekking and so on, but with Yao Ming maneuvering in the back streets of Houston and Texas, the company intends to drive home the message that GPS has indeed hit the mainstream and could be used by everybody to make their lives simpler.

Although brand Yao has yet to attain its full potential, it has achieved both on-field and off-field popularity and impact. The basketball star has a team of professionals to manage the marketing of the Yao brand. Team Yao consists of a veteran NBA agent, a University of Chicago professor, and Yao's agent, a Chinese entrepreneur who is also Yao's relative. Team Yao commissioned eight Chicago business school students to develop a 500-page formal marketing plan. Team Yao screens each endorsement deal to ensure an ideal collaboration between Yao and the brand by carefully following the plan to avoid overexposure of Yao.[37]

Yao's prominence as a brand endorser lies with his popularity in both Western and Asian societies. Although there have been other Chinese basketball players drafted in to the NBA, no on else has been voted three-time NBA all-star.

Although he started slowly, Yao has surprised people with his performance on the court. Yao's international success serves as a role model for his fellow Chinese and generates a lot of pride. He symbolizes a new generation of

Chinese who are capable of competing in one of the toughest sports that require big, tall, powerful men – not the typical image of Asian males.[38]

Yao, who shows genuineness, humility, sincerity, and patriotism is a hardworking basketball player. At 7ft 5ins, Yao is one of the tallest players in the history of the NBA. But unlike other big players, he is remarkably agile. With China hosting the Olympics in 2008, Yao will have ample opportunity to further extend his celebrity status for a host of brands.

Celebrities in India

India's Bollywood has an audience of approximately 3.6 billion globally compared to 2.6 billion for Hollywood. This fact gives enormous power to the big and mighty Bollywood stars as they chart new territories beyond Indian soil. Amitabh Bachan, a demigod in India, and Shah Rukh Khan (or King Khan as he is fondly called) are the new power centers. Aishwarya Rai, a former Miss World, and one of the leading actresses in Bollywood and now the Indian face in Hollywood, has also become one of the most sought-after celebrities. They have tremendous power at their disposal to influence the public. With a strong list of achievements in their respective fields, these personalities are the new weapons of companies in branding and marketing their offerings.

Moreover, these Bollywood personalities have such a huge fan base that it has become the norm for them to endorse a wide portfolio of products and brands. The spectrum spans fast moving consumer goods, consumer electronics, cars, cosmetics and leisure destinations.

Another category of celebrities in India are cricket players, especially those who play for Team India. It is surely not an overstatement to say that cricket is one religion that unites the diverse landscape of India. Its popularity is so enormous that literally the entire country shuts down when India plays against its neighbor Pakistan – such is the power of cricket in the Indian mindset. Realizing this power and the loyalty that cricketers command, companies have used them as spokespersons for their companies' offerings since the early 1970s. Even here, the portfolio of products that cricketers endorse is very wide and often the endorsers have nothing to do with the products they endorse. But given the nature of awareness and recall that these endorsers generate, companies appear to be willing to play along.

The huge population in India and the Indian diaspora in almost every other country in the world also enhance the reach and power of these Indian celebrities. Indian movies typically depict extended families who are attached to their roots and an Indian youth who is struggling to find the right balance between traditional values and the allure of westernization, themes that cut across many developing countries. Indian films resonate as much in Nigeria, Mali and Morocco, as they do in Russia, Nepal, Pakistan, Singapore and Malaysia. Viewers in these countries are not just aware of Bollywood but actively watch, memorize, and adore the films and their stars. With such a tremendous audience reach, Indian movie stars command a powerful following.

Conclusion

This chapter has discussed celebrity endorsements as an effective possible channel of communication and branding for companies in Asia. The frameworks presented serve as useful guidelines for companies in making crucial decisions about celebrity endorsement strategies. The following presents a brief 10-step guideline.

---

10 steps to celebrity endorsements

1. **Consistency and long-term commitment:** As with branding, companies should try to maintain consistency between the endorser and the brand to establish a strong personality and identity. More importantly, companies should view celebrity endorsements as long-term strategic decisions rather than short-term tactical decisions which could be changed on a frequent basis.

2. **Three prerequisites to selecting celebrities:** Before signing on celebrities to endorse their brands, companies need to ensure that they meet three basic prerequisites, namely the endorser should be attractive, have a positive image in society, and be perceived as having the necessary knowledge (although it might be difficult for a celebrity to meet all three prerequisites).

3. **Celebrity–brand match:** In line with the model described earlier, companies should ensure a match between the brand being endorsed and the endorser so that the endorsements are able to strongly influence the thought processes of consumers and create a positive

---

perception of the brand. They should enhance the consumers' perception about their lifestyle and elevate them emotionally.

4. **Constant monitoring:** Companies should monitor the behavior, conduct and public image of the endorser continuously to minimize any potential negative publicity. One of the most effective ways to do this is to ensure that celebrity endorsement contracts are effectively drafted, keeping in mind any such negative events. These contracts should guide companies and celebrities alike about their overall conduct in relation to the brand.

5. **Selecting unique endorsers:** Companies should try to bring on board those celebrities who do not endorse competitors' products or other quite different products, so that there is a clear transfer of personality and identity between the endorser and the brand.

6. **Timing:** As celebrities command a high price tag, companies should be on the constant lookout for emerging celebrities who show some promise and potential and sign them on in their formative years if possible to ensure a win–win situation.

7. **Brand over endorser:** When celebrities are used to endorse brands, one obvious result could be the potential overshadowing of the brand by the celebrity. Companies should ensure that this does not happen by formulating advertising collaterals and other communications. Moreover, the brand scope and policy should dictate the kind of celebrity to be hired and vice versa.

8. **Celebrity endorsement is just a channel:** Companies must realize that having a celebrity endorsing a brand is not a goal in itself; rather it is one part of the communication mix that falls under the broader category of sponsorship marketing. Therefore companies should back up celebrity endorsements with several communications activities to obtain greater effect for the brand.

9. **Celebrity ROI:** Even though it is challenging to measure the effects of celebrity endorsements on companies' brands, companies should have a system combining quantitative and qualitative measures to measure the overall effect of celebrity endorsements on their brands.

10. **Trademark and legal contracts:** Companies should ensure that they hire the celebrities on proper legal terms so that they don't endorse competitors' products in the same product category, thereby creating confusion in the minds of the consumers. Comprehensive legal contracts must govern the endorsement deal in all aspects to avoid any disputes.

Notes

1 "Chinese youth aren't patriotic purchasers. Most favour brands such as Coke and Nike over local rivals", *Advertising Age*, 5 January, 2004.
2 http://www.hongkongdisneyland.com.
3 "HK Songtress Kelly Chen to perform in Genting", *The Star Online*, 15 April, 2005.
4 Friedman, Hershey, and Linda Friedman. (1979), "Endorser effectiveness by product type", *Journal of Advertising Research*, **19**, 5 October, pp. 63–71.
5 "A force to reckon with", *Time Asia*, June 7, 2004.
6 http://news.naver.com.
7 Kamen, Joseph M., Azhari, Abdul C., Kragh, Judith R. (1975), "What a spokesman does for a sponsor", *Journal of Advertising Research*, **15**, pp. 17–24.
8 http://www.loreal.com.
9 "Aishwarya Rai: Back in the groove", *Hindustan Times*, 17 April, 2005.
10 Friedman and Friedman (1979), op. cit.
11 Kahle, L. R. and Homer, P. M. (1985), "Physical attractiveness of celebrity endorser: a social adaptation perspective", *Journal of Consumer Research*, **11**, March, pp. 954–61.
12 Speck, Paul Surgi, Schumann, David W., and Thompson, Craig. (1988), "Celebrity endorsements – scripts, schema and roles: theoretical framework and preliminary tests", *Advances in Consumer Research*, **15**, pp. 69–76.
13 "Star marketing", *The Korea Economic Daily*, 27 October, 2003.
14 "Celebrity goldminers", *ACCJ Journal*, April 2004.
15 Erdogan, Zafer B. (1999), "Celebrity endorsement: a literature review", *Journal of Marketing Management*, **15**, 291–314.
16 Hamlin, Michael Alan (2004), "Celebrity branding", *TeamAsia*, September 20, 2004.
17 "Bajaj 'discovers' Jackie Chan", October 9, 2004, Business Line (*The Hindu*).
18 http://ir.zaobao.com.
19 Press Release: "Superstar Gong Li is new celebrity face of healthy lifestyle specialist OSIM", January 16, 2003.
20 Author interview with company management.
21 "Yue Sai Kan: the face of modern China", Kim Barnet, 1 April 2002, Brandchannel.com.
22 "Holding up half the sky. Five Chinese women: Some are smart, rich, and running the show; others just want a piece of the booming economy", Annie Wang reporter associates, Barney Gimbela; Zhang Dahong, 4 October 2004, *Fortune*.
23 "South Korean actor Bae Yong Joon arrives to tumultuous welcome", *Japan Today*, 17 April 2005.
24 "South Korean star sparks tourist boom", CNN.com, 13 March, 2005.
25 "Adjusting McLuhan's reception of hot and cool media", *The Japan Times*, 12 September, 2004.
26 http://www.mofa.go.jp/region/asia-paci/future/address0406.html.
27 Erdogan, B. Zafer (1999), op. cit.
28 http://in.rediff.com (accessed 22 April 2004).
29 McCracken, Grant (1989), "Who is the celebrity endorser? Cultural foundations of the endorsement process", *Journal of Consumer Research*, **16**, 310–21.

30 Beech, Hannah, "From heroes to brands", *Time Asia* , May 31, 2004.
31 Gardyne, Tom Bruce, "Will a celebrity bond with your brand?" *Director*, September, 2004.
32 Huang, Patricia, "Pouring it on", *Forbes*, March 28, 2005.
33 Kafka, Peter, "Celebrity by the share", *Forbes*, March 21, 2000.
34 Tripp, Carolyn, Jensen, Thomas D. and Carlson, Les, (1994). "The effect of multiple product endorsements by celebrities on consumers' attitudes and intentions", *Journal of Consumer Research*, **30**, 535–47.
35 Lowry, Tom, "How big is Yao Ming?", *Business Week*, October 25, 2004.
36 Hesseldahl, Arik, "Garmin signs NBA's Yao as pitchman", *Forbes*, April 13, 2004.
37 Lowry, Tom and Roberts, Dexter, "Wow! Yao!" *Business Week*, October 25, 2004.
38 Luo, Michael. "Yao Ming boosts ethnic pride." *Times Union*, Albany, New York. February 9, 2003.

CHAPTER 6

ASIAN BRAND STRATEGY

You can analyse the past but you have to design the future.

Edward de Bono

It takes time to build brands and the successful path can take many avenues depending on the product, service, category, market, the company heritage and many other factors. At one end of the brand building spectrum is the physical product and service with its tangible descriptors, and at the other end the intangible descriptors, with associations and perceptions linked to the values and personalities of the brand in the minds of consumers. Where does the boardroom start the process, and what is the right direction? There is no single answer to this. Most companies started with products and services, and slowly they migrated into brands over time, as more and more associations were attached to the original products and their names.

It is the responsibility of the boardroom to facilitate and manage this process, set the direction of the brand or the portfolio of brands, and ensure that adequate resources are available to support the growth.

Aligning the brand

It is crucial to establish a common brand vocabulary within the corporate management team and also the entire organization to ensure that issues are discussed and communicated at a common level. The two essential terms in the brand vocabulary that organizations need to understand and which are the starting points before commencing a brand process are brand identity and brand image:

- **Brand identity:** describes the company's strategic intention for the brand, its uniqueness, meaning and values, and how the brand aims to be positioned in the marketplace. It projects how the boardroom wants the brand to be perceived by customers and other stakeholders. Brand identity is the strategic charter for the brand and links closely to the overall business strategy.

- **Brand image:** the picture of the brand in the minds of customers and stakeholders. It refers to the way customers and stakeholders decode all the signals provided by a given product, brand, company or even country. The brand image is a result of many external factors of which marketing communications is just one.

The primary task of the boardroom is to develop and manage a sustainable brand identity on one hand and ensure a balanced alignment between the brand identity and brand image on the other.

The marketplace is dynamic and changes constantly. The competitive environment and its direction should thus be taken into consideration on a regular basis to ensure that the intentions described in the brand identity are well suited to compete in the marketplace at any given time. Companies must ensure that identity, image and market space serve a common purpose, as shown in Figure 6.1.

It needs to be noted that as brand identity is the strategic charter, it has a perspective long term. Although there may be changes in the marketplace, the brand identity does not often change. However, the way it is communicated might change regularly, within the limits and boundaries described in the brand identity.

Figure 6.1 Brand alignment model
Source: VentureRepublic

Brand management model

The brand management model describes a six-step model for building, managing and evaluating strong brands (Figure 6.2). It helps Asian board-

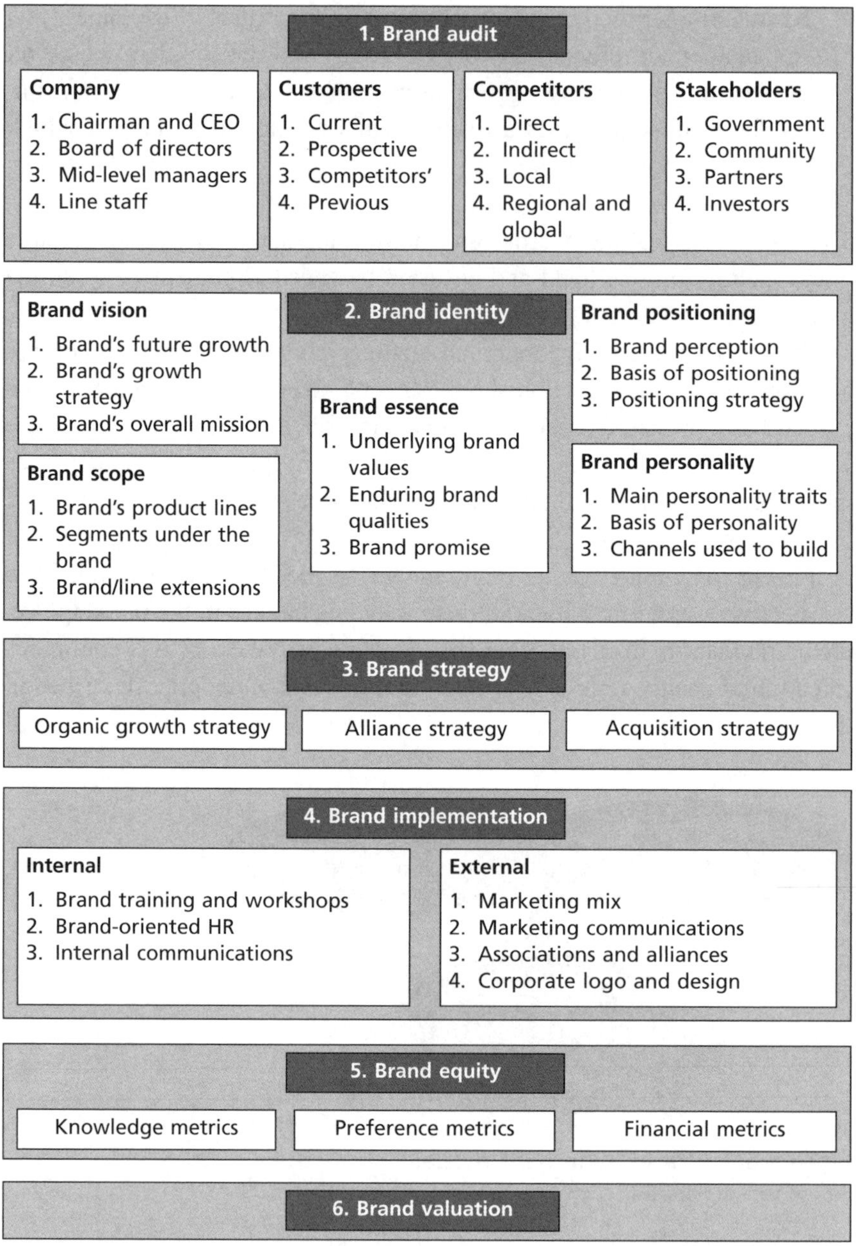

1. Brand audit			
Company	**Customers**	**Competitors**	**Stakeholders**
1. Chairman and CEO	1. Current	1. Direct	1. Government
2. Board of directors	2. Prospective	2. Indirect	2. Community
3. Mid-level managers	3. Competitors'	3. Local	3. Partners
4. Line staff	4. Previous	4. Regional and global	4. Investors

2. Brand identity

Brand vision
1. Brand's future growth
2. Brand's growth strategy
3. Brand's overall mission

Brand scope
1. Brand's product lines
2. Segments under the brand
3. Brand/line extensions

Brand essence
1. Underlying brand values
2. Enduring brand qualities
3. Brand promise

Brand positioning
1. Brand perception
2. Basis of positioning
3. Positioning strategy

Brand personality
1. Main personality traits
2. Basis of personality
3. Channels used to build

3. Brand strategy

Organic growth strategy	Alliance strategy	Acquisition strategy

4. Brand implementation

Internal
1. Brand training and workshops
2. Brand-oriented HR
3. Internal communications

External
1. Marketing mix
2. Marketing communications
3. Associations and alliances
4. Corporate logo and design

5. Brand equity

Knowledge metrics	Preference metrics	Financial metrics

6. Brand valuation

Figure 6.2 Brand management model
Source: VentureRepublic

rooms to focus their processes and efforts in the right direction. In building strong brands, companies need to follow six important tasks:

- **brand audit** (profound understanding based on data, experience and other insights)

- **brand identity** (the strategic charter of the brand)

- **brand strategy** (intended direction linked to corporate strategy)

- **brand implementation** (the messages and channels of communication)

- **brand equity** and **brand valuation** within a brand management driven boardroom (systematic and organization-wide framework).

Each element is now discussed in detail.

Brand audit

The brand audit is the first essential step for Asian companies in the brand building process. It is a comprehensive process that involves four major phases: company analysis, customer analysis, competitor analysis and stakeholder analysis. The purpose of the brand audit is to provide the management with an overall analysis of the brand from internal and external sources. By carrying out the brand audit, companies can obtain several benefits, as shown in Table 6.1.

TABLE 6.1 **Benefits of a brand audit**
■ Have a better idea about strengths and weaknesses of the current brand portfolio
■ Determine their current positioning in the market and formulate the desired positioning
■ Evaluate any gap in brand perceptions between internal and external stakeholders
■ Determine the relative position of the company in relation to its competitors
■ Understand customers' needs, preferences and priorities in the specific market
■ Build associations and personalities that would be relevant to and desired by the customers' preferences and would strongly resonate with them
■ Formulate strategies that will assist them to outsmart their competitors

Source: VentureRepublic

The brand audit provides a structured framework and a firm foundation on which companies can define brand identities and strategize their future actions. Companies normally have a wealth of data about their customers, distribution channels and competitors. This information can be collected through desk research and interviews with staff throughout the organization and preferably also with external stakeholders.

To obtain an unbiased view of the market and the brand, companies can benefit from using external brand research. It is usually a combination of qualitative and quantitative techniques. Based on respondents' answers to various questions, multiple sets of data are collected through in-depth interviews, focus groups, surveys and questionnaires. Sophisticated statistical tools like conjoint, factor and regression analysis are then used to analyze and structure the often large amount of data to present findings in various user-friendly formats and levels of details. Other commonly used methods are cluster analysis, multidimensional scaling and correspondence analysis.

Brands can potentially consist of multiple, sometimes even innumerable, tangible and intangible features and benefits, and the interdependencies between them are often complex. The most successful brands emphasize features, benefits and emotional aspects, because they are not only important to customers, but also help the brand to differentiate itself from those of its competitors. These are called "brand differentiators" and are critical for building brand equity.

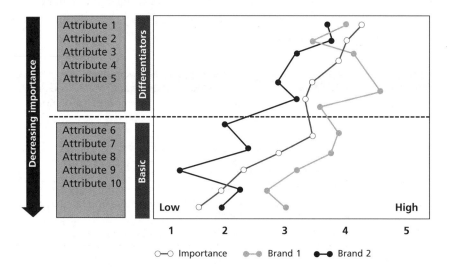

Figure 6.3 Brand performance analysis chart
Source: VentureRepublic

An example of a brand and how it performs against its brand attributes as well as competing brands is shown in Figure 6.3. Brand attributes can comprise features, benefits and emotional aspects or a selection of them, depending on the research setup. Figure 6.3 illustrates how respondents rank various attributes in decreasing order of importance, and also how they rank various brands on the same attributes. The top attributes are the brand differentiators as they are most important, according to respondents, followed by the basic attributes. Figure 6.3 illustrates the potential gaps in brand performance as the gaps between the importance curve and the brands, and also between the brands themselves. These gaps can indicate where a brand can focus to improve customer perceptions and competitiveness.

Figure 6.3 is just one example of how data can be analyzed and presented to assess and benchmark the current brand performance. The multivariate statistical tools mentioned in this section can help to determine brand differentiators from basic brand attributes, and how to employ them successfully.

Successful branding is more than gut feeling and great creative ideas. Asian companies can benefit from a rigorous and fact-based approach to branding. Cost-effective brand building depends on deep insight into customer needs, preferences and other market insights to tailor the brand successfully. Some of these insights might be available internally, while others are found externally. The results from these different research measures provide management with real data, knowledge and insights.

The brand audit is an important platform for building and managing the brand identity as discussed in the following section.

Brand identity

As mentioned earlier, the brand identity is the *strategic charter* that guides the company and customers. The identity of a brand serves two main purposes. Internally, the identity guides all the strategic decisions regarding the brand, such as the communication, brand/line extension, brand architecture, and association and partnering decisions. Externally, it provides customers with a clear sense of what the brand stands for, its essence, promises and personality – depending on how well the company expresses and delivers on the promises from the brand identity.

Therefore, brand identity not only serves as a direct link to the corporate strategy of the company internally but also serves as the crucial link between the brand and the customers externally. Given the enormous significance of the brand identity, corporate management must spend considerable time and effort to develop relevant, sustainable and resonating brand identities.

Although there are many factors that influence the creation of a brand identity, the internal processes around creating the brand identity are as important as the results themselves. The process itself enables corporate management to discuss and decide the intention and direction of the brand. This inevitably leads to discussions about other internal functions and their alignment in relation to branding in order to optimize the delivery of brand promises.

Companies should always consider the following five important factors when developing the brand identity:

1. **Brand vision:** an internal document that clearly records the future path and growth for the brand as envisioned by corporate management. This document clearly lays down the future direction for the brand and the desired role and status that the brand hopes to achieve in the stated time. It defines the strategic and financial objectives of the brand.

2. **Brand scope:** a more specific subset of the brand vision document. This describes in detail the growth opportunities for the brand in line with the brand vision. Among other information the brand scope outlines the market segments and product categories the brand can enter into.

3. **Brand positioning:** the place that every brand strives to occupy in customers' minds. Positioning is all about the perception of the brand. Companies should decide on the brand positioning based on the market segment that it is targeting, customer dynamics and the competitors' positions in the market. All brands strive to communicate one single idea and occupy a unique position in their customers' minds. Brand positioning enables customers to make an easier assessment of their wants and needs, and it helps them to minimize their risks when selecting the brand.

4. **Brand personality:** the set of human characteristics associated with a brand.[1] Through its own characteristics and features, marketing communications, mental associations, usage patterns and partnerships, a brand can take on a certain personality. This helps the customer to connect emotionally with the brand. A strong brand personality also helps customers to express their own beliefs and attitudes by associating themselves with that particular brand.

5. **Brand essence:** the heart and soul of the brand – usually stated in two or three words. It encapsulates what the brand is all about, what it stands for and what makes it unique. This is an internal tool and is never communicated as part of the external brand building effort. It serves as an internal anchor in the company and illustrates the core of the brand and its meaning.

Using the above five factors, corporate management can construct a brand identity for their brand which will direct company actions toward the objective of evoking unique impressions in customers' minds and building competitive advantage.

Brand strategy

The brand research and identity processes build a strong foundation from which companies can devise suitable strategies for their future growth. Global brands in many industries across the world have used many tried-and-tested growth options for a long time. Many have religiously followed the differentiation path, some have been the cost leaders, while others have tried to combine these two dominant strategies.

Before expanding internationally, Asian companies must achieve global standards of competitiveness and distinct capabilities in their core activities. A McKinsey study of global leaders found that they brought their key processes up to or above global benchmarks before they globalized. An example is Asian Paints from India which reduced its working capital turns below most of its global competitors.[2]

Companies in Asia are increasingly meeting the competitive pressure of serving the price-sensitive and hard-to-reach consumers who are more demanding than their peers in the developed economies.[3] An example is India's second-largest bank ICICI Bank, which developed the capability to earn profits from small transactions by handling money transfers for a highly mobile middle class. It later used this capability when expanding internationally.

Secondly, Asian companies must focus on the corporate culture and their distinct values as an important part of building a strong international brand. The adequate organizational structures and the talent pool of executives with the right skills and experiences are crucial for expansion into diverse markets. The structure must allow for a certain degree of autonomous decision making to suit specific local tastes and requirements and yet be part of the overall corporate direction. Similarly, employees must be strong brand ambassadors, contributing to the overall performance and the local company culture.

According to McKinsey, companies expanding from emerging markets are successful when they first leverage their distinct capabilities and corporate cultures and subsequently adapt and change where needed.[4] HSBC is an example of a brand which has successfully followed this strategy (see box).

Building the world's local bank

In 1865, the Hong Kong Shanghai Banking Corporation (HSBC) was established in Hong Kong to finance the growing trade between China and Europe. It developed distinct trade finance capabilities, operational discipline and gained skills in handling cross-border transactions and complex networks. In Hong Kong, its home market, the bank had to cope with the relatively small deposits of the local customers, which taught it to operate with a cost-to-income ratio lower than that of US and European competitors.[5] HSBC hires top talent and trains future executives through international programs as preparation for global positions. In the 1980s and 90s, HSBC expanded into several international markets through organic growth and acquisitions. It has become one of the world's largest and most successful financial institutions, with 9,800 offices in 77 countries and territories serving over 110 million customers.[6]

Asian companies need to resist the temptation to simply imitate the strategies that western brands have followed. Asian companies have some inherent, unique advantages. Asia is a continent not only of different countries, but essentially very strong and unique histories, cultures, mindsets, and practices. They need to leverage these and come up with options that will enable them to grow robustly.

Most of the brands that are emerging from Asian countries are strong within their countries but not regionally throughout Asia or internationally. These companies can choose between expanding to different countries within Asia and then going beyond that, or expanding simultaneously to all regions. Asian boardrooms will be confronted with two main challenges when deciding on future brand growth strategies:

- **Management control:** Building a successful brand is about investing resources (financial and organizational) on a continuous basis and maintaining the consistency of the brand in the market. These decisions can easily be made when the management has full control over the brand. But when a company operates beyond national boundaries, it can either decide to grow its own brand portfolio or possibly ally with other brands or acquire brands. This alters the level of control that management has over the brand, which can be a great challenge, but is a choice that must be made.

- **Time-to-market:** With growing competition in literally every industry and the proliferation of products and services as well as brands, the time taken by a company to launch and grow its products and brands becomes extremely crucial for success. This is something else for companies to consider before they can choose from the many strategy options available. Some options may seem obviously better than others, but viewed within the constraints imposed by time-to-market, things may appear different.

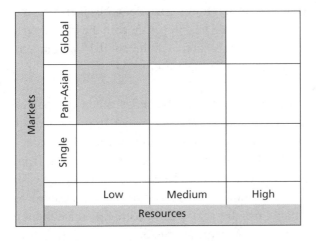

Figure 6.4 Asian brand growth matrix
Source: VentureRepublic

Figure 6.4 illustrates the possible growth strategies for Asian brands across different markets. The matrix has management control and time-to-market as the main factors underlying it. The horizontal axis measures the resource availability of Asian companies (financial and organizational resources) and the vertical axis looks at the market reach these companies aspire to achieve. The availability of resources along with management control and time-to-market determines the overall brand strategy of Asian companies.

Challenges in moving along the vertical axis: When companies move beyond their home markets to venture into new territories, it often turns out to be a two-edged sword, with opportunities and challenges in equal measure. Given the distinctly different dynamics of Asian countries, companies expanding beyond their national markets face some obvious challenges:

- **Lack of customer knowledge:** As different countries have different cultures and dynamics that underlie customer behavior patterns, new entrants will find it hard to decipher this and build a competitive edge.

- **Lack of distribution network:** Despite Asia's booming growth, in many countries, distribution is the name of the game. Usually local companies would have entrenched distribution networks, with long-term relationships and personal rapport. This makes it difficult for new entrants from other countries to gain access to distribution networks.

- **Increased competition:** Expansion to different countries increases the competition as the companies would be competing with the incumbents of the particular market. It not only increases the number of competitors, but also increases the level of competition.

Challenges in moving along the horizontal axis: When companies decide to extend beyond their national markets, either into regional or global markets, it becomes a question of resource availability. Companies either have their own financial resources or they can seek funding from external channels. Their own resources could be cash assets or strong cash flows that can be used for expansion plans, while companies that choose to raise money from the outside usually seek public listing or raise money through investors, private equity companies or funds.

Internal funding and strong resources basically provide better management control, and the company can decide with a fair degree of freedom on strategies and objectives, and align their own expectations with regard to profitability, growth rates and time horizons.

External funding can dilute the company interests and prove challenging in some cases. Success here depends on whether investors believe in intangible assets like branding, and whether they understand the difficulties in building and managing brands. Investors also need to understand that it takes resources and time to align the brand promise and its delivery throughout the entire organization. Finally, they need to accept the time horizon required before they can expect positive returns from their brand investments.

With these opportunities and challenges and the underlying constraints in mind, boardrooms need to decide how to grow their brands, using the following three brand growth strategies:

- Organic growth strategy

- Alliance growth strategy

- Acquisition growth strategy.

Depending on the life-cycle stage of the companies and their brand(s), companies can select one or more strategies in combination to suit their needs and requirements as time progresses. The three strategies are discussed in the following sections.

Organic growth strategy

An organic growth strategy is where companies grow their brand portfolios without leveraging the equity of any other brands. Companies strive to grow organically by expanding in the same market or other markets by having full management control over their brands. This strategy has its own advantages and disadvantages. As the company is the sole owner of the brand, it gives the company a lot of leeway to decide on its positioning and personality. It also provides companies with the freedom to invest in and continuously manage the brand across all touch points.

A classic example of the organic growth strategy is Singapore Airlines which has grown organically since its inception in 1972. Despite an infusion of capital from shareholders, management control over the brand has been strong throughout the entire life cycle of the brand, resulting in a successful balance between brand promise and brand delivery.

The disadvantage of this strategy is that companies potentially might not be able to extend their brand beyond a certain set of product categories and market segments due to high resource requirements. This makes it challenging for companies to launch new brands as the investments are significant. Moreover, as the brand would have built in certain entrenched personalities in consumers' minds, branching out into different product lines could prove challenging, depending on how large the resource requirements are in order to establish and communicate this.

Trung Nguyen: Vietnam's very own Starbucks

One of the best-known brands within Vietnam is its own version of Starbucks: Trung Nguyen. Started in 1996, today it operates more than 400 outlets in the country, and many more in countries such as Japan, Singapore, Malaysia, China, Taiwan, Hong Kong, and even the US, Canada, Australia and Russia. What started as a small venture to exploit the growing coffee drinking needs of Vietnam's people has grown into a multi-country brand.[7]

Trung Nguyen has adopted a distinct expansion strategy since its inception. It has taken the franchising path to expand beyond Vietnam. Since the mid-1990s, the brand has been successful in franchising both domestically and internationally. Moreover, the company wants to extend its brand into Singapore with a chain of coffee shops and it has invested US$73,000 for this purpose.[8] It recently sold the rights to use its brand for US$50,000 to a Japanese company and for US$30,000 to a Singaporean company. This strategy has helped the brand to establish its name in different markets.

Leveraging on this brand equity, Trung Nguyen has also ventured into the tea business in Vietnam, the country being one of the largest tea exporters in the world. Trung Nguyen has spent almost US$1.3 million on the 'fairy tea house', which offers customers the experience of enjoying Vietnamese coffee and tea and immersing themselves in the local culture.[9]

As the brand plans on further expansion into other markets and other product categories, it needs to ensure that its trademark is well protected and its brand name is not misused by any other businesses. As Vietnam still has a long way to go in implementing strong intellectual property rights law, Vietnamese companies must take special care to protect their brand names.[10]

When South Korean companies first branched out internationally, their early marketing strategies were based on entering other developing countries, which required fewer resources compared to targeting the larger and more developed markets. Many Chinese companies are using the same tactics. Geely Auto, a smaller Chinese car brand with 4 percent local market share, is entering the Middle East. Huawei, a large and rapidly expanding Chinese telecom equipment manufacturer, is ambitious about establishing its brand internationally through a similar strategy. The company spends more than 10 percent of revenues on R&D,[11] and is competing with the likes of heavyweight Cisco, which in 2003 filed a suit against Huawei for breach of intellectual property rights (IPR). Huawei is looking at extending into consumer brand opportunities and already provides handsets and television products.[12]

Alliance growth strategy

An alliance growth strategy is where companies tie up with other companies in a strategic alliance, whereby both companies benefit from their combined strengths, and the product or service being offered leverages the brand names of both companies.

A classic example is the motorbike market leader in India, Hero Honda. This is one of the most successful co-branding activities in India between the local Hero group and Honda of Japan. The Hero group has the local contacts, local market knowledge, distribution networks, and knows how to create the relevant marketing communications, with the right feel for the local market. Honda has cutting-edge, Japanese technology and gains access to the extremely lucrative, Indian two-wheeler market, with the high brand recognition of Hero in the Indian market to leverage on.

The strategy has inherent advantages and disadvantages. When two companies decide to combine two distinct brands (or a portfolio of brands), both companies reap the advantages of access to new markets, distribution channels, customer segments and products. But on the downside, it faces the risk of confused positioning, and ineffective management of the brand's identities. This happens especially when the two brands stand for two distinct things in the marketplace, catering to two distinct customer groups.

Thus, for companies opting to grow successfully through the alliance strategy, effective brand management practices become crucial. Companies must ensure that there are regular brand tracking procedures to assist in maintaining a proper balance in the alliance between the two strong brands, and that customer perceptions support the intentions of the alliance.

Another example is TCL, a Chinese electronics brand, which started making mobile phones in 1999. Today it has become one of the largest manufacturers, selling 60 million handsets in 2004. From almost no recognizable market share in China, local Chinese handset brands have captured almost 50 percent share, competing head-on with global mobile phone brands. To grow further outside China, TCL set up a venture with Alcatel's mobile phone business in 2004. Similarly in 2003, TCL and Thompson from France decided to merge their television businesses to become the largest television manufacturer in the world. TCL will use Thompson's RCA brand in the US, and the Thompson brand itself in Europe.[13]

As these examples show, the alliance strategy usually takes place between companies that want to explore new territories but lack certain key ingredients and experiences to make that move.

Acquisition growth strategy

Acquisition growth strategy is where companies acquire other companies or brands as a means to grow. There have been many examples of both successful and unsuccessful cases of mergers and acquisitions (M&A). As with any business decision, companies need to evaluate the benefits against the costs. A study among 45 companies with M&A experience in Asia Pacific showed that retention of key talent, communication, retention of key managers and integration of corporate cultures were the four most critical areas for the successful integration of companies.[14]

An example of the acquisition strategy comes from Hong Kong. Shiriro is a 90-year-old family business, producing and distributing several well-known, worldwide brands and with a turnover of more than US$300 million. In 2003, it acquired Hasselblad from Sweden, one of the most prominent camera brands preferred by professional photographers all over the world. Hasselblad is known for outstanding quality and durability even under extreme conditions. In 1969, the brand was part of the legendary Apollo 11 mission to the moon.[15]

The acquisition strategy might prove useful for companies that are venturing into new territories outside home markets. As foreign companies would not have a deep understanding of local practices and market mind-sets, and it would take a long time to develop that competence from scratch, one of the best ways for companies to leapfrog would be to acquire local firms or their brands. This strategy would allow the acquirer to tap into the brand equity of an already established brand, and benefit from its customer base and distribution networks.

An example is Procter & Gamble (P&G) acquiring Gillette Company for a whopping US$57 billion in 2005.[16] Both companies have powerful brands. Gillette is a powerful branded house (single corporate brand structure) against P&G which is a powerful house of brands (multiple product brand structure). By acquiring Gillette, P&G has obviously gained access into new product lines, market segments and customer profiles. But it required huge resources on the part of P&G to acquire Gillette.

The acquisition strategy will mostly be adopted by companies which have strong financial resources at their disposal. Although at the outset the acquisition strategy seems rosy, it has its own inherent disadvantages. One of the biggest challenges in an acquisition is the issue of integration. This comprises the integration of people, resources, policies and procedures and, most importantly, the integration of brands and brand management practices. It also requires cost savings and economies of scale to become successful and accepted from a financial point of view, so an acquisition is often a decision that comprises more than merely the brand advantages.

Star Cruises: acquisitions on the high sea

Leading the Asian market with an 80 percent share in the region and around 900,000 people sailing its ships a year, Star Cruises is surely cruising its way into the global high seas. A part of Resorts World, a Kuala Lumpur listed company, which in turn is a unit of the Malaysian listed casino group Genting Berhad, Star Cruises has been on the acquisition route to gain global dominance.[17]

Star Cruises acquired the larger-than-itself Norwegian Cruise Lines (NCL) in March 2000, to become the fourth largest cruise operator in the world, with a fleet of 17 ships. This acquisition has given Star Cruises a direct entry into the markets of North and South America, Antarctica, Alaska, the Caribbean and Europe. By riding on the strong brand equity of the acquired brand, Star Cruises has been able to grow beyond Asia much faster than by the traditional methods.[18]

With the Asian cruise market valued at a mere US$1 billion out of the total world cruise market of US$14 billion, there is lot of scope for Star Cruises to grow.[19] With this in mind, Star Cruises is leaving no stone unturned. Recently Star Cruises picked up a 20 percent stake in the Singapore-based budget airliner Valuair for an estimated $20 million. Valuair is planning on expanding its routes across Asia including cities in China and Japan. This plan fits well with Star Cruises' strategy as the alliance will provide multiple opportunities for both brands to offer joint air/cruise packages.[20] Star Cruises serves as a good example of following the acquisition strategy to take an Asian brand beyond Asia and gain geographical reach and scope within a limited time horizon.

Brand implementation

The final step in building a brand is the brand implementation process. The previous two steps of brand research and brand identity will enable the company to establish the foundation of the brand and its intended direction. The brand implementation phase is where all the formulated strategies are put into practice in the marketplace. It brings the brand to life and this is where brand associations ultimately start to form in the mindset of customers.

The brand audit identified the brand differentiators and basic brand attributes on which the brand can be built. These are delivered through many touch points. A *touch point* is generally defined as a point of interaction between the company and its stakeholders: internal or external. From a branding perspective, a touch point can be defined as an interaction between the brand and its stakeholder where the brand has an opportunity to make an impact. These touch points give the brand multiple avenues to communicate its value proposition to its target audience and make strong impressions if delivered right (Figure 6.5).

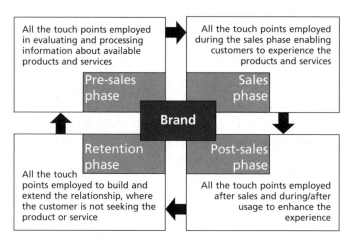

Figure 6.5 Touch point model
Source: VentureRepublic

It is the sum of all the experiences that customers have through these touch points that ultimately builds strong brand equity. This clearly demonstrates that branding is more than just marketing communications. The entire company has to operate successfully around the brand. The touch point model is useful for aligning brand promise and brand delivery.

Companies must ensure that all possible customer touch points are methodically taken care of in the brand implementation process, so that customers actually experience what the brand promises across all interactions with the company.

Touch points can be defined for each function of the company, for example marketing, sales, HR, finance and purchase. All these function interact with stakeholders at some point in time. To make an impact successfully, management must chart all the possible touch points for the brands and formulate the best ways of interaction for each of the functions and touch points. This is easier said than done as it involves extensive cross-functional management discussions in order to make decisions on operating procedures and work flows involving potential strategic tradeoffs.

As represented in Figure 6.5, touch points are classified in four phases: pre-sales, sales, post-sales and retention. These phases also represent the customer purchase life cycle. Each phase provides a unique occasion for the brand to make an impact. As each phase has different levels of awareness, involvement, and significance for customers and stakeholders, companies need to choose the right way of delivering the touch point depending on the occasion.

The touch point model can be used both internally and externally for brand implementation, and this is now discussed.

Internal implementation

The touch points provide a tool for Asian companies to structure, direct and lead the organization and its activities in line with the branding strategy. The tool will also help the buy-in, consent and participation of all employees toward living the brand. The company can implement the following measures to align the organization around the brand:

■ **Brand training and workshops:** Internal stakeholders ranging from senior management to frontline staff must understand and buy into the brand for a successful delivery of the brand's promises. This can be ensured by having structured training programs and brand workshops where employees are educated about the brand, its components and promises. This not only educates the organization as a whole but also makes every individual realize the importance of their contributions to make the brand a success.

- **Brand-oriented HR:** The brand will be successful when everyone works toward its growth and strength. Contribution to the overall brand growth and profitability must be a key factor when defining job profiles and responsibilities. It should also be a basis for appraisal and performance purposes of all employees including the management. This will ensure commitment from the entire organization as performance is linked to financial rewards.

- **Internal communications:** One of the most effective ways to ensure the success of internal brand alignment is to keep all employees informed and updated with the brand, its intention, its challenges, and its external status and image. The entire organization must be aware of the brand promise, how it is being positioned in the market, the entire marketing communications package and the latest updates related to the brand and its strategy. By being on the same page as external customers, every employee will be able to act in tandem with the brand identity and contribute to overall success.

External implementation

Externally, the touch points provide companies with structured plans about the multiple avenues where the brand is in contact with the customers and how the brand can make an impact by choosing the right channel and message. The brand management model (Figure 6.2) illustrated the main external implementation methods, which are discussed in more detail below:

- **Marketing mix:** Externally, the company should ensure that all the marketing elements are in line with its overall brand identity. This includes the quality of the product, the price points and choice of distribution channels among other elements. All these will affect the brand image and positioning in the market. Companies must ensure that all these aspects are constantly monitored, adjusted and optimized for better impact.

- **Marketing communications:** A main element in implementing the brand strategy is the use of marketing communications. The success of a brand will depend on how effectively the message is conveyed to customer segments, distribution channels and many other stakeholders.

The brand positioning, personality and values of a brand will prove futile unless they are communicated through the right media channels, making use of a comprehensive mix of verbal, visual and audio conduits to make a strong impact. Companies should select from the various communications channels available to ensure that brand messages reach the customers, despite the high level of competing messages and noise in the marketplace.

Innovative communications

English Premier League football is one of the most watched foreign sports in China – 100–360 million people watch the games on TV. In 2003, the mobile company Keijian, from Shenzhen, aimed to position its brand as healthy, energetic and upmarket. It decided to sponsor Everton Football Club from the Premier League and the company was also involved in a player exchange program involving players like Li Tie.[21] It was not new to have Chinese football players in foreign leagues, but it was the first time for a Chinese brand to sponsor a club in a foreign league. Everton players had the Keijian name and logo on their shirts, and the company would attach football to everything, building up to the Beijing Olympics in 2008. Instead of buying expensive TV advertising, Keijian hired a Chinese journalist in Liverpool to produce football stories for distribution to Chinese TV stations and sports websites.[22] The case is interesting, as until then Everton had been mid-table and with a limited fan base. But overnight, they became the most popular British football team in China. Initially, Keijian had no intention of entering the British market. Its goal was purely to create awareness and affinity at home, and it just needed an avenue to advertise.

- **Associations and alliances:** Another possible vehicle for building the brand is through partnerships with other brand owners, organizations and distribution channels. Every entity that a brand interacts with will have an influence on its image. Therefore companies should ensure a proper evaluation process when selecting partners through associations and alliances. The outcome can be effective leverage of brand equity from partners that fits well with the brand, while being cost-effective compared to traditional communication channels. A classic example is collaboration between an airline and a credit card company.

- **Corporate logo and design:** A brand must have a simple, appealing, exciting and durable visual aspect. The entire design scheme, including corporate and brand logos, plays an important part. Companies must ensure that the design and logos are relevant to their respective target customer base, reflect their aspirations and effectively convey the brand identity, personality and values in a clear manner. Strong design schemes and logos serve as important identifiers of brands when brand associations and values are attached to them over time, as evidenced by the enduring nature of Nike, Coca-Cola, Mercedes-Benz and McDonald's.

For the successful implementation of brand identity, both internal and external factors must be carefully monitored and managed. Figure 6.6 is an example of how the touch point model can be developed and implemented in an airline company. It illustrates where and when a given customer interacts with the airline.

By utilizing different channels to communicate the brand proposition and effectively reach the customers, the airline can use the touch point model to offer optimum and consistent brand experiences across its customer segments and markets.

As the entire interaction cycle between the customer and the brand is structured into four different stages, it enables companies to manage a focused and actionable approach. It helps companies to optimize their resources by aligning brand promise with brand delivery.

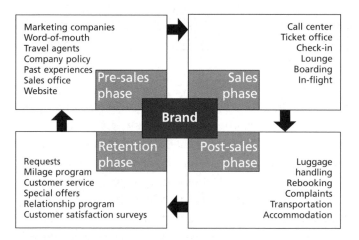

Figure 6.6 Example of a touch point model for an airline company
Source: VentureRepublic

Brand equity

There is no universally accepted definition of brand equity. The term means different things for different companies. Many definitions are focused primarily on consumer responses, but can benefit from being attached to the financial performance, and hence reflect the sole purpose of branding, that is, to drive a profitable business and provide shareholder value.

However, there are several common characteristics of the many definitions used today. Professor David A. Aaker, a leading academic in brand management, defines brand equity as:

> a set of assets (and liabilities) linked to a brand's name and symbol that adds to (or subtracts from) the value provided by a product or service to a firm and/or that firm's customers.[23]

The Marketing Science Institute defines brand equity as:

> the set of associations and behaviors on the part of the brand's customers, channel members and parent corporation that permits the brand to earn greater volume or greater margins than it could without the brand name and that gives a brand a strong, sustainable and differentiated advantage over competitors.[24]

There are other definitions of brand equity, but the above two more or less capture its overall essence.

There are several stakeholders concerned with brand equity, such as the firm, the customer, the distribution channels, media, and other stakeholders like the financial markets and analysts, depending on the type of company ownership. But, ultimately, it is the customer who is the most critical component in defining brand equity as it is his/her choices that determine the success or failure of the company. Customer knowledge about the brand, its perceived differences and its effects on purchase behavior and decisions lie at the heart of brand equity. The knowledge and associations attached to the brand result in choices which have a direct impact on the brand's financial performance.

Brand equity is the combined measure of brand strength and consists of three sets of metrics – knowledge, preference and financial. The brand equity model in Table 6.2 is a useful guide for corporate management to benchmark the objectives and performance of their own brands as well as competitor brands. These metrics are now discussed in more detail.

TABLE 6.2 **Brand equity model**		
Knowledge metrics	**Preference metrics**	**Financial metrics**
Brand awareness	▪ Familiarity	▪ Market share
▪ Recognition	▪ Consideration	▪ Price premium
▪ Unaided recall	▪ Purchase	▪ Revenue
▪ Aided recall	▪ Usage	▪ Transaction value
▪ Top-of-mind recall	▪ Loyalty	▪ Lifetime value
		▪ Growth rate
Brand associations		
▪ Functional		
▪ Emotional		

Source: VentureRepublic

Knowledge metrics

Brand knowledge refers to brand awareness (whether and when the customer knows the brand) and brand image (what associations customers have with the brand). These metrics capture how the brand is perceived in the customer mindset (awareness, feelings and perceptions). As discussed earlier, a brand would select and use the relevant communication channels and touch points to successfully communicate its brand identity to its customers. The direct result of these activities would be to create brand knowledge.

Brand awareness can be measured through brand recognition and brand recall. Knowing about the brand as a result of many past actions, interactions and experiences with the brand is referred to as "recognition". Relating and recalling the brand from memory whenever any related dimension is mentioned, such as the product category, occasions of use and so on is referred to as "recall".[25]

As the basic knowledge of the brand drives all the other customer interactions with it, customers must be aware of the brand. But mere awareness is not sufficient to drive brand equity. Customers should be able to relate the brand to product categories, the needs it fulfills, the occasion of use and so on. This ensures that the brand is in the customer's repertoire. Simply put, recognition without recall is less efficient, and companies must seek high recall for their brands. Usually recall is measured in three levels:

▪ **Aided recall:** customers recall the brand when prompted with some cues. Customers are aware of the brand but are not readily able to relate the brand to any specific dimensions (product category, needs, usage). Companies need to ensure that the brand message and its value propositions are communicated effectively so that it becomes one with its dimensions and customers are able to recall it without any cues.

- **Unaided recall:** customers recall the brand without the help of any cues about the brand. Whenever the related dimensions (product category, usage, needs and so on) are mentioned, customers can relate them to the brand. This reflects a high level of recall. Customers are aware of the brand and able to retrieve it from memory when needed, which is important in many purchase situations. Companies can achieve this by constantly communicating the relevance of the brand and delivering on the brand promise to keep it in the minds of the customers.

- **Top-of-mind recall:** the ideal stage of recall that all brands aspire to achieve – the brand is at the top of customers' minds in the respective product categories. Without any cues, they are able to mention the name of the brand as the first choice when the category or other cues are mentioned.

Another measure of brand knowledge, as important as awareness metrics, is the associations built around the brand to define its character. Associations are formed and attached to brands by usage and over time.

In his book *How Brands Become Icons,*[26] Professor Douglas Holt describes how four different "authors", namely companies, popular culture, customers and others influencers (like media, opinion makers and so on) shape opinions about the brand and fill it with meaning. A brand culture is established as the "authors" use, discuss and monitor the brand as part of their daily lives and as they interact with the brand at various stages and levels of involvement over time. A brand can therefore be viewed as the *culture* of a product or service, and products and services can become cultural artifacts. Hence brands play a strong role in society and in popular culture.

Relationships or mental bonds are developed and formed between brands and their customers' minds in many ways as mentioned before. One of the ways is when the company conveys attributes and benefits through various means of communications channels and touch points. It can be purely functional where brands seek to base the associations on basic attributes (design, quality, price points and so on). It can also be emotional associations where brands build on factors in addition to the basic attributes (image, prestige, and so on) to allow customers to make a statement, feel good, and express their personality by associating themselves with the brands.

The research from the brand audit will help companies to identify the brand differentiators and basic brand attributes to obtain a relevant and optimal mix. Successful branding means emphasizing those features, benefits and emotional aspects which are important to customers, while differentiating them from those of the competition.

Companies must seek to build strong associations which are in line with the overall brand positioning. The touch point process clearly demonstrated the importance of managing these interactions to shape and sharpen the brand experience. All associations that the brand aspires to develop should be credible, unique and, most importantly, relevant to customers.

Functional associations are connections that brands build with customers based on certain tangible and basic attributes that constitute the brand. For example, BMW's functional associations could be German engineering, precision technology, tested quality and long-term durability. All these are attributes that make up a BMW car. They are tangible and can be measured and evaluated in quantifiable terms. Although these associations are relatively easy to establish, they tap into the basic level of brand building. They might also run the risk of becoming generic over a period of time. For example, an airline which emphasizes safe flights will not be able to reap any special benefits as flight safety has become a generic attribute in the airline industry. This attribute does not differentiate it from the competition.

Functional associations are relatively easy for competitors to copy and they would often be able to claim the same for their own brands. Therefore brands must aspire to create additional associations that appeal to human emotions to ensure a stronger bonding with the customer.

Emotional associations are connections that brands establish with customers based on factors appealing to their own mindsets, beliefs and personalities. These associations are intangible in nature and relate to factors like status, prestige, aspirations, values and personality types. In the BMW example, the emotional associations could be prestige and social class, and the status associated with owning a BMW. The brand could fit and support an individual who is in charge of his life. Hence the brand plays an important role for the customer to express his personality, beliefs and desired status.

Emotional associations are much stronger than functional associations as these tap into the emotional aspects of customers, but they take longer to establish as the products and services are filled with meaning over time. The associations attached to the brand are conventions shared collectively by groups and networks of people. Brands with strong emotional associations create switching costs for customers by becoming part of their lives and experiences. It is relatively complicated for customers to switch brands as it could mean abandoning the shared conventions in the groups and networks.

By having a longer life in customer minds, emotional associations provide competitive advantages by creating barriers for competing brands to replicate the trusted relationship between the brand and its customers.

Knowledge metrics form the initial component of brand equity, with their focus on awareness and the associations created around the brand. They lay the foundation for further interactions with customers and other stakeholders – a strong connecting link between marketing actions and various customer responses.

Preference metrics

These metrics describe and track customer actions based on the awareness and associations created in the previous phase. Preference is a generic term that refers to the level of liking toward something and it can range from mere liking to a deep loyalty with repeat actions over time. Preference metrics include all those different levels of liking and actual customer behavioral patterns as a result of the awareness and associations that are created:

- **Familiarity:** a level of awareness where customers are more knowledgeable about the brand than, for example, just the brand name itself.

- **Consideration:** customers are interested in the brand. After acquiring basic knowledge about the brand, customers evaluate the brand benefits and attributes against other brands in the same category. They narrow down their list of brands to consider. This becomes the repertoire of brands from where any further purchase decision is probably made.

- **Purchase:** the brand is sought and purchased. It could also be referred to as trial.

- **Usage:** customers decide whether to stick with the brand or switch to a different one. This is crucial and depends on the usage experience that customers have.

- **Loyalty:** the ultimate testimonial for any brand seeking to create loyal customers. Success is tied closely to how well the brand aligns the promise and delivery. The loyalty stage is where customers have deep and meaningful relationships with the brand. Measures of loyalty are customer satisfaction and retention, for example.

Preference metrics help a company to assess the equity of the brand in terms of marketing metrics. Additional metrics could be customer leads and acquisitions to illustrate the pipeline of future revenues.

Figure 6.7 illustrates how preference metrics could be applied to three different brands. It shows the value of each of the preference metrics, and also tracks the conversion rate between the stages for each brand. A benchmark of conversion rates is important as it indicates possible bottlenecks which need to be addressed with specific marketing actions. It could also highlight stages where certain touch points have to be evaluated for future relevance or emphasized more than at present. For example, brand B has a lower conversion rate from the familiarity to the consideration stage compared to the two other brands (40 percent against 75 and 70 percent respectively).

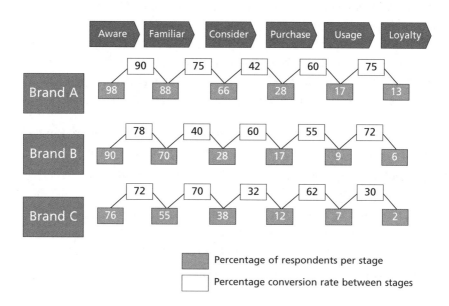

Figure 6.7 Brand metrics performance model
Source: VentureRepublic

The chart can be used for other variables and could include customer segments, distribution channels and other factors which can help the company to accomplish a complete picture of the preference metrics and their impact on business. Benchmarking against brands, segments and distribution channels is important as it reflects dynamics over time and will track the level of progression.

It is important to note in this context, that business-to-business (B2B) brands have a considerable advantage over many consumer brands. B2B brands know their customers directly and interact with them frequently. They can therefore employ metrics like acquisition, retention and loyalty with precision, as the data needed are drawn directly from the customer level instead of the aggregate level. Many consumer brands base their metrics on an aggregate level and have less direct interaction with customers.

Financial metrics

These metrics measure the financial implications of brand equity linked to marketing metrics:

- **Market share:** quantifies the brand's share of the market and can be divided into customer segments, product segments and geographical markets. It is an indication of the brand's ability to retain and, more importantly, attract new customers.

- **Price premium:** the financial advantage of a strong brand is its ability to command a price premium in the market. Measuring the differential price points between the brand and competing brands indicates the level of value creation and the premium adds to the overall brand equity. Price elasticity measures can also be included.

- **Revenue:** the average annual revenue per customer divided into segments, product segments and geographical markets. The trend of this metric illustrates whether the brand extracts more value from customers on an annual basis.

- **Transaction value:** the average transaction value per customer divided into segments, product segments and geographical markets. The trend of this metric shows how well the brand develops its customers, for example in the form of cross-selling and/or upselling to other products and brands.

- **Lifetime value:** the average lifetime value of customers divided into segments, product segments and geographical markets. The trend of this metric illustrates whether the brand extracts more value from customers throughout their entire life cycle with the brand.

- **Growth rate:** the level of brand strength and its equity in the market along with the level of loyalty among customer segments and the pipeline of prospective customers determine the growth opportunity of the brand. The ability of the brand to drive growth adds to its overall equity.

Financial metrics measure the overall value that a company generates from investments made in building and managing brands. Companies need to make sure that business drivers and marketing metrics are aligned, so that the impact of brand equity on the financial outcome is maximized.

Based on the detailed analysis of brand equity, it should be quite clear that brand equity is not just about top line growth but also the bottom line. Although brand equity gives companies tools to measure the overall equity, the actual value of a brand, considered for accounting and M&A purposes, is based on different methods. The final step of the brand management model covers this aspect.

Brand valuation

Brand valuation is a relatively new development in the practice of brand management. For most of marketing history, marketers were not able to justify fully the financial implications of marketing and branding-related expenses. Until the 1980s, tangible assets like manufacturing plants, land, property and also financial assets were perceived as the main source of business which could be accounted for in financial terms on the balance sheet. There was a common acceptance that intangible assets like brands generated a large part of shareholder value, but there was no generally accepted method of how to account for these assets on the balance sheet.

During the 1980s, two major factors drove the increasing recognition of the intangible assets valuation. Firstly, the gap between company book values and market value in, for example, their stock listings was continuously widening. Secondly, the many M&As of the 1980s saw a huge increase in the premiums paid over and above market value for companies.

A leading UK food conglomerate was one of the first companies to independently assess its brand value in order to fence off a potential hostile takeover attempt, and in 1989 this early method of valuation was endorsed by the London Stock Exchange by allowing the inclusion of intangible assets in the class tests for shareholder approvals during takeovers.[27] This led to the development of more sophisticated methods during the 1990s and the discipline is still work in progress by academics and practitioners.

The purpose of these various methodologies, all with different steps, has been to put a financial value on the brand. One method is based on predicting the future earnings derived from the brand and capitalizing the earnings by applying a multiple in the form of a discount rate, hence calculating the net present value (NPV). This approach combines brand equity measures and financial measures, and has become the most widely recognized methodology for brand valuation.

The brand equity measure relates to how brands drive customer demand and also influence long-term loyalty (as discussed earlier in this chapter). The financial measure is the NPV of expected future earnings which is a common concept in business and within the financial community. This method includes the following three steps for brand valuation (Figure 6.8):

1. **Financial analysis:** identifies and predicts revenues and earnings from intangibles related to individual brands or the entire brand portfolio. The analysis can be further divided into various segments, such as types of customers, distribution channels, markets and so on, and then calculated into a total sum. The intangible earnings are calculated as brand revenues minus operating costs, a charge for the capital employed and taxes. This method is similar to the net economic value added (EVA), which represents the cash flow from an opportunity adjusted for the cost of resources used to generate the cash flow.[28] Therefore, a capital charge is included in the calculation.

2. **Brand contribution:** assesses how much the brand contributes to drive demand, thereby measuring the extent to which the brand contributes to intangible earnings. The brand contribution can be measured in various ways but the association and preference metrics discussed earlier are the most common factors for determining the proportion of intangible earnings related to the brand. The brand earnings are calculated by multiplying the brand contribution (for example as a percentage or an index factor) by the intangible earnings from the financial analysis.

3. **Brand value:** calculates the NPV of the expected future brand earnings discounted by a discount rate which best reflects the risk of the future brand earnings. In other words, the discount rate takes into consideration the strength of the brand equity and its expected potential to generate future brand earnings. The brand discount rate is estimated as the current, risk-free rate adjusted for any risk involved in the form of the expected volatility of future brand earnings. In principle, strong brand equity can accelerate and enhance cash flow, and can lead to less volatile and vulnerable cash flows and vice versa.[29] The brand value is a calculation of the NPV of the expected future brand earnings from the selected periods, discounted by the brand discount rate. As the brand is also expected to generate earnings after these periods, an annuity component should be added to reflect this. The annuity estimates the value of brand earnings after the forecast period.

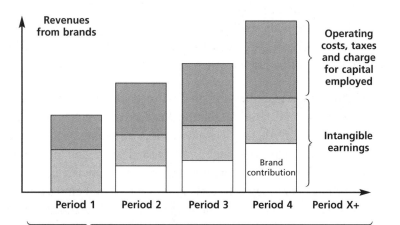

Figure 6.8 Illustration of the net present value brand valuation method

Conclusion

Over the past decade, a number of approaches for brand valuation have been developed by different brand and management consulting firms. Interbrand was one of the first consultancies to develop and further refine the principles of the valuation method of discounted brand earnings. It has almost become the industry standard, with many global corporations using it and the US GAAP (Generally Accepted Accounting Principles) and The International Accounting Standards recognizing it. The Appendix describes the brand valuation method proposed by Interbrand in detail.

Recognition by the above standard accounting procedures extends credibility to the various brand valuation methods. Therefore, any boardroom can commission a brand valuation study in the knowledge that accounting companies, auditors, local accounting standards boards, tax offices and stock exchanges will accept the brand value as calculated when it appears as part of their financial statements.[30]

Despite these developments, all valuation methods, including brand valuation, have an inherent element of subjectivity in them. Several factors such as the length of the time horizons for the future earnings, the size of the operating costs, the measure of how much the brand contributes to intangible earnings and the estimation of the brand discount rate are all subject to individual assessments.

Brand valuation can be applied for two major purposes. It provides the company with an internal tool and framework for strategic brand management and determines the financial outcome of the marketing actions, hence helping to assess the profit generation of the brand. Brand valuation is also applicable for accounting and financial purposes, such as M&As, licencing, joint ventures, alliances, collateral for debt and many other applications.

Notes

1 "Dimensions of brand personality", Jennifer L. Aaker, *Journal of Marketing Research*, **34**, August 1997, 347–56.
2 "Global champions in emerging markets", *McKinsey Quarterly*, (2), 2005.
3 *McKinsey Quarterly*, (2), 2005, ibid.
4 *McKinsey Quarterly*, (2), 2005, ibid.
5 *McKinsey Quarterly*, (2), 2005, ibid.
6 http:// www.hsbc.com.
7 "Business: Trung Nguyen coffee wins ASEAN Young Business Award", 29 July 2004, Vietnam News Brief Service.

8 "Coffee giant to pour into Singapore", 14 March 2005, *Vietnam Investment Review*.
9 "Trung Nguyen officially inaugurates its fairy tea house", 21 March 2005, *Saigon Times Daily*.
10 "Café chain cites rival rip off", 23 April 2001, *Vietnam Investment Review*.
11 "China power brands", *Business Week*, 8 November 2004.
12 "China offers brand new opportunities", *Financial Times*, 22 April, 2004.
13 *Business Week*, 8 November, 2004, op. cit.
14 "Executive Summary of Watson Wyatt Worldwide's M&A Survey – Asia Pacific", 1998, Watson Wyatt Worldwide.
15 "Shiriro acquires Hasselblad", press release, 30 January, 2003.
16 http://phx.corporate-ir.net.
17 "Star Cruises rebounding from Tsunami blip", Kelvin Wong, 31 January 2005, *Straits Times*.
18 *Winning in Asia*, Peter J. Williamson, Chapter 5, p. 141.
19 Kelvin Wong, 31 January 2005, op. cit.
20 "Fly-cruise deals from Star Cruises, Valuair", 21 December 2004, *Straits Times*.
21 "Everton paid nil in Li Tie's transfer?", *China Daily*, 14 August, 2003.
22 "Chinese phone maker's fancy footwork", BBC News, 27 October, 2003.
23 *Building Strong Brands*, David A. Aaker, Free Press, 1996.
24 *How Consumers Identify Good Brands*, Alastair Gordon, AC Nielsen paper.
25 *Strategic Brand Management*, Kevin Lane Keller, 2nd edn, Prentice Hall, 2003.
26 *How Brands Become Icons*, Douglas Holt, Harvard Business Press, 2004.
27 Jan Lindemann (2004) "The Financial Value of Brands", in *Brands and Branding*, The Economist/Bloomberg Press.
28 "The EVA style of investing", James A. Abate, L. Grant and G. Bennett Stewart III, *Journal of Portfolio Management*, Summer 2004.
29 "Market-based assets and shareholder value: a framework for analysis", Rajendra K. Srivastava, Tasadduq A. Shervani and Liam Fahey, *Journal of Marketing*, **62**, January 1998.
30 Author interview with Renzo Scacco, director of brand valuation, Interbrand Australia.

CHAPTER 7

SUCCESSFUL ASIAN BRAND CASES

*The West underestimates the potential power of the East and the
shift of wealth that is taking place already.*[1]

Sir Martin Sorrell, CEO, WPP Group

Branding is the face of a strong business strategy

Brands will become a prominent business driver and a strong source of
sustainable competitive advantage and financial value in Asia during the
next two decades for the reasons discussed so far. The region is going
through an era of renewed growth, development and prosperity. This has
resulted in a new and profound confidence throughout Asia. The booming
economies of China, India, Thailand and Malaysia have resulted in the
emergence of millions of middle-class consumers with an increasing
disposable income. This rising disposable income will not only buy them
basic products but will also enable consumers to buy brands. This potential
consumer power can serve as a strong platform for building and managing
brands in the region.

This chapter looks at some of the successful Asian companies which
have established themselves as strong brands throughout the region and
many of them well beyond Asia. By combining a classic Asian business
heritage with unique insights into their industries and strong management,
these companies have built successful brands which others can learn from.

The different brands portrayed in this chapter are inspiring examples of
how companies from highly diverse beginnings and heritage have created
successful brands. It describes their brand journey, their reasons for tread-
ing this path, their brand management processes and the major challenges
they face in the future.

There are many factors (internal company issues, macroeconomic,
market and industry issues) that determine the success of brand strategies.
Successful brands are dependant on the right mindset, beliefs, skill sets and
resources, as discussed previously. But the one single issue that stands out

amongst all is the commitment and dedication of the boardroom in creating, managing and nurturing brands as part of driving shareholder value.

Despite the individual character of the boardrooms of the companies portrayed in this chapter, they share one common theme which is also one of the strongest reasons for their success: their commitment to branding. These boardrooms strongly believe in the importance of branding and brands, the ability to drive value from brand strategies, and the criticality in managing branding processes at the boardroom level led by the CEO and corporate management.

Another common characteristic of the brands depicted in this chapter is their strategy of using branding as one of the key strategic pillars right from their inception. This is in great contrast to the usual Asian bottom-up approach to marketing and branding. The difference in beliefs, style, strategies and results among the two types of boardrooms clearly suggests that a management-driven approach to branding is a key success factor. Any Asian company that aspires to build strong brands can indeed learn a thing or two from the following case stories.

CASE 1
Singapore Airlines – an excellent Asian brand

Think about one of the strongest brands from Asia, and chances are that Singapore Airlines (SIA) and its long-serving, almost iconic Singapore Girl, comes to mind first. SIA has consistently been one of the most profitable airlines globally, and has always had the reputation of being a trendsetter and industry challenger. There are several good reasons for this. Most relate directly to strong brand management driven primarily by the SIA boardroom and corporate management, and the healthy brand equity as the result of a dedicated, professional brand strategy throughout a diversified and global organization.

The Singapore Airlines brand has been instrumental to the airline from the very start. It serves as one of the leading brand cases from Asia for other established brands as well as any aspiring brands. Unlike many other Asian companies, the Singapore Airlines brand is unique in that the boardroom takes dedicated leadership of the brand strategy.

Background

Singapore Airlines traces its beginnings back to 1947 as Malayan Airlines, a joint venture between the Malaysian and Singapore governments, serving primarily the Southeast Asian region. In 1965, Singapore separated from Malaysia, and the two governments agreed to set up separate airlines. Singapore Airlines came into its own in 1972.[2]

Singapore Airlines was in a different position from most other airlines at the time. As there were no domestic routes to serve, it immediately started competing on the international playing field, in terms of international air traffic rights, access to airports, securing flight slots and landing rights, and attracting a new customer base. Unlike most state-owned entities, Singapore Airlines was subject to heavy competition from the onset and this tough start created a driving spirit to compete and a dedicated approach by the boardroom to build a strong brand. These factors have prevailed within the organization since then, and served the airline well, as the following will illustrate.

Brand philosophy

Singapore Airlines decided on a fully branded product/service differentiation strategy from the very beginning. Innovation, best technology, genuine quality and excellent customer service were to become the major drivers of the brand.

Throughout the course of its 33-year history, Singapore Airlines has remained true to its brand attributes. It has pioneered many in-flight experiential and entertainment innovations, and strived to be best in class. SIA was the first to introduce hot meals, free alcoholic and non-alcoholic beverages, hot towels with a unique and patented scent, personal entertainment systems, and video on demand in all cabins. The company keeps driving innovation as an important part of the brand, and the cabin ambience and combined experience are key factors of their success.

On the technology side, Singapore Airlines still maintains the youngest fleet of aircraft amongst all major air carriers, and keeps to the stringent policy of replacing older aircraft for newer, better models. It has always been first in line to take delivery of new aircraft types like Boeing 747 jumbo jets, Boeing 777, and it will become the first airline to fly the Airbus super jumbo A380 in 2006. At one stage, even the aircraft were sub-

First to Fly A380

SINGAPORE AIRLINES

EXPERIENCE THE DIFFERENCE IN 2006

Singapore Airlines will be the first commercial airline to fly the Airbus A380

Courtesy Singapore Airlines

branded, for example the 747 Megatop and the 777 Jubilee, to further distinguish SIA and its brand from competitors.

Singapore Airlines also flew the Concorde between Singapore and London in the late 1970s in collaboration with British Airways (BA). The aircraft was painted with SIA's colors and logos on one side, and BA's on the other, and it carried crew from both airlines.

The strategy behind the technology program is clear – it enhances cost efficiency to use the latest aircraft. An example of this was the new non-stop services to Los Angeles and New York launched in 2004, which attracted huge publicity in the global media and kept the brand's innovation promise alive. It is the world's longest commercial passenger flight between Singapore and New York, lasting for more than 18.5 hours.[3] The special aircraft for these long-range routes (Airbus 340-500) have been sub-branded Leadership to further distinguish the brand promise. An advantage of SIA's constant first mover introductions is the significant impact from substantial media exposure and international recognition.

Singapore Airlines recognizes that each innovation has a relatively short life span. Once other airlines adopt it, it is no longer considered "innovative". Therefore, SIA continues to invest heavily in R&D, innovation and technology as an integrated part of the business strategy to further differentiate itself.[4]

When the tsunami struck across Asia in December 2004, SIA engaged in aid transport through its global network and within three weeks the company's cargo subsidiary had shipped 325 tons of supplies. SIA staff collected US$110.300 and the company contributed US$183,000 to the Red Cross.[5]

The Singapore Girl

The personalization of the Singapore Airlines brand is the mixed male and female cabin crew, where especially the flight stewardesses, commonly referred to as Singapore Girls, have become very well known. SIA engaged French haute couture designer Pierre Balmain at the inauguration of the airline in 1972. He designed a special version of the Malay sarong kebaya

Singapore Airlines' main brand ambassadors, the Singapore Girls, in Central Park, New York City
Courtesy Singapore Airlines

Ms See Biew Wah, SIA check and training stewardess, gets that Balmain touch from the French couturier and Madame Madeleine Kohler, Balmain's director of creations and special projects. The uniforms made their debut in 1968
Courtesy Singapore Airlines

as the uniform which later became one of the most recognized signatures of the airline – a very specific and visual part of the entire brand experience.

The Singapore Girl strategy turned out to be a powerful idea and she has become a successful brand icon, with an almost mythical status and aura around her. The Singapore Girl encapsulates Asian values and hospitality, and can be described as caring, warm, gentle, elegant and serene. It is a brilliant personification of SIA's commitment to service and quality excellence. The icon has become so strong that Madame Tussaud's in London started to display the Singapore Girl in 1994 as the first commercial figure ever.

Singapore Airlines also runs one of the most comprehensive and rigorous training programs for cabin and flight crew in the industry to ensure that the SIA brand experience is fully and consistently delivered. The company runs an internal training academy in Singapore where all levels of staff are trained, retrained and evaluated regularly. Cabin crew are evaluated at least four times a year to ensure that the brand delivers, from service and food issues to emergency procedures.[6]

Brand communication

Singapore Airlines has been as consistent in its communication vehicles as in its brand strategy. The primary message, Singapore Airlines – A Great Way to Fly, has been consistently conveyed in exclusive print media and also in selected TV commercials of high production value to underline the quality aspirations of the brand. All communication messages are featured through the iconic Singapore Girl in different themes and settings in various locations around the world.

When Singapore Airlines recently launched their comfortable "space bed" seats in business class, they ran a 60-second commercial of a highly emotional and mythical character to underline the aspiration of the brand and the Singapore Girl, and to set their airline brand apart from the competition.

Interestingly, Singapore Airlines has chosen to focus on one aspect of the experiential brand strategy – in-flight hospitality and warmth featured by the Singapore Girl – rather than trying to communicate the entire brand benefits through its messages; a dangerous trap, which many other brands often fall into in their efforts to communicate everything at once. This has led to a focused and consistent message for SIA during the last 33 years. This in itself is a great achievement for any brand, as changing marketing staff throughout a company's life span often feel inclined to change the communication platform by putting their own fingerprints on their work.

The Singapore Girl has contributed immensely to the success of Singapore Airlines' brand strategy and its entire positioning around customer and service excellence.

Brand strategy

While other airlines have also pursued high service/quality brand strategies, none has been able to match Singapore Airlines in consistency, commitment, and true permeation of the brand in every facet. SIA has been able to maintain its brand advantage by not wavering from its brand strategy. This is a particularly difficult position to maintain in a highly cyclical industry where the competition seems to react on a daily basis to changes in performance. This type of commitment takes dedication from the board, CEO and senior management team, and strong faith in the brand's ability to pull through bad times. The management team and shareholders must maintain a longer term outlook to avoid making short-term, reactionary decisions which dilute the brand. A testimony among many others to this fact was given when Cheong Choong Kong, former CEO of SIA, was made Asia's Business Man of the Year in 2002.[7]

For example, pressure on US airlines stemming from low-cost carrier competition has caused a number of the full-service airlines to begin charging for on-board services which used to be free. Historically, business travelers were willing to pay a premium for full-service airlines, essentially because they provided these services. By abandoning their customer service strategy, even on restricted flights, the premium US airlines are diluting their brand in search of short-term profitability. This is creating a circular effect where the premium airlines are losing cost-sensitive customers to low-cost airlines, which causes them to reduce price to retain these customers. This in turn creates more cost pressure. This cost pressure causes them to start reducing the premium services which made them distinct from the low-cost airlines in the first place.

Singapore Airlines has been able to deliver some of the best results in the industry by avoiding this type of reactionary behavior.

Developing cost advantages

Singapore Airlines' brand strategy is, in theory, a relatively high-cost strategy. Each brand benefit requires significant investment, careful management and detailed implementation programs to live up to the brand promise. Singapore Airlines has carefully built a financial and fixed cost infrastructure which allows it to continue investing to support the brand while challenging the competition on costs.

First, the strong cash position allows Singapore Airlines to internally fund purchases of new equipment and airplanes with cash and in large numbers to get discounts, and limit interest costs.[8] SIA is not locked into long-term leases, and can easily accommodate newer, more fuel-efficient equipment which also minimizes maintenance costs and avoids expensive aircraft downtime.

A second benefit of SIA's infrastructure is the age of its fleet. Maintaining the youngest generation of aircraft provides SIA with some of the lowest fuel costs in the industry. This is significant since an airline's fuel costs constitute 15–20 percent of the total costs. On top of this, SIA has a policy of hedging up to 50 percent of its fuel contracts two years in advance to avoid cyclical and often large volatility in fuel prices – a task carried out by in-house trained specialists.[9]

Finally, the financial and cash position has allowed SIA to weather the short-term dips in the industry better than the competition.

The brand delivers results

Singapore Airlines has maintained its position as one of the best-known and best-performing brands in Asia, and remains one of the few consistent performers in an industry where established brands are struggling to stay alive. SIA has followed a simple management formula to achieve outstanding results:

Revenues: Command a price premium through consistent brand benefits and avoid reactionary pricing behavior in order to condition the customer not to wait for price matching.

Costs: Tight control of costs through ownership of the most cost-efficient aircraft, hedging against fuel price increases, agile management of the entire company and so on.

Profits: Run the business with a long-term outlook. Be consistent. Stay true to the brand.

Future challenges

The last three years have seen a dramatic shift in the airline industry. There have been major shakeouts and loose consolidation amongst premium, full-service players and a wide expansion in the low-cost carrier market – not least in the, until recently, highly regulated Asian airspace. Air travel is becoming a commodity and most major routes are saturated with fierce competition. The low-cost carriers have significantly influenced consumer behavior for cheap price bargains among leisure travelers. Increasingly, business travelers are doing the same on short- and medium-haul routes in order to save company costs.

SIA has already jumped ahead, launching its own carrier for local and short-haul routes, Tiger Airways, to stay at the forefront of competition. The aim is to avoid dilution of the core premium brand, Singapore Airlines.

Singapore Airlines' strongly embedded positioning and commitment to the brand has positioned it well to compete in the new landscape. The challenge is to stay true to the brand and keep delivering on the fairly high-cost promise of quality, innovation and service. This requires heavy, ongoing investments and healthy cash flows which can only be achieved through a continuous price premium strategy and satisfactory passenger load factors. In other words, customers' perception of the price/value equation, their future buying behavior (partly to be influenced by the low-cost carriers) and loyalty, among other factors, are crucial for the future.

In most industries, there are always segments willing to pay for quality brands. Therefore, the question is not whether there are customers in the market for higher value airlines, but rather the ability for SIA to constantly nurture the brand promise, keep innovating and capture the overall value of the brand in the minds of the customers.

The strong brand equity of Singapore Airlines is one of the most valuable assets for the company and its cash-rich balance sheet. Singapore Airlines is an interesting business case from Asia demonstrating the importance of having strategic branding on the boardroom agenda. The airline can serve as valuable inspiration for other Asian companies trying to build and extract value from their own brands. Singapore Airlines is among the top companies globally that are truly able to control the brand through every interaction and experience. SIA has become a hugely rewarded innovator and industry leader: "A Great Way to Fly".

CASE 2
Amanresorts – the unbranded brand

Amanresorts is one of the iconic brands to have emerged from Asia.[10] Widely acclaimed as the best luxury resort brand in the world, Amanresorts is known for ultra-premium service and luxury, high-profile clientele and the most exotic locations. True to the meaning of its name – Aman means peace in Sanskrit – Amanresorts has built up a reputation of providing a divine and peaceful experience by maintaining exclusivity and being totally discreet about its clients, among them many famous celebrities. A magazine once referred to Amanresorts as being "faultlessly discreet".[11]

Despite not going down the path of traditional brand building (discussed later), Amanresorts has managed to build one of the strongest brands in the hospitality industry across the world. Creating a perfect blend of a resort

Paradise on earth – sea, sun, and luxury at Amanwella (Sri Lanka)
Courtesy Amanresorts

experience with the local history, culture and heritage, Amanresorts has been able to create a real world paradise. As with most iconic brands in the world, Amanresorts was also guided by its visionary founder and chairman, Dutch-Indonesian Adrian Zecha, and his clear-cut business strategy right from the start.

The brand equity was built by creating a strong and distinct personality in line with the organization's philosophy. The management team, led by Adrian Zecha, has ensured a continuous investment in all aspects of the brand to ensure consistent delivery of Amanresorts' brand promises.

Background

Amanresorts was born out of Adrian Zecha's strong contempt toward the corporatization of the hotel and resort industry. The first of the Amanresorts was started in Phuket, Thailand in December 1987 and it was called Amanpuri. Based on its founding philosophy, Amanpuri had fewer than 50 rooms as against the over 400-room norms of the big hotel chains. This was part of the strategy. By having fewer than 50 rooms in each of the Amanresorts, the company has been consistently able to provide a world-class personalized service to every guest. Amanresorts runs one of the highest yields per room in the entire industry.

As Adrian Zecha once said: "The whole point is to keep things as not institutional as possible."[12] The strategy has been so successful that today Amanresorts has its "pieces of paradise" spread across 11 countries – France, Indonesia, French Polynesia, Thailand, Cambodia, Morocco, Philippines, USA, India, Bhutan and Sri Lanka, with more in the pipeline.

The right location is the key factor in the hotel industry and, particularly for a luxury brand like Amanresorts, it simply defines the success of the company. Adrian Zecha is known for being a great site locator and has an impeccable nose for future sites. He said Croatia would become the next hot destination in Europe while the Balkan war was still tearing countries apart. Many of the greatest and often hidden locations in the world reside with old families who only rarely consider selling their heritage jewels. When they do decide to sell, it is very likely Zecha will get the first call, due to his reputation and exclusive network. Said Anil Thadani, Amanresorts' co-founder: "If someone called from Brazil for example, and said that they had a beautiful site, Adrian Zecha would not hesitate to fly off to see the location the same day. He is known for that."[13]

Brand philosophy

Amanresorts has emerged as one of the iconic brands of the global hospitality industry. Apart from a proactive and supportive top management, the other main factor contributing to the brand's success has been a dedicated alignment of the corporate vision with the branding strategies and programs. Amanresorts' corporate strategy and hence its branding strategy has been built on four main pillars:

- Keeping the resorts non-institutional

- Providing guests with a luxury private home and not a mere hotel

- Offering its visitors a holistic holiday experience by combining luxury with the unique heritage and culture of the resort location

- Maintaining a high level of exclusivity.

Non-institutional

Right from the start, Amanresorts has striven to be as unlike a typical commercial resort chain as possible. The owners' aversion toward the corporatization of the hotel industry has led to a unique work culture and atmosphere within Amanresorts. With the objective of providing an excellent personalized service to all its guests, staff members are constantly urged to be as innovative and creative in their service as possible to make every interaction with the guests a memorable experience. Most of the managerial and other staff that Amanresorts recruits are primarily people who have had no experience in the hotel industry but possess the right attitude and the ability to conform to the Amanresorts' culture. This is strictly adhered to, as Amanresorts believes that people with no experience come without any hang-ups about doing things in a particular way and without rigid mindsets. This fits in well with Amanresorts' philosophy of creative and innovative service.

The right attitude was the key point when Adrian Zecha and Anil Thadani once stumbled upon a great front office desk clerk in a Sydney hotel whom they subsequently hired to run Amanpuri. He later developed into one of the best performing managers at one of the resorts.[14]

Furthermore, there is no written manual describing standard operating procedures (SOPs) nor are there any set ways of doing things. Sharon Howard, who has been associated with Amanresorts for the last 13 years training its staff, said: "Every employee is trained to be intuitive, to watch body language and not intrude, and it's exciting that there's no set way to do the job."[15] Managers and staff are asked to run the resorts as if they were their own companies. This unique work culture has enabled Amanresorts to delight its high-paying guests ever since the inception of the brand.

Luxury private home

When Adrian Zecha started Amanpuri with just 40 rooms it was evident that it was going to target the ultra-premium customer segment of Hollywood stars, pop singers, sports icons and wealthy businesspeople. Given the limited number of rooms and the expensive luxury facilities provided, it had to be priced at the very upper end. This justified its target customers. Another main attribute was the strategy of providing ultra-premium and extremely personalized service to the limited number of guests at each resort. This belief was well captured when Adrian Zecha said: "Amanresorts is not a hotel company. We are a lifestyle company. When you visit, you should feel like you are staying at a very beautiful private home".[16] At some properties, Amanresorts maintains a 6:1 employee guest ratio, something that is unheard of in the hotel and resort industry.[17]

Every customer is treated the same, regardless of star, VIP or any other status. Ordinary people's dreams of luxury and mingling with the stars are fulfilled by Amanresorts as comfortably as the VIPs' desire to travel discreetly and incognito, and be treated like anyone else. This is often difficult to provide with other large hotel chains.

With such a high commitment on delivering the brand promises, it is not surprising that Amanresorts has maintained a highly loyal customer base that keeps returning to one of the 15 Amanresorts to experience the paradise once again. They are also referred to as "Aman Junkies" and would come back year after year and/or try the latest resort regardless of its location.

One with nature – luxurious Aman-i-Khás (India)
Courtesy Amanresorts

Holistic experience

The next main pillar of the branding strategy has been the holistic holiday experience, offered by blending comfort, personalized service and luxury with the culture and heritage of the locality. One of the main characteristics of any Amanresorts is the fact that the location of all the resorts has some historical background and importance. Amanresorts offers special guided tours to the surrounding areas of the resorts to explore the local traditions and culture through interaction with the local population. It also takes its guests on unique travel journeys around the resort. Before the opening of Aman-i-Khás in India, the French manager spent six months exploring the neighborhood for a radius of some 20 kilometers around the resort on a motorbike. He showed Anil Thadini, the co-founder of Amanresorts and himself a native Indian from the region, an abandoned village from the 12th century that everyone had forgotten about.[18]

The affluent guests at Amanresorts are used to all sorts of haute cuisine in their daily lives and most travel extensively on business, staying at hotels and eating at restaurants all year round. Therefore, Amanresorts provides no fancy food, but instead simple local cuisine prepared with fresh ingredients served by local cooks to maintain the authenticity of the locality – to the great satisfaction of the guests who finally get a "home-cooked" meal. Most guests do not leave the resorts to eat outside.

Exclusivity

The final brand pillar has been the exclusivity of Amanresorts. Given the high profile of Amanresorts' clientele, it would have been easy for Amanresorts to capitalize on the presence of celebrities to gain worldwide publicity and media coverage in the global press. But in line with its overall strategy, Amanresorts has refrained from doing so. Amanresorts was never meant for the mass public and will never become so. It has been created for people who pay a high premium to have an experience of a lifetime. So the company has maintained a strict policy of exclusivity.[19] This policy has added to the overall brand equity of Amanresorts and its 100,000 plus repeat customers.[20]

The company has put in place a system whereby all employees act as brand ambassadors. It has managed to do this not through any brand manuals (by and large Amanresorts does not use manuals), but by being a responsive and caring employer. A case in point was when the bombs went off in

Bali in 2002, devastating the local tourism industry. Despite a financially crippling occupancy rate of 6 percent as a result of the terrorist acts, Aman-resorts did not lay off any staff. The management sent a clear signal to the organization and the local community that Amanresorts valued their contribution to the overall success of the company. Amanresorts has also invested a lot of time and effort in nurturing the leadership in its organization by regular training programs. In fact, each resort manager has become so attached to the resort that it has created a self-fulfilling culture.[21] With these measures, the management has been successful in aligning its entire staff with the activities of the organization. This will show companies aspiring to build successful brands the importance of balancing internal and external branding.

Amanresorts, by religiously practicing and consistently delivering on all four of its brand promises externally and aligning the commitment of its staff to its brand promises internally, has been able to build an almost iconic brand with a loyal customer base without resorting to the traditional ways of brand building.

Brand communication

Amanresorts is probably the only resort brand in the world to have achieved this iconic status with absolutely no advertising since its inception. Being true to its underlying philosophy of exclusivity, Adrian Zecha and his team decided against any form of advertising right from the start. The company does not send out press releases. The only brand communication that Amanresorts has made use of in the last 15 years is word of mouth. Ninety days before the opening of every Amanresort, the company sends out postcards to its list of approximately 120,000 recipients with the new beautiful location shown but without mentioning the actual place, to tease the prospective customers in advance and create attention about the new resort. In addition, loyal guests receive a periodic newsletter, Amannews, with descriptions of new properties and news about interesting historical or cultural events at existing properties.

In addition, Zecha invites a close circle of friends to experience the resort before it opens. This way news about the resort spreads quickly within the target segment of Amanresorts' customers and also reaches exclusive travel media like Condé Nast *Traveler* and Andrew Harper's *Hideaway Report*. This exclusivity in itself entices more customers toward the Amanresorts' brand. With leading Hollywood stars, pop singers and sports personalities visiting these resorts, it creates a desirable attribute for the brand in the eyes of prospective customers.

Future challenges

Company culture

With its iconic status and following from all over the world and the cream of society being die-hard patrons of the brand, it seems that nothing will be able to challenge Amanresorts' positioning. The biggest challenge will be to sustain the unique company culture and commitment to delivering the brand promise without manuals and detailed management practices. With success comes the obvious threat of copycats – different hotel and resort chains starting their own version of Amanresorts in an effort to give a similar paradise experience. Although so far no other resort chain is mentioned in the same breath as Amanresorts, it will indeed be a threat worth keeping an eye on.

Management

Another challenge will be to nurture a solid line-up of capable and passionate leaders who will be well equipped to carry the Amanresorts' spirit forward after the first generation of managers led by Adrian Zecha fade out. He turns 73 in 2006. This will probably be the most important crucial challenge for the management, as the success of Amanresorts is totally dependent on the organization's unique culture and philosophy. In addition to this, Adrian Zecha himself personifies the brand and is much admired and loved by the many loyal Aman junkies. Instilling this guiding philosophy in the next generation of leaders, who must not only abide by it but also be passionate about it, will decide the continuing success of Amanresorts in the future.

CASE 3
Shiseido – the Asian cosmetic giant

Of the handful of Asian brands that have made it into the global brand rankings, most, like Sony, Canon, and so on, originate from Japan. Japan has long been known for its prowess in technology, production efficiency, and superior quality. So it comes as no surprise that Shiseido, one of the strongest Asian cosmetic brands, also comes from Japan.

Shiseido has been one of the few non-technology brands from Japan that has made it big in the global fashion, beauty and cosmetic scene. Leveraging its unique heritage and the positive effects of its country of origin, Shiseido has been able to penetrate markets around the world by offering high-quality, relevant and exciting products. Early on, Shiseido realized the importance of offering a highly differentiated experience to customers and continually exciting them with innovative and high-quality products.

There are several reasons for the enduring success that Shiseido has enjoyed since its inception a century ago. But in the recent past, one of the main reasons for its success has been its well-managed brand management practices. The commitment from the company's management has seen a continuous investment in brand building activities.

Breaking into the fashion and beauty market, traditionally dominated by European and US brands, and establishing a brand name is no easy task. Shiseido truly stands apart as a great example for many aspiring cosmetic brands from Asia to become international players.

Background

Shiseido was started in 1872 by Arinobu Fukuhara as Japan's first Western-style pharmacy in Gizna, Japan's fashion and cultural hub. Shiseido started out as a pharmaceuticals company when herbal medicine was the order of the day in Japan. But it outgrew its initial business quite soon when it formulated the winning concept of blending oriental mystique and aesthetics with the technology and science of the Western world. This combination became a strong advantage for Shiseido right from its early days. Soon Shiseido diversified from its pharmaceuticals business.

As early as 1888, it launched Japan's first toothpaste, and in 1897 it ventured into the cosmetic business by launching Eudermine, a cosmetic product. In 1918 Shiseido launched its first perfume, and by 1937 it came out with its first line of cosmetics. Since then, Shiseido has transformed itself into a fully fledged cosmetics company with a wide product line encompassing various aspects of cosmetics, from skin care, to beauty products, to general cosmetics. By the late 1970s, Shiseido started penetrating foreign markets in Europe and the United States with specific product lines.

Although the unique concept of blending Eastern aesthetics with Western science provided Shiseido with a strong differentiating factor, it had to extend this beyond a mere concept. Shiseido relied on its core philosophy for guidance. From the beginning, Shiseido based its philosophy on five core management principles which were enunciated way back in 1921. They were: quality first; co-existence and co-prosperity; respect for customers; corporate stability; and sincerity.[22] Shiseido also crafted brand identities for all its products and aimed at positioning them toward different customer segments.

Shiseido has based its brand building on five key points:

- Creativity and innovation in all its product offerings

- Unique blend of oriental mystique and sensitivity with Western fashion values

- Application of clinically tested formulae to create products that would enhance skin care and beauty

- Ability to customize its offerings to its different markets by constantly analyzing market trends

- Strong distribution strategy.

Shiseido has also developed a brand architecture system in line with its aspiration to serve several segments of the market. With constant investment in brand management, Shiseido has been able to successfully serve both the premium as well as the value segments in many markets around the world.

Shiseido was one of the first Asian brands to adopt the acquisition strategy to grow beyond its home market. Acquiring rival firms in global markets has served two purposes. On the one hand, it gained an easy entry into the market and, on the other, it helped Shiseido to gain customers' acceptance. This strategy, along with a strong brand management practice followed religiously throughout the organization, has contributed to Shiseido's emergence as an international brand.

Brand philosophy

From its inception, Shiseido has managed to build its image as an innovator and a market leader. When it ventured into the cosmetics business from its core pharmaceutical business, it leveraged this very perception to the fullest. It came out with unique fragrances and cosmetics made from natural flowers to maintain its uniqueness. It was easy for Shiseido to gain a high level of acceptance in its domestic market as the heritage of the brand was already well known.

The company faced many challenges when it decided to venture out of Japan in the early 1970s. This was the period when brands like Sony and Canon were still establishing their brand names in the global market. Moreover, Japan was more well known for its production efficiency, technological prowess and high-quality electronics than it was for cosmetics and beauty products. This made it an uphill task for Shiseido. The fashion, beauty and cosmetics business was dominated by brands from Europe, particularly France and the United States. Therefore Shiseido faced the challenge of breaking into the global cosmetic industry, gaining acceptance and building a strong brand.

One of the strongest advantages for Shiseido when it entered the cosmetics business was the fact that it was an Asian brand venturing into Western markets. It used the mystique and aura of a distant land, with its oriental tradition, color, smells and aesthetics, to its advantage. Its first product for the global market, Zen, was launched in 1964. Shiseido packaged it using traditional lacquer designs from 16th-century motifs of Kyoto temples. This not only gave it a distinctive appearance but also created an aura of mystique around it.

In 1997, Shiseido was awarded the US Fifi Award, the most authoritative fragrance industry award, for a new fragrance that it had created using aromacology.

Shiseido has always used R&D to introduce new products based on clinically tested formulae. The vision behind Shiseido's R&D has been "creative integration". This vision called for an integration of function with sensitivity. In line with this vision, Shiseido has introduced many products aimed at enhancing the beauty of its customers. An example was Shiseido's first anti-aging skin care line called Benefiance in 1982, the Shiseido relaxing fragrance cultivated with a new aromacology. This initiative has given Shiseido credibility in new markets. By bringing together rational elements backed by scientific proof and aspirational as well as emotional elements backed by a strong brand image and personality, Shiseido has been successful in positioning itself in many markets globally.

Another important pillar of Shiseido's brand philosophy is its flexibility in modifying and customizing its offerings. It not only does this in different markets in line with its unique needs, cultures and so on, but also in its brand management practices. One of the reasons for Shiseido's success is that the brand has been able to span markets from the premium segment to the value segment by creating distinct brand identities and personalities for its product lines. A case in point is its strategy in the Chinese market. When it entered China in 1981, it introduced a sub-brand called Aupres, and positioned it as an elite brand. It was catering only to the top 1 percent of the market. Later on, when Shiseido decided to target the mass market, it came out with another brand extension called Za. By tracking the trends of the customers and the associations that they had about certain products with certain places, Shiseido created their distinct stories. For example, for makeup products, customers preferred an elite image and that was conveyed by creating a brand personality with an American undertone. For skin care products, customers preferred quality and reliability which was conveyed by creating a brand personality with a Japanese undertone with the brand Pure & Mild. This kind of flexibility in its brand management model has helped Shiseido to take on different market segments in different markets quite successfully.[23]

Finally, Shiseido has developed a strong distribution network in Japan, across Asia and in all its major markets across the world. Shiseido adopted the three main channels:

- Department store for luxury products along with personal counseling to customers

- Shiseido licensed store (chain store) selling luxury and also middle-level products along with personal counseling to customers

- Convenience and drug stores through which it sold middle- to mass-market products by launching self-cosmetics (no counseling provided).

This strategy has proved successful for Shiseido as it has been able to market the entire product portfolio through leveraging multiple channels.

Brand strategy

Shiseido has followed a strategy which is uncommon for Asian brands expanding beyond the region. Shiseido has used acquisitions as a main channel to gain a foothold in the crucial cosmetics markets of Europe and the United States. As cosmetics is an industry driven by aspirations, lifestyle issues and images, Shiseido decided on the acquisition path to gain visibility, acceptance and access to established customer bases in new markets rather than spending years trying to establish the Shiseido brand from scratch.

In order to gain entry into the French and thus the European market, Shiseido acquired the Carita brand and prestigious salon on the Faubourg St. Honoré in Paris in 1981. The salon, with it distinguished and rich clientele of royalty and celebrities, commanded a unique position in the French market. To gain entry into the North American market, Shiseido acquired Unilever's Helen Curtis in 1996.[24] These acquisitions gave Shiseido an opportunity to build on something already strong in those markets.

Another major strategy of Shiseido has been the setting up of two brand holding companies. It established InterAct Co. Ltd. to market new imported non-Shiseido brands, and AXE Co. Ltd. to market brands which are developed by Shiseido but operate as independent brands in the market, without Shiseido's name to them. This strategy helped Shiseido in many ways. It has been able to bring a lot of new brands into the market which have been quite different from its own brands. This has given it the leeway to address the latest emerging trends without having to worry about the possible effects on customer perceptions or any potential dilution of its brand equity. At the same time, the opportunity to import and market non-Shiseido brands has given Shiseido a chance to test the market for newer tastes, trends and so on without taking too much risk.

Future challenges

Despite Shiseido's enduring success, it faces a new set of challenges as it travels ahead into new markets with different demographics, increased competition and multiple segments.

Continue the Asian/Western blend

One of the main challenges for Shiseido in the future will be to maintain the blend that it created between oriental mystique and Western science and technology. It becomes significant as Shiseido has been acquiring brands in the US and Europe with their own heritage and unique brand stories. Given this, it will be a challenge for Shiseido to carry on with the blending as that is one of its strongest differentiation factors.

Consistency in positioning

Shiseido has positioned itself predominantly as a high-end premium and luxury brand in the US and European markets and it spans the entire market spectrum from low-end, through value and middle to luxury segments in Asia. With customers traveling around the world, a global media landscape and internet making information flows across countries much easier, Shiseido should take steps to ensure that it conveys its varied positioning carefully in its different markets.

Maintaining a strong brand architecture system

Managing the brand architecture could prove to be a challenging task for Shiseido. Shiseido has been engaged in three main activities:

■ Acquisitions of brands in Europe and the US

■ Importing new non-Shiseido brands into Japan through the brand holding company

■ Introducing multiple brand extensions in the market.

Given the diverse market segments that Shiseido's brand extensions serve, these brand extensions will obviously have their own brand image and personalities. Integrating them with the parent brand and managing their interactions with the parent brand will be challenging.

Developing the corporate brand in the Western world

Although Shiseido has been successful in following the acquisition strategy, it has yet to build a strong corporate brand in the US and European markets. As it has been acquiring brands with a loyal customer base, modifying the brand identity and personality of the acquired brand to suit the overall Shiseido brand architecture could prove challenging. Developing a strong corporate brand with a unique identity and personality will be crucial for Shiseido's long-term success.

CASE 4
Samsung – the Asian global brand

Think of any high-end consumer durable like a camera, MP3 player integrated mobile phone, plasma television, or even camcorders, and it is only natural that Samsung comes to mind, along with Sony and a few others. Samsung, the South Korean behemoth, was ranked the 20th most valuable brand in the world in 2005, with a brand value of US$14.96 billion, by Inter-brand Corp., an international brand valuation firm, in its annual ranking of the world's top 100 brands.[25] Much like the hallowed GE, Samsung has a diversified empire with interests in electronics, heavy industries, financial services and trading. With a vision of being a global leader in most of the industries that it operates in, Samsung booked world record profits of over US$10 billion in 2004. Beating global leaders like Intel (with US$7.5 billion in profits) and Microsoft (with US$8.1 billion in profits), Samsung became one of only ten companies in the world to record US$10 billion profits.[26]

These achievements are outstanding testimonials to Samsung Chairman Kun-Hee Lee's vision of taking Samsung from a manufacturer of cheap versions of Japanese products to a global leader in digital convergence. With a business strategy spun around building a top-notch brand, the company invested billions of dollars to reposition Samsung into a respectable brand, with innovation, cutting-edge technology and world-class design as its trademark characteristics. From being on the verge of bankruptcy during the Asian financial crisis of 1997, Samsung has grown into a truly world-class business empire.

With its commitment to building a strong brand, Samsung serves as a strong example of brand building and brand guardianship among Asian companies.

Introduction

Samsung started as Samsung General Stores in 1938 in the Northern province of Kyungsang in South Korea. Till the early 1970s, it was involved in businesses ranging from commodities, wool, and insurance to fertilizer manufacturing and broadcasting. Samsung was better known as a company that produced cheap copies of Japanese electronic goods.

The foundations for today's Samsung were laid by the current chairman Lee when he took over the management of the company in 1993. His declaration of new management principles put intellectual capital, organizational creativity, technological innovation and employee empowerment at the center of Samsung's business philosophy. This philosophy saw Samsung focusing on a couple of core businesses. Samsung Electronics is one such key business unit that produces world-class mobile handsets, wide-screen plasma television screens, digital camcorders and other household appliances. Samsung Electronics, established in 1969, generated a net profit of

US$6.8 billion in 2004.[27] This has been the flagship division within the Samsung Group. *Business Week* ranked Samsung Electronics as the number one in the information technology global ranking in 2002. With more than US$100 billion of sales, US$70 billion of assets, net profits of US$10 billion, and brand equity valued at US$12.6 billion, Samsung is fast catching up with its major rivals Sony, Canon and other consumer electronics giants.[28] The success of Samsung is to a large extent based on its brand management processes. From its early days of repositioning the brand from a cheap manufacturer to a brand of class and quality, Samsung has had a consistent policy of basing all activities in line with its brand strategy. The management of the company has set an example for the whole industry in brand stewardship, with the chairman himself taking the lead in constantly managing and nurturing the Samsung brand.

Brand philosophy

One of the main reasons for Samsung's global success is its deliberate branding strategy. From the beginning, Samsung had to fight hard to change customers' perceptions of it as a manufacturer of cheap electronic goods. Starting in 1993, with the new Chairman Lee, Samsung has adopted an aggressive branding and advertising strategy. The branding philosophy of Samsung has been built on five main pillars: innovation; cutting-edge technology; world-class designs; recruiting the world's best talents; and internal branding.

For the past five decades, Sony has been the undisputed brand leader in the consumer electronics industry worldwide. When Samsung started out on its branding journey, one of its initial goals was to emulate Sony and its best practices. Being a competitive industry, one of the best ways for Samsung to capture customers' attention was to come out with innovative products, as Sony did with its Walkman and recently with Play Station. With standardized products and relatively short product life cycles in the consumer electronics industry, Samsung Electronics wanted to put its innovation into building new features, creating new categories of appliances and usage. Samsung understood quite early on that for innovation to be successful and profitable it had to be constantly backed by superior technology and the best designs.

Samsung has believed that the surest way to beat the market leaders is to adopt the latest cutting-edge technologies and bring out superior products before its competitors. In line with this strategy, Samsung has invested heavily in R&D to churn out new technologies which can be used in various products. In 2003 alone Samsung Electronics spent around US$2.3 billion on R&D – 8 percent of its revenue. With nearly one-fourth of its workforce working as researchers in 15 R&D centers around the world, Samsung is totally committed to developing cutting-edge technology.[29] Another case in point to prove its commitment to technology is the fact that Samsung Electronics took the sixth place by the number of patents registered in the United States in 2004. With a goal of being one of the top three patent registering companies by 2007, Samsung is committed to its investment in technology.[30]

Samsung also realized that it needs to be the best in designing its products in the market. Ultimately, it is a game to woo the consumers. Backed by innovation and cutting-edge technology, the latest, trendiest and coolest designs have given Samsung a unique position in both the market and the minds of consumers. With cut-throat competition, the visual treat offered by Samsung's products has acted as a marked differentiator from its strong rivals. In line with this thinking, Samsung started Innovative Design Lab of Samsung, an in-house academy to teach and study design. With support from Chairman Lee, this serves as the design laboratory for all future Samsung product designs. Samsung also started comprehensive training courses for all its design employees to learn the latest trends in designing, along with courses on ergonomics and mechanical engineering. By looking at the art, culture and sculpture of many countries, the design lab trains its design engineers to be the best in the field. Today, with around 380 design engineers working out of four design centers outside Seoul in San Francisco, London, Tokyo and Los Angeles, Samsung has indeed incorporated design into its corporate and brand strategies.[31]

For Samsung to achieve its lead in either cutting-edge technology or leading designs, it needed the best talent available. Acknowledging this basic fact, Samsung has been, for quite some time, a leading recruiter from many of the top-tier business schools around the world. This is evident when Hak Soo, the COO and the vice president of Samsung says: "People are Samsung's biggest challenge. We need to hire and train the best talents from all over the world because we are a global company, not just a Korean company."[32]

Samsung has been able to attract the best of the industry and business schools alike by providing exciting opportunities in a global market.

By practicing the brand strategy based on these five pillars, Samsung has been successful in repositioning its brand in the global market. Now, Samsung stands for a brand that is known for innovation and world-class, quality products.

Brand communication

Samsung has used all possible channels of communication to convey its brand's positioning and personality. Mass media advertising, public relations, event sponsorship, sports events, product placement, and the Samsung experience gallery have been the major channels that Samsung has used for its brand communication.

The brand communication had two main objectives. Firstly, to reposition Samsung as a premium, world-class brand offering quality, credibility and design and, secondly, to be seen and accepted as a brand on a par with the likes of Sony – to be the top consumer electronics brand across the world.

With these two huge objectives on one hand and formidable competitors like Sony and Canon on the other, Samsung had to use all possible channels to communicate its superior positioning in the consumer electronics industry.

Samsung used its technological prowess combined with its design and innovation to gain attention in the industry. Products like the world's first wristwatch clamshell rotating camera phone, the largest plasma TV, the largest LCD display, and the color wrist phone, all conveyed Samsung's technological leadership to a global audience. This was just the first step. These products also gave Samsung a lot of media coverage from international business magazines like *Business Week* and the *Wall Street Journal* to technology magazines and websites like CNET.com and others. These, along with the many awards that Samsung has won for its design and use of technology to create better products, acted as credible third-party endorsements. Once again these gave Samsung credibility for its repositioning effort.

Samsung wanted to take advantage of the technological breakthroughs of the 1990s, mainly digital convergence. With its leading technology in the fields of wireless communication, memory chips and plasma screens, Samsung saw a great opportunity. Instead of going for leadership in each of the product categories, Samsung wanted to position itself as a leader in digital convergence – making products which combined wireless communication with photography, music and video. This philosophy has guided Samsung in all its communications for the past seven to eight years.

The year 1997 saw Samsung's first global campaign: Challenge the Limits. The main aim of this campaign was to position Samsung as a leading company that aimed to reach heights beyond mere technology. With the same aim, Samsung sponsored events such as the Olympics, the winter games and extreme sports. This was in contrast with other global brands like Nike which sponsored individual sports personalities. In line with its personality, Samsung wanted to convey a team spirit, healthy competition and global convergence. The next major global campaign was in 1999 when Samsung came out with DigitAll: Everyone's Invited.[33] Through this campaign, Samsung wanted to reiterate its leading position in the digital convergence era. It wanted the world to see it as a company which had the capabilities to provide the best digital products and experiences.[34]

These campaigns were the integrated media events that Samsung created to communicate its positioning to the world. Simultaneously, Samsung used all the other channels to consistently communicate its positioning and personality.

Event sponsorships

Samsung has been using international electronics, games and technology events to showcase its product range and offer the Samsung experience by sponsoring these events. Events like the World Cyber Games, CeBit, Comdex, IFA and the Consumer Electronics Association provide Samsung with access to its core target customers – both businesses and consumers alike – where it can educate and entertain them. An event like the Consumer Electronics Association held in Las Vegas, Nevada, for example, attracted some 130,000 visitors from over 110 countries to watch the spectacle spread over 1.4 million square feet of space. By being the chief sponsor of such events, Samsung has been able to consistently project and bolster its own brand image.

Sport sponsorships

With a mission to become a global leader in consumer electronics, Samsung had to communicate to a global audience. What better way than sponsoring international sporting events to achieve a global awareness? Samsung has been the chief sponsor of the 1988 Seoul Olympics, the 1990 Beijing Asian Championship, the 2000 Sydney Olympics, the 2002 Salt Lake Winter Games, and also the Olympics in Athens 2004. By setting up a 1,064 square meter entertainment complex within the Olympic sports complex called An Olympic Rendezvous, Samsung was successful in attracting over 300,000 visitors to showcase not only its current portfolio of products and offer the Samsung experience, but also its futuristic, pipeline products.[35] Samsung's affiliation with international sporting events has added a positive feel to its personality as a company with a competitive spirit competing on a global level with world-class competitors. These events have also helped Samsung to increase awareness levels in prospective consumer groups across the world.

Samsung experience

The North American market is an important market for Samsung. Being the most important playground for all major global players to prove their mettle, winning the markets and consumers' minds in the US is crucial for any global company. With this intention, Samsung created the Samsung experience in New York City. It opened the 10,000 square feet gallery at the Time Warner Center in Manhattan in September 2003 full of its latest technology. To date, Samsung operates this as a pure gallery – a place to offer customers an experience, not to sell products. With an excellent combination of technology, people and ambience, Samsung has been successful in creating a positive image in the minds of US customers.

Product placement

With movies reaching a global audience, Samsung successfully managed to place its high-tech gadgets in the cult movie *The Matrix*, giving Samsung an excellent opportunity to gain the attention and curiosity of millions of people worldwide. With its emphasis on technology appealing especially to youngsters, teenagers, and young adults, the association with movies like *The Matrix* has helped Samsung to convey its positioning strongly to a potential customer base.

With such dedicated and targeted brand communications, Samsung has been able to narrow the gap between itself and the industry leader Sony in just one decade. Although Samsung has been doing all the right things, it will indeed be a challenge to continue to keep up the consistency in the future.

Future challenges

As the market leader in semi-conductor chips, the third largest cellular handset maker in the world behind Nokia and Motorola, and the largest manufacturer of flat display screens in the world, Samsung has indeed come a long way from its humble beginnings of 1983. But Samsung faces some tough challenges in the future.

Maintaining consistency

Samsung has invested billions of dollars in global advertising and brand building activities. Given its presence in multiple industries on the one hand and its consistent investment in R&D on the other, it will be difficult for Samsung to sustain its investment in branding activities. But Samsung must not be complacent and reduce the brand budget. It has not yet reached a position where the brand can live independent of its products as Sony does. Therefore, it will be extremely important that Samsung continues to build and nurture its brand in a consistent manner.

Spreading the corporate brand too thinly

Even today, the Samsung name is found on literally everything from ships, memory chips, to mobile phones and camcorders. Although the company is leveraging its brand to build new business and gain considerable advantage in existing businesses, this can prove dangerous to the corporate brand. As Samsung has been trying hard to position itself as a premium lifestyle brand worldwide, many of the businesses in the Samsung portfolio do not match this positioning. Therefore, although it might appear as an advantage at the outset, spreading the corporate brand too thinly across a wide array of businesses might prove costly to Samsung in the long run.

Local and international competition

Today Samsung is faced with never-seen-before competition in the consumer electronics industry. Not only should it fight the leaders like Sony and Canon, but also the new crop of companies which are following the Samsung path to compete with Samsung, the most significant one being the LG Group of South Korea and potential competitors from China and Taiwan. Although Samsung has a comfortable lead time due to its top-notch technology and constant innovation, this should not lead to any sort of complacency. Samsung should continue investing in technology and design capabilities on the one hand and marketing and brand management activities on the other to maintain the lead over its rivals that it has so tirelessly built over the past decade.

Managing the Samsung brand architecture

The Samsung name is used to represent every business unit of the Samsung group, as mentioned earlier. Even though the trend of late is to nurture a strong corporate brand, as Unilever and P&G have been doing, Samsung lacks the necessary similarity between its various business units. Therefore, Samsung should develop a strong brand architecture system which will define and monitor the interaction of various brands within the Samsung portfolio with the corporate brand. This will be easier said than done, given the extremely diversified business units of the chaebol (Korean business conglomerate).

The brand architecture would also guide Samsung in acquiring new brands to enter the value segments of different markets, as LG has done with the Zenith brand in the US to target solely the value segment. With the millions of dollars that Samsung has spent over the past decade to build the Samsung brand, it will be a major challenge to put in place a strong architecture system which will help the branding practices of Samsung going ahead.

Creating the Samsung personality

Most great brands are those that have strong personalities, with Apple iPod being the latest proof. But Samsung seems to have ignored this crucial aspect in building its brand. Although Samsung has been doing all the right things in its communications, it has not focused on creating a strong personality for its brand. It does not own anything specific in the consumers' minds, like a Harley-Davidson standing for the rugged independence of western America or a BMW standing for the ultimate driving experience. As has been well recorded in the branding literature, a successful brand not only provides the customers with functional benefits, but also emotional and self-expressive benefits.[36] So far, Samsung has emphasized the functional benefits of leading-edge technology, contemporary designs and exciting features. It needs to go beyond this and create a cult following for its brand, like the Apple iPod has done. Samsung needs to ensure that its brand can live on independently of its products. This could prove to be a major challenge.

Notes

1 "Sir Martin's shopping spree", *Business Week* online, 4 October, 2004.
2 www.singaporeair.com.
3 "Singapore Air makes longest flight", CNN.com, http://edition.cnn.com/2004/BUSINESS/06/28/singapore.airline.
4 Author interviews with current and former SIA staff.
5 *SilverKris*, Singapore Airlines in-flight magazine, XX, 2005.
6 Author visit to the training academy 2003.
7 *Fortune Magazine*, "Asia's Business Man of the Year", February 7, 2002.
8 *Fortune Magazine*, February 7, 2002, ibid.
9 *Asian Wall Street Journal*, "Flying in the face of fuel costs", October 15, 2004.
10 For further reference to iconic brands, see Douglas Holt, *How Brands Become Brands*, Harvard Business School Press, XXXX.
11 *AsiaWeek*, "Paradise regained", June 15, 2001.
12 "Welcome back to paradise", Wendy Kan, Phuket, April 2001, *Time Asia*.
13 Author interview with Anil Thadani, chairman, Schroder Capital Partners and co-founder of Amanresorts.
14 Ibid.
15 Morocco's New Paradise, www.travelandleisure.com June 2000.
16 *AsiaWeek*, June 15, 2001, op. cit.
17 Author interview with Anil Thadani.
18 Ibid.
19 Jackson Hole, *Wyoming's Amangani Resort: Aman America*, www.travelandleisure.com, February 1999.
20 *TimeAsia*, "The kingdom of the Divine", July 26–August 4, 2004.
21 Author interview with Anil Thandani.
22 Company website.
23 "When Chinese desire transcends politics", David Pilling. *Financial Times*, 1 April 2004, page 11.
24 Company website.
25 "Global Brands, *Business Week*/Interbrand rank the companies that best built their images – and made them stick", Richard Berner and David Kiley, July 2005, *Business Week*.
26 Sang-Hun Choe, Associate Press writer, 19 January 2005.
27 "Can Samsung keep soaring?" Assif Shameen, *Asia Inc*, 1 June 2004.
28 *Asia Inc*, 1 June 2004, ibid.
29 "Samsung Electronics – As good as it gets?" *The Economist*, 15 January 2005.
30 "Samsung eyes third position in US patents race", Bang Sung-hoon, Chosun Ilbo, 17 January 2005.
31 Samsung's lessons in design, http://www.cdf.org/9_1_index/samsung/samsung.html.
32 Assif Shameen, *Asia Inc*, 1 June 2004, op. cit.
33 http://www.samsung.com.
34 "Samsung's DigitAll tag takes a democratic turn", Elkin, Tobi and Snyder, Beth, *Advertising Age*, **70**(10), 77, May 2005.
35 "The 2004 Olympic torch relay: The first global roadshow, Samsung gets up close and personal", *M2Presswire*, 5 August, 2004.
36 *Building Strong Brands*, David Aaker, The Free Press 1996.

CHAPTER 8

ASPIRING ASIAN BRAND CASES

*The purpose of price is not to recover costs, but to capture the
value of the brands in the minds of consumers.*

Akio Morita, Founder, Sony

The successful case stories of Singapore Airlines, Amanresorts, Shiseido
and Samsung have indeed laid the blueprint for branding success in Asia.
As is evident from the brand stories in the previous chapter, the main reason
for their success has been the continuous support from corporate management, including the chairman and CEO.

It is indeed good to see these Asian brands becoming successful well
beyond Asia. But with two-thirds of the global population, growing
economies, and a rapidly growing middle class with an increasing disposable income, Asia still boasts only a handful of powerful brands, which is a
cause for concern.

Despite Asia's historical focus on manufacturing and trading activities,
the global landscape could potentially face a wealth of new Asian brands
in the coming years. Every country in Asia has its own list of aspiring
brands just waiting to cross the local borders. In literally every industry
sector, many companies are realizing the potential value creation that
they might be forgoing due to a lack of branding. These companies are
gradually making a mark in the region, having been inspired by the
industry leaders. But, as yet, not many have managed to attain international recognition.

Even governments of Asian countries are providing incentives for
companies to adopt the right brand management practices to move up the
value chain. A case in point is IE Singapore's (a government institution in
Singapore tasked with internationalizing domestic businesses) initiative to
educate and encourage Singaporean companies to build more successful
brands. Authorities in Taiwan, Malaysia and Hong Kong are looking at
similar initiatives. With these initiatives, a large number of companies
across Asia are already somewhere on the branding journey.

In the next 10–20 years, Asia will definitely contribute to the next generation of internationally recognized brands. This chapter examines four of these aspiring brands that could make a mark in the global brandscape.

CASE 1
Jim Thompson – the Asian silk brand[1]

The Jim Thompson Thai Silk Company from Thailand is one of the well-known Asian brands with great potential to emerge as a strong international lifestyle brand. Known for its silk fabrics, clothing, accessories and, lately, home furnishings, it has been one of the few brands endorsed by Thai royalty and celebrities for its quality, designs and Asian feel. The brand has come a long way since the company was established in 1951 by Jim Thompson, an American soldier who settled in Thailand.[2]

The company operates 50 retail stores in Thailand, Singapore, Malaysia, Dubai, Brunei and Japan. Jim Thompson has established a strong name for itself locally and regionally, with US$50 million sales and US$10 million profits in 2003. The company employs 3,000 people and the brand has its presence in 30 countries across the world.

Background

When Jim Thompson resigned from the American armed forces and decided to settle down in Thailand, he spent his initial days traveling around the country. It was during one such visit that he came across the fledgling Thai silk cottage industry. Although Thailand had had a strong silk industry, by the early 19th century it had deteriorated badly as cheaper fabrics from Japan and the West forced traditional weavers out of business.[3] Jim Thompson came across the Ban Krua community, renowned for its hand-woven silk fabric. Jim Thompson strove to revive this declining Thai silk industry and the result was the founding of the Jim Thompson Thai Silk Company in 1951. By establishing personal and close ties with this weaving community (the weavers still have a small stake in the company), Jim Thompson was able to produce some world-class silk

fabric. It stood out from the rest in the market as it had the charm and feel of being hand-woven and the quality was far superior to any other silk product.[4] For example, Thai silk is different from Chinese silk. Thai silk is inconsistent and has "humps and bumps" and iridescent colors (changing colors depending on light). Also, Thai silk is not good for garments but ideal for soft furnishing materials.

To ensure 100 percent control on the quality of the output, Jim Thompson is vertically integrated in its production. Although in 1967, 100 percent of materials were hand-woven silk, today only 50 percent are hand-woven silk and the remaining 50 percent are of other materials. But, according to William Warren, a Jim Thompson biographer based in Bangkok:

> it took years of experiment, frequent frustration and plain hard work first to persuade a handful of remaining weavers to increase production on better looms, using color-fast chemical dyes instead of traditional vegetable colors, and then open up foreign markets where none had existed before.[5]

The founder Jim Thompson was successful in taking this Thai silk beyond Thailand by leveraging his contacts in the United States and other countries. It gained international recognition in *Vogue* and in 1951 it was featured in a Broadway production.[6] The company also benefited a lot from the personal charisma and personality of Jim Thompson. Although his efforts to set up the Thai silk company proved to be a major profit earner, he also single-handedly revived the almost dead Thai silk industry. This gained him a lot of respect and adulation. In 1967, Jim Thompson disappeared mysteriously in Malaysia's Cameron Highlands and was never found again, dead or alive. His previous connections to the CIA gave rise to many theories about the sudden disappearance, and since then have added tremendously to the legend of the brand and created a strong myth.

Today, almost 54 years since its inception, Jim Thompson continues to grow with the same kind of zest and passion. Although it started out with just silk fabrics, by leveraging its brand equity and the Thai heritage, the company has now diversified into many other related product lines, the latest one being home furniture. In 2001, it signed up Ou Baholyodhin, the renowned London-based Thai designer known for his clean designs strongly influenced by Asian cultures, to craft the new furnishing line.[7]

Jim Thompson's future strategy is to focus on finished products for the home. Given its brand equity in different markets, the company is focusing on retail products in Asia where it has strong brand equity. As the brand is strongly linked to the Thai experience, buying Jim Thompson products for tourists relates to taking back home a piece of Thai culture. This is the reason why 40 percent of retail customers in Thailand are Japanese who buy gift items when returning from Thailand. Even in Singapore and Malaysia, 80 percent of sales are for Japanese. But, on the other hand, in Europe, where the company is building its brand, this connection with Thailand and the direct experience with Thai culture may not be possible. Therefore, the company is focusing on finished products for the home which are distributed through local distributors.

Jim Thompson also collaborates with Ed Tuttle, a leading American designer. Through this collaboration, Jim Thompson provides custom-made fabrics (Rue de la Paix, Vendome and Chenille Canvas) for his architecture and design projects which include Amanresorts and Park Hyatt Hotels among others. As design is a vital part of the company's success, these collaborations with external consultants also provide external views on the latest, upcoming trends from the West.

Brand philosophy

The company has built its brand primarily on three pillars. First is the myth surrounding the founder Jim Thompson. Second is the unique blend of Eastern (Thai) tradition and heritage with Western contemporary designs. Third is the elevation of the brand from a mere cottage industry product to a lifestyle concept.

Jim Thompson has built a story of the brand surrounding the founder, his origins, his contributions to the Thai silk industry and his eventual mysterious disappearance. Jim Thompson's journey to revive the Thai silk industry and his drive to involve the weaving community as strategic partners in the business is itself a legend in Thailand. By leveraging this connection, Jim Thompson has been able to blend into the social fabric of the country.

Jim Thompson has been successful in differentiating itself by uniquely blending the Thai tradition and the feel of Western contemporary designs. The brand has collaborated with leading designers to develop appealing and upmarket designs, colors and fabrics.

Finally, Jim Thompson has created a lifestyle concept centered around silk and contemporary designs. Although the company started out with silk fabrics, it has successfully expanded into home furnishings and even into restaurants, with three restaurants operating in Bangkok and one in Kuala Lumpur, which opened in spring 2005. These two brand extensions have enabled Jim Thompson to create an emerging, premium lifestyle concept.

These three brand pillars have enabled Jim Thompson to maintain its differentiation in the marketplace and build a strong brand.

Brand strategy

Well known for its quality, design and Asian feel, Jim Thompson has been widely acknowledged by leading brands in the hospitality industry. The brand's furnishing materials have been widely used by many of the luxury hotels including The Oriental, Amanpuri, the Regent, Conrad and the Sukhothai. In Europe, the Park Hyatt Paris and Park Hyatt Milan hotels among others have been attracted to Jim Thompson's furnishing materials. The Park Hyatt Paris has used 9,000 square meters of furnishing materials alone. These clients among many others serve as strong testimonials to the brand.[8]

It is normal for a strong brand to leverage its brand equity and diversify into related market segments, and Jim Thompson has also followed this path. Today, its portfolio consists of many additional product lines apart from silk fabrics. It has scarves, handbags, textiles, clothing, and accessories for home furnishings. In fact the home furnishings line, comprising sofas, armchairs, dining chairs, dining and coffee tables and lamps, has become such an important part of the whole business that it contributes almost 30 percent to the total business and 90 percent of the total exports.[9]

Although this is a bit far from its core business, Jim Thompson has been able to extend its brand personality, its design and sophistication and extend successfully in related segments. With the business appearing to be focusing on the lifestyle concept, it recently opened a boutique at the prestigious Empire Hotel and Country Club in Brunei. This physical structure is even better than the other 55 such boutiques around the world, as it provides a comprehensive experience to customers by showcasing the entire product portfolio of the brand.[10]

Brand communication

Jim Thompson has selectively used mass communication channels to build its retail brand. The company employs other communication channels like

Jim Thompson's main store in Bangkok, Thailand
Courtesy Jim Thompson Company

fairs and exhibitions to create awareness about its professional brand. It showcases its products during these events and generates considerable interest in the brand. By leveraging the unique designs of its retail stores, where it showcases its entire product portfolio, the company offers a comprehensive experience for its customers. As Jim Thompson does not own retail outlets outside Asia, it works closely with its international distribution partners.

Many resources are spent on internal marketing which involves educating the channel partners about the brand, the product features and benefits. Jim Thompson also maintains a list of its 55,000 customer names in Thailand for local promotions. As these 55,000 customers have already purchased Jim Thompson merchandise at least once, they also act as strong word-of-mouth marketers.

Finally, as the brand is strongly associated with its founder and with Thailand, it has preserved the Jim Thompson House in Bangkok as a private museum open to the public. The Jim Thompson House belongs to the James HW Thompson Foundation. It displays Thai art and crafts along with the entire product portfolio of Jim Thompson. On peak days, it has more than 1,000 visitors adding significantly to the promotion of the brand to foreign tourists, including keeping the myth around Jim Thompson's disappearance alive as part of the brand story. This not only helps to build awareness among its prospective customer base but also reiterates its strong link with Thailand's heritage and culture.

Future challenges

Creating a strong brand identity and personality

Jim Thompson's myth about its founder and its brand is widely popular in Asia among retail customers. But in Europe, the company deals with hotels, designers and interior decorators. Thus, at an aggregate level, Jim Thompson operates as a B2C brand in Asia and a B2B brand in Europe. Given this, a major challenge is to create a consistent brand identity that resonates across regions and customer segments, while catering to the specific needs of one particular customer segment.

Installing a brand management system

As the brand grows, it becomes crucial to constantly monitor and hone the brand to reflect the market demands. With any retail brand, the brand promise and brand delivery must be equally balanced. Service, for example, is an important element. Jim Thompson only owns retail outlets within Asia. This necessitates the channel members being properly trained in executing the brand promises outside Asia. To maintain such a training system, the company must ensure consistent support from corporate management and continuous investment of resources.

Expansion beyond Asia

Jim Thompson's brand equity within Asia is, to a large extent, related to the myth of the founder of the company. But outside Asia, this myth is less known and may not be relevant. Moreover, an Asian brand with a Western name might confuse customers. Given these impediments, Jim Thompson should strive to create a brand with an appealing identity that is not only relevant to customers across regions but also captures the unique Asian heritage. Taking a brand to multiple markets and sustaining the investment in brand building can take a toll on the resource capabilities of the company.

Interior of Jim Thompson's house in Bangkok, now a public museum
Courtesy Jim Thompson Company

Moreover, most resources are utilized for operations and production. Jim Thompson needs to consider these factors before venturing into multiple markets and product segments.

Single brand company

Another major challenge will be to leverage the Jim Thompson brand name and potentially introduce new brands in the market. Till now, Jim Thompson has been a single brand company. Going ahead, the challenge will be to cautiously leverage the brand equity through brand or line extensions to explore new opportunities, either by introducing new brands to cater to new segments or venturing into new product categories. Jim Thompson must be cautious in carrying out this exercise as it might result in a possible dilution of brand equity as a result of brand stretch. Finding the right balance between expansion and protecting the brand equity from dilution will prove to be a considerable challenge.

CASE 2
Li Ning – anything is possible

Li Ning is one of the star brands emerging from the Chinese landscape. Competing head-on with the likes of Nike, Adidas and Reebok in China, Li Ning is a company which deals in shoes, sportswear and sports accessories. Li Ning belongs to the new generation of Chinese companies that have realized the importance of branding and have started to consciously invest in building their brands. Along with the leading Chinese computer company Lenovo and leading Chinese consumer electronics company Haier, Li Ning belongs to the list of Chinese corporations that have not only provided tough competition to the global brands in their respective industry sectors but also managed to gain a market leadership, initially in China, against the foreign brands.

Courtesy Li Ning Company

Although Li Ning was the domestic market leader in its industry for some time, recently it lost the leadership position to Nike and lost the 2008 Olympics sponsorship to Adidas, which won it with a US$80 million bid.[11] Moreover, Li Ning's patriotic and nationalistic appeal lost out to the "cool" factor of Nike. By spending almost 10 percent (US$12.08 million) of its US$120 million revenues on marketing and branding in 2003, Li Ning has surely realized the importance of building a strong brand based on a unique identity and personality.[12] But in terms of market share, it still needs to fight it out with Adidas for the second position behind the market leader Nike. For the last five years, the turnover of the Li Ning Group has been growing at a rate of more than 45 percent on average and in 2004 it had sales of US$226.9 million (47.2 percent increase year on year) and a net profit of US$16.12 million (42 percent increase year on year).[13]

More importantly, Li Ning needs to understand that customers' purchase decisions are not always based on rational factors. This in turn means that Li Ning, like any other brand, should strive to create excitement around the brand by making it relevant to its target customers, and build proper associations related to lifestyle so that the brand resonates with its target customers.

Background

Li Ning Sports Company was started in 1990 by Li Ning, an Olympic gymnast who became the most honored athlete in the 23rd Olympic Games at Los Angeles in 1984. Having won seven out of the eight gold medals in the men's category, in the Sixth World Cup Gymnastic competition in 1982, he became an instant sporting icon in China. After retiring from professional gymnastics, he channeled his passion for sports into setting up a professional sports goods company producing footwear, clothing and other accessory products for a range of sports from basketball, football and tennis to swimming, fitness and sports fashion.

For Li, the defining moment of his life was not when he stood at the Olympic podium to receive his medals. Instead, it was in July 1989, when, in nationwide advertisements, he announced to the Chinese public that he was founding his own company and requested help for a logo. By August, he had received more than 20,000 entries from peasants, workers and many others. Despite this, he had to hire artists to develop the fox-tail-like logo derived from his initials L and N. Even when Li Ning travels today, people still come to him and say they participated in the contest back in 1989.[14]

Almost 15 years since its inception, Li Ning has emerged as one of the more promising brands from the Chinese landscape. It was proven with the successful listing of Li Ning on the Hong Kong stock exchange in early June 2004, through which it raised around US$67.9 million for its further expansion.[15]

One of the key success factors of Li Ning in China to date has been the charisma and iconicity of its founder Li Ning and the company has leveraged this fact to the full, although he is now becoming a little passé for the younger customers. Furthermore, Li Ning, following the footsteps of Nike and Adidas, began sponsoring sporting events from quite early on, despite the fact that only around 15 percent of Chinese aged 15–35 actively play any sport, compared to America's 50 percent, as academic achievement and commercial success are still the main factors that drive Chinese people.[16]

Li Ning's success so far has been based on four major factors: Li Ning's personal charisma and popularity giving the brand its initial credibility and acceptability; a strong distribution network covering many of the remote Chinese cities; sponsorships of some key sporting events involving Chinese sports stars; and finally the luring value proposition of providing shoes of quality on a par with those of Nike, but half the price of Nike and similar foreign brands. These factors have boosted Li Ning's growth till now. But Nike's resurgence in 2003 poses a strong threat to Li Ning and highlights the importance of having the right branding practices in place for these Chinese companies that aspire to challenge the experienced global brands.

Brand philosophy

Unlike most of the leading brands in the sports product category like Nike, Adidas and Reebok, Li Ning's success is not because of its brand management practices, although in the last two years, Li Ning has been doing the right things toward building a brand. So much so that Li Ning topped the list of China's own cool brands along with Haier and Lenovo, with a 49 percent backing in a survey.[17] Li Ning has been able to grow into a market leader in its category because of the four non-brand factors mentioned earlier.

One of the strongest advantages that the Li Ning sports company had when it started in 1990 was the brand equity of its founder, the star gymnast, Li Ning. Having scaled great heights both in the World Cup gymnastic competition and in the Olympic Games, Li Ning had become a

Li Ning's store front in Wuhan, China
Courtesy Li Ning Company

national sports icon in China. This popularity and the national pride were translated into the Li Ning Company. This association not only made it easy for the company to gain high levels of awareness in the marketplace, but also brought in high levels of acceptance from its target market. This was Li Ning's first major differentiating factor.

In a country like China, where there is a huge imbalance between urban and rural cities, in terms of infrastructure, employment, income and spending levels, one of the major challenges is to reach the far-flung areas that have huge chunks of population. Most of the global brands like Nike and Adidas have traditionally concentrated on the urban cities like Shanghai, Beijing and Guangzhou, where people have considerable disposable income. In contrast, from the beginning Li Ning recognized the importance of reaching those people in the far-flung rural pockets. With a strong local knowledge, established contacts and relationships with people at ground level, Li Ning has been able to set up stores and distribution networks throughout China. In the absence of a single distributor with a national presence, these established channels of distribution work as a competitive advantage. This has been another major factor contributing to Li Ning's success to date.

Taking a page out of Nike and Adidas's branding activities, Li Ning, quite early on, adopted sports sponsorship as an important part of its overall marketing activities. Both Nike and Li Ning were pitted against each other when they sponsored national teams in the 2004 Olympics with Nike backing the Chinese national team and Li Ning the Spanish team in basketball.[18] Apart from sponsoring the national teams in many events like diving and gymnastics, Li Ning has also sponsored international teams like the French national gymnastic team, the Spanish national men's and women's basketball teams and Russian delegations at 2001 and 2003 Universiade and has been a partner and sponsor to the national Chinese Olympic teams for a number of years. Although this has helped Li Ning, there is a catch here. While Li Ning sponsors all these events, the events that resonate the most amongst consumers are the NBA and the English Premier League and Li Ning has not been a major sponsor of these events like Nike and Adidas.[19] This pushes Li Ning to re-examine its sponsorship strategies. But in January 2005, Li Ning became a strategic marketing partner of NBA in China.[20]

The other major factor that has contributed to Li Ning's success is its value proposition. Li Ning has conveyed a value proposition to its customers that is a combination of quality comparable to Nike's products and a price that is close to half of that of Nike's. This has been a winning formula for Li Ning until recently. Nike and Adidas have traditionally priced their products quite high and have targeted the urban rich in cities like Shanghai, Beijing and Guangzhou. Against this, Li Ning, by combining its strengths in the distribution network, the popularity of its founder, references to patriotism and finally with this value proposition, has been able to capture a much larger market.

Given this potent combination of factors, Li Ning has managed to carve out a niche for itself in the intensely competitive Chinese market. But as the events of the past two years show, these factors alone cannot sustain its initial success. With Nike recapturing its market leadership from Li Ning, and Adidas having bagged the sponsorship for the 2008 Chinese Olympics, it is time that Li Ning gave a fresh look to its overall branding strategies.

Brand communication

Li Ning has used sports sponsorships and mass media television advertising as its two main communication channels to reach the Chinese public. With China's CCTV reaching a majority of the population, it is a powerful channel for any brand to connect with its customers.

In its television advertising, Li Ning has projected the national pride, patriotism and made-in-China themes quite forcefully. Li Ning with its ad agency Leo Burnett has come up with television commercials which highlight the country of origin to provoke a sense of national pride among its customers.[21] With this strategy, Li Ning is not only differentiating itself from the other global brands by implicitly saying that it knows the Chinese market much better, but is also knocking on its customers' emotional reservoirs to associate the brand with the country. Especially with the Olympic Games to be held in China in 2008, this strategy could prove successful. But, on the way, Li Ning seems to have overlooked one crucial factor that propelled Nike into the leadership position: the hunger among the Chinese people for Western gear and the growing sense of individualism. Even though Li Ning has redirected its focus toward highlighting individualistic and cool characters – sponsoring sports like basketball, running and soccer – it should have a fully fledged revisit of the brand communications strategy.[22]

On the other hand, in the sponsorship channel, Li Ning is not only sponsoring Chinese national teams, but also other international teams like the French team at the Sydney games. By doing this Li Ning plans to gain international exposure and wider acceptance of the brand.

Thus, Li Ning is cashing in on the Olympics craze to evoke national pride and oneness among customers to bond with the brand. Although this strategy might seem perfect at the outset, it does come with its own set of baggage.

Future challenges

Creating a distinct brand personality

Li Ning has not been able to create a strong brand personality for its products as successfully as Nike or Adidas. It is common knowledge that providing good functional benefits in today's market is the cost of entry. What makes a company and its products resonate with its customers is a strong identity and personality. Li Ning lags behind in this respect. For many years it has played the 'founder's-charisma' card to entice the customers. But given the current crop of sports stars, this proposition seems to be losing steam. By trying to do all things for all people, Li Ning has not been successful in communicating its personality to its consumer base properly. With Nike and Adidas catching up on the distribution network on one hand and deciding to venture into the mass market beyond the urban cities on the other, they are threatening Li Ning's position. Therefore, Li Ning needs to establish and build more emotional bonds by creating a strong brand personality which could prove to be a strong source of sustainable competitive advantage.

Overemphasis on patriotism and national pride

With the Bejing Olympic Games in 2008 round the corner, Li Ning has concentrated on projecting Chinese national pride and patriotism in its mass communications. But a recent survey, conducted by WPP Group's Ogilvy & Mather Worldwide and the research firm Synovate, showed that customers are less concerned about the origin of the brand than the brand itself. The survey results showed that the consumers did not see any direct relationship between patriotism and buying national brands over international ones.[23] Given this, Li Ning needs to find a fine balance between projecting patriotism and being relevant to its target market. Li Ning cannot afford to do one thing, when in fact the research and facts on ground suggest something totally different. Maintaining this fine balance will be a huge challenge for Li Ning because it has by default created a pseudo personality in the minds of its customers by projecting the made-in-China tag line so aggressively.

Clear positioning

Positioning seems to be the biggest challenge for Li Ning as the company has positioned itself in a confusing manner between sports and leisure. One of the fundamental steps toward building a strong brand is to have a strong positioning in the marketplace. With a price point that is close to half of that of Nike, it wants to project the value-for-money concept. But with high-profile sponsorships, extension of product lines and competing with the likes of Nike and Adidas, it also aims to project the premium concept. This creates confusion. Li Ning has to sort this out by deciding on a clear positioning strategy. Moreover, with the current generation of customers preferring Western brands amidst a growing sense of individualism, and Li Ning still not able to match up the quality and technological innovations of Nike, Reebok or Adidas, it has an enormous task of doing its homework right and coming out with a resonating positioning.

Li Ning has enjoyed success by combining some crucial factors which at once proved to be a competitive advantage. With the decades-long investment of Nike and Adidas paying off, those factors have ceased to provide any competitive advantage to Li Ning. Now it seems that Nike and Adidas have the advantage, with their strong brand names that resonate well with Chinese customers. If Li Ning is to recapture its leadership position, it should start on a targeted brand building journey. By combining its unique history and legacy with clear positioning and relevant sponsorships, Li Ning surely stands a chance of reclaiming its leadership position in the Chinese market.

CASE 3
Jet Airways – a powerful Indian brand

Jet Airways, the largest Indian domestic carrier, is one of the country's strongest brands. Jet Airways has built up a strong reputation for offering a great flight experience by combining world-class service, reliable operations and on-time performance. Although there are several reasons for Jet Airways' success, the main reason is the unflinching support from management toward building a strong brand. By having a clear-cut branding strategy built on the four pillars of world-class service, on-time performance, reliable operations and customer responsiveness, Jet Airways has been successful in carving out a strong presence in the Indian market and in customers' minds.

Background

Jet Airways was started by Naresh Goyal in 1993. With the Indian airline industry thrown open for private players by the Indian government, Jet

Airways was one of the 17 airlines that entered the market. With the cut-throat competitive pressures and capital constraints of the industry, only 2 of those 17 managed to stay alive – Jet Airways and Air Sahara. From then on, Jet Airways has come a long way in the last 10 years. Today it operates 270 flights daily to 44 destinations across India and commands a total market share of nearly 43.1 percent.[24]

THE JOY OF FLYING

Courtesy Jet Airways

The success of Jet Airways is a standing tribute to the commitment and investment of its corporate management in driving a strong management team coupled with cost-effective and robust operation systems to build a strong brand. Right from the start, the mission of the company has been to be the most preferred domestic carrier in the country. The entire corporate and brand strategy of Jet Airways has been based on this under-lying mission.

Brand strategy

Jet Airways has built its brand by focusing on the ingredients required to realize its stated corporate mission – to be the most preferred domestic airline in India. When Jet Airways entered the market, Indian Airlines was the market leader and was a virtual monopoly as it was state-owned. Indian Airlines had built a reputation for providing pathetic service, delayed flights, bad food and grumpy and irresponsible staff.[25] These things initially made it quite easy for Jet Airways. Understanding the concerns and require-ments of Indian customers, Jet Airways took steps to address those concerns. Flight safety, on-time flights, world-class service, sumptuous food and friendly and responsive staff were to become the foundations for the Jet Airways brand.

Jet Airways began by flying what was then, and still is, the newest fleet of airplanes in India, which provides two benefits. First, it was able to instill confidence in consumers about flight safety because of the technical superiority of the new aircraft and, second, it was able to optimize the fuel costs. The technical superiority has helped Jet Airways to maintain 99.6 percent technical dispatch reliability, to have 83 percent of all its flight departures within 15 minutes of schedule as against 65 percent of flights for Indian Airlines. Fuel cost constitutes the biggest portion of any airline's costs. With a modern fleet, Jet Airways was able to reduce its fuel costs to 26 percent of its total cost as against 40 percent for other airlines.[26] Jet Airways also placed strong emphasis on recruiting well-trained and efficient pilots by conducting extensive in-house training to all of its pilots to ensure safer flights.[27]

Till the late 1990s, the majority of people who opted for air travel were business executives. With air tickets being so expensive, air travel was beyond the reach of the common man. This prompted Jet Airways to set a high standard of in-flight service. As the company professes, it wanted to be the "Businessmen's preferred airline". This objective has led to many service innovations like the first in-flight mail order shopping program called Jet Mall,[28] a frequent flyer program called Jet Privilege, offering frequent flier rewards, special deals for vacations, hotels and *The Economist*, and a co-branded credit card with Citibank to provide the best of both the big brands,[29] to name a few.

Jet Airways has also established a benchmark in ensuring on-time flights, something that was a major concern of passengers with Indian Airlines. To complete the service experience, Jet Airways has been proactive in ensuring a friendly and responsive customer service on the ground. From cancellations, rescheduling of tickets, frequent flyer programs, to garnering feedback from customers during baggage collection to constantly pushing its own limits, Jet Airways has been a pioneer. All this has endeared Jet Airways to its core segment of travelers – business executives. Now, with more leisure travelers also opting for air travel, Jet Airways has once again taken the initiative to delight them with its promotional packages, seasonal discounts, apex fares and so on.

Jet Airways focuses extensively on the service aspect to distinguish its brand from other local competitors
Courtesy Jet Airways

Brand communication

Jet Airways has not followed the traditional rules of brand building by spending huge sums of money on advertising. Instead, it has depended heavily on third-party endorsements like national and international awards, public relations and word-of-mouth publicity. This communication strategy has worked well for the airline.

Right from the start, Jet Airways captured the attention of all major awards for all the right reasons. It has won awards in literally all major categories – from the best domestic airline in Asia Pacific by TTG Asia, best technical dispatch reliability award from Boeing Company, air transport world market development award for market development, to being declared a "superbrand" by the international Super Brands Council.[30] These awards have communicated Jet Airways' emphasis on its core brand promise and its consistent delivery in a credible and efficient way more than any advertisement could have ever done.

While the initial endorsements built the brand awareness in the market, the subsequent brand experience that passengers had with Jet Airways helped to cement close ties. This positive experience spread by word of mouth among the various segments of the market. It created a buzz about Jet Airway's impeccable service, its friendly staff and its on-time flights. All of this enhanced Jet Airways' image in the eyes of its prospective customers.

With this positive buzz going on in the market, the media was not to be left behind, and there were articles and stories in the press based on the writers' own experiences. With prominent newspapers and magazines giving positive reviews about Jet Airways, its equity with the public rose even higher.

Jet Airways was successfully able to leverage its positive image by consistently delivering on all its promises. Thus Jet Airways was able to build strong brand equity without going the usual and expensive advertising road.

By building a successful brand, Jet Airways has achieved tremendous success in the last 10 years of its existence. It has the leading market share in the domestic airline industry with 43 percent as against 38 percent of Indian Airlines and 13 percent of Air Sahara, the other two major domestic carriers.[31] Jet Airways has managed to have a seat factor of 65 percent when 61 percent would enable it to break even.[32] It has won major international awards which has helped the airline to increase its awareness beyond Indian borders. This will be important, given Jet Airways' plans to fly on more international routes. It already operates flights to Colombo, Kathmandu, Singapore, Kuala Lumpur and London.

Future challenges

Despite all the success Jet Airways has enjoyed, the coming years will bring some unique challenges. Jet Airways has to remain focused on its mission of being the most preferred airline and the consistent delivery of its brand promises if it is to stay ahead of the increasing competition.

The emergence of low-cost carriers

The biggest challenge will be the emergence of the low-cost carrier which threatens to alter the dynamics of the domestic airline industry in India.

Carriers like Air Deccan that have entered the market are offering air fares at almost one-third of Jet Airway's prices. Although Air Deccan is only operating on some selected routes, it is just a matter of time before it expands nationally and competes head-on with full-service airlines like Jet Airways. With many more budget airlines scheduled to make an entry in 2006, Jet Airways has to get its house in order and come out with a robust strategy to tackle this threat.

Brand dilution because of brand stretch

Jet Airways has responded to the threat from the low-cost carriers by coming out with various schemes like "Everyone can fly" and the "Low night fare" to lure budget travelers. Jet Airways is trying to be everything to everyone. Although it operates a business and an economy class with different prices, competing with a low-cost carrier on price despite being a full-service airline could prove challenging and dangerous for the brand. Jet Airways has regularly come out with discount schemes to attract budget travelers, but risks diluting the brand equity. It must find a balance between catering to businessmen at the higher end and budget travelers at the lower end.

Competing with international airlines

Having been given a license to operate on international long-haul routes, Jet Airways faces further challenges. Although it has good customer perception and response to its services inside India, it will be a major challenge for Jet Airways to offer the same levels of services on medium- and long-haul flights and maintain the consistency which made it known in the first place. Like other Asian brands, Jet Airways has to find an optimum balance between the unique Indian tradition of hospitality and culture and the best practices of the airline industry to appeal to a global audience. Another challenge for Jet Airways would be to build its brand in the international arena. Mere PR and endorsement might not be sufficient. Jet Airways will find it challenging to generate and maintain high levels of awareness and recall initially and strong loyalty over time.

Professional management team

The management style at Jet Airways has been a topic of debate in the popular press and also in the Indian aviation industry. Jet Airways has had two CEOs leave the company in a matter of three years. Many have attributed this to the conflict in working styles between the Chairman Naresh Goyal and the CEOs. It has also been alleged that the chairman interferes in all matters of corporate governance and also runs the organization as a family fiefdom.[33] In the future, Jet Airways will be compelled to change its style of governance, as it has become a publicly listed company following its blockbuster IPO on the Indian stock market in March 2005.[34]

CASE 4
Giordano – the Asian clothing brand[35]

Giordano is one of the better known clothing brands to originate from Asia, operating in more than 20 countries across the region and the Middle East. As a retailer of casual wear, it offers customers good value for money by combining trendy, comfortable and good quality clothes at affordable prices.

Background

Giordano was founded by Jimmy Lai in 1980. The name was intentionally selected to add an international dimension to the brand. Giordano initially started out selling clothes manufactured for the US market as a wholesale trade. In 1983, Giordano started selling products under the brand name Giordano with its own retail outlets. Faced with intense competition, from its inception Giordano has emphasized the value-for-money concept. Especially during the Asian financial crisis in the 1990s, Giordano was able to sustain and grow due to its philosophy, as more and more customers became price and value conscious.

Giordano repositioned itself in 1987 toward a retailer of discounted casual unisex clothes, having previously offered only men's clothes. The repositioning was in line with its value-for-money concept.

Brand management structure

The Giordano brand portfolio consists of four brands: the corporate brand,

The signature store front of Giordano
Courtesy Giordano

Giordano, which also serves as the core brand, Giordano Ladies, Giordano Junior and Bluestar Exchange.

- Giordano Ladies is the high-end premium brand. Targeted at 20–40-year-old working women, it provides "career wear" at an affordable price, although it is priced around 30 percent higher than the core Giordano brand. Giordano Ladies is sold through 24 exclusive retail outlets and contributes 4 percent of the turnover.

- The core Giordano and Giordano Junior brands are the mass market brands offering good quality casual wear. With 1,384 retail outlets, these two brands contribute 88 percent of the overall company turnover.

- The Bluestar Exchange brand, which is priced around 30 percent lower than the core Giordano brand, is targeted toward the low-end, price-conscious budget customers. It operates through 121 retail outlets and contributes 8 percent of the overall turnover.

Giordano manages its brand centrally from headquarters in Hong Kong. Recognizing the uniqueness of various markets in Asia, it also allows for sufficient leverage for the country teams to handle the day-to-day management. Giordano manages the entire product portfolio by classifying them as core, movable and icing items:

- *Core items* (40 percent) such as T-shirts and trousers are sourced, manufactured and distributed centrally.

- *Movable items* (40 percent of the portfolio) consist of approximately 200 stock keeping units (SKUs) of seasonal fashion products, centrally designed and developed and from which regional teams select based on local market preferences.

- *Icing items* (20 percent) are developed by regional and country markets.

In line with this strategy, Giordano also allows considerable leeway for the regional teams to come up with region-specific promotional activities that are sensitive to the local culture and mindset. By combining centralized management with localized micro-marketing and considerable leeway for regional teams, Giordano has been able to stay relevant to customer needs.

Brand philosophy

Giordano won the first round of competition by being the first mover in the value clothes segment in Asia. The Asian financial crisis gave Giordano an opportunity to consolidate its positioning. Although these factors helped Giordano to grow, one of the more important reasons for its success has been its relentless drive to build a strong brand based on its corporate values and vision: "To be the best and biggest world brand in apparel retailing." The branding philosophy is based on excellent customer service, quality merchandise, product innovation and a value-for-money positioning. All these values have resonated within the many Asian markets that Giordano operates in. Giordano traditionally has been a heavy advertiser, using outdoor media among others to communicate its value proposition. In 2005 it came out with a "World without strangers" campaign, depicting people from different countries around the world, to drive home the point that Giordano aspires to be a global brand.

Customer service

From the beginning, Giordano has used service as one of its main differentiating factors. Giordano has integrated the front and back end of providing services in a successful manner. To provide excellent service, a company needs to have professionally trained personnel. Giordano has put in place a structured training program called "attitude training" which not only trains Giordano's staff, but also assists in recruiting the right type of people who fit the corporate culture. In recruiting people, Giordano selects those whose attitudes match the company's corporate culture. This selection criterion ensures that customers are provided with the best service. By having specially designed training rooms equipped with two-way mirrors, video cameras, training consultants and full-time training staff, it spends considerable time and effort in training every employee. By introducing many training modules on different aspects of service, Giordano also provides flexibility to its employees to choose from those modules to gain expertise in certain specific aspects.

In recognition of its efforts to build up an army of well-trained and service-minded employees, Giordano has been awarded a certification of merit: "Grooming Future Leaders: Giordano Trainee Program" by the Hong Kong Management Association for Excellence. Giordano has also realized that training alone will not motivate employees to perform to their best. In this regard, Giordano has been able to attract and retain the best talent in the industry by paying good wages to its employees in the retail industry. As Giordano moves into newer markets in Asia and beyond, providing customers with this superior service would prove crucial.

The service campaign was started in 1989 when Giordano came up with the "Giordano means service" badge that all the staff wore. This enabled Giordano to proclaim three main aspects: "We allow unlimited try-ons, we exchange – no questions asked and we serve with a smile". The company launched two initial campaigns that were deemed to be very successful. One was the campaign asking customers to fix the price for a pair of jeans and then it was sold at that price. The other was where Giordano gave T-shirts to customers for every fault the customer pointed to in Giordano. These two gestures endeared Giordano to its customers, and helped the brand to build a strong reputation around trust and deliverable service.

One of the main factors for this enduring service orientation has been the solid support from corporate management. One example is that the entire management and staff at the headquarters in Hong Kong serve at a Giordano outlet during the Christmas and Chinese New Year break to drive home their commitment to customer service. This also ensures a strong feedback loop to corporate management.

Quality merchandise

Giordano has been offering clothing that reflects a contemporary and easy living lifestyle by combining simplicity in design and quality in its workmanship. By providing appealing designs in vibrant colors for each of the segments in its brand portfolio, Giordano has been able to maximize its revenue generation. Moreover, by managing its inventory and stock levels through just-in-time and quick response inventory systems, Giordano has been able to respond quickly to changes in trends that are crucial in the retail industry. By communicating the quality aspect of the brand, Giordano has created a sense of security in customers' minds by consistently meeting their expectations.

Product innovation

Bringing in new features and materials and making them affordable to its customer segments has been the trademark of Giordano. A case in point here is the DryTech product that Giordano introduced. This fabric, with its moisture management property, was similar to that being used by Nike in its sportswear products. By exploiting the nature of this fabric and making multipurpose clothing for different occasions, Giordano created avenues to bring innovative products into the value-for-money mass market. Consistent with its innovation, Giordano is introducing CoolMax, a specialty fabric, to the mass market in 2005. By consistently coming up with new products, Giordano has been able to create an image of a brand that is proactive, fresh, and contemporary.

Value-for-money positioning

Giordano positioned itself as a value-for-money clothes retailer during the late 1980s and reinforced it again during the Asian financial crisis. With the customers becoming more value- and price-conscious, this was an ideal positioning for Giordano. Despite selling value-for-money clothing, Giordano has been able to maintain its quality perception.

Giordano came up with a sub-brand called Bluestar Exchange specifically to target budget customers who were price-conscious. Targeting the mid- to lower-income working-class people, Bluestar Exchange provided them with a range of colors and prints in a narrower assortment to keep the design and production costs lower. To serve the young career woman with "career wear", Giordano came up with Giordano Ladies brand. This almost created a new market space for the brand. While Zara and Mango operate with clothes for a similar segment, the price points differentiate Giordano Ladies. Although Giordano Ladies is priced almost 30 percent higher than the core Giordano brand, it still provides a value-for-money perception in that specific segment by combining quality with affordability. This again has stressed the overall positioning.

By being consistent in practicing their corporate values and the Giordano brand's essence, Giordano has been able to maintain its growth in the market, with turnovers of US$406 million and US$480 million in 2003 and 2004 respectively, an 18.1 percent increase year on year.

Giordano's competitors

Although Giordano has been the first mover in the value-for-money casual-wear segment in Asia, there have been many who have challenged Giordano's position and are competing head-on against the brand. As Giordano operates in multiple segments, it directly or indirectly competes against many players. Bossini, Hang Ten, Esprit, G2000 and Gap are some of the more well-known competitors.

Bossini and Hang Ten are direct competitors for the core Giordano brand. These two players, with similar positioning and product portfolios, have been targeting similar customer segments. But Giordano, with its emphasis on friendly service and higher quality, has been able to maintain its edge.

Esprit, with its fashionable and more edgy image, is positioned higher than the core Giordano brand. With its appealing advertisements and an international image, Esprit poses a threat to the Giordano Ladies brand.

Giordano is embarking on moving the entire Giordano portfolio a notch higher. The company is moving the core Giordano brand to a slightly higher positioning and bringing the Bluestar Exchange brand to the mass market level. This move would put a lot of pressure on Giordano as that market space already has many entrenched players.

Future challenges

Sustaining innovation and quality

Up till now, Giordano has been able to sustain the levels of innovation along with quality that it has come to be known for. But, given Giordano's expansion plans within and beyond Asia, there will be a severe pressure on resources. Moreover, with many Asian countries, including China and India, allowing more foreign investment in the textile and retail industry, it is only a matter of time before the competition intensifies even more. Given these changing market dynamics, it will be a challenge for the brand to sustain its current advantages.

Establishing a clear positioning

Giordano has been consistent in its value-for-money positioning since its inception. But with sub-brands like Giordano Ladies and Bluestar Exchange catering to distinctly different market segments, it would be worthwhile for Giordano to re-examine its overall positioning. As the core Giordano and Giordano Junior brands still contribute a huge bulk of the overall business, it should not jeopardize the overall positioning and wander off in a different direction.

Creating a strong brand personality

As clothing is so visible, this makes it the best product category to build resonating and exciting brand personalities, because the merchandise can be used powerfully by customers to express their identities. Traditionally, Giordano has emphasized the functional attributes of quality, value and design. But with the upward positioning of the entire Giordano portfolio being planned, Giordano should develop a more emotional and personality-based positioning to compete against the likes of Gap and Esprit.

Expansion plans

One of the main advantages of Giordano has been its deep understanding of Asian market dynamics and customer mindsets. As it plans to expand into India, Russia, North America and European markets, it will find it difficult to gain a firm foothold, as each of these markets is culturally unique and poses distinct challenges. Giordano should counter this by establishing strong relationships with local distribution networks and recruiting local people who have a good understanding of local market dynamics.

Notes

1 A substantial part of this case is based on the author's interview with the company management.
2 "Disappearance of Jim Thompson: The silk magnate mystery/30 year puzzle", Michael Richardson, 26 March 1997, *International Herald Tribune*.
3 Michael Richardson, 26 March 1997, *International Herald Tribune*, ibid.
4 "New hand behind Jim Thompson's legacy", 26 May 2002, *The Nation* (Thailand).
5 Michael Richardson, 26 March 1997, *International Herald Tribune*, op. cit.
6 "Mystery of Jim Thompson's disappearance", 1 February 2004, *New Sunday Times*.
7 "Inspired by Asian cultures", 23 December 2002, *The Nation* (Thailand).
8 23 December 2002, *The Nation* (Thailand), ibid.
9 23 December 2002, *The Nation* (Thailand), ibid.
10 "Jim Thompson boutique to open its doors at Empire", 31 August 2004, *Borneo Bulletin*.
11 "Beijing: Adidas to sponsor Chinese Olympics", 4 February 2005, *Campaign*.
12 "Just do it Chinese-style", 2 August 2003, *The Economist*.
13 http://www.lining.com/EN/investors/inside-4_1.html.
14 "Movers & shakers", *Asia Inc*, December 2003/January 2004.
15 "China firm faces sneaker rivals on home court", Leslie Chang, 23 June 2004, *Asian Wall Street Journal*.
16 2 August 2003, *The Economist*, op. cit.
17 "Chinese brands raise 'cool quotient'", 28 April 2004, *Wall Street Journal*.
18 "Beijing: Adidas to sponsor Chinese Olympics", 4 February 2005, *Campaign*.
19 Leslie Chang, 23 June 2004, *Asian Wall Street Journal*, op. cit.
20 Author interview with Li Ning management.
21 "Li-Ning taps into patriotic fervour", White, Amy, *Media Asia*, 15621138, 8/13/2004.
22 "How Nike figured out China", Matthew Forney, Daren Fonda, Neil Gough, 25 October 2004, *Time* US edition.
23 "Study: Chinese youth aren't patriotic purchasers; Most favor global brands such as Coke and Nike over local rivals", Normandy Madden, 5 January 2004, *Advertising Age*, **6**, **75**(1), English.
24 Author interview with the company's management.
25 Jordan, Miriam, (1994), "India's skies, filled with competition, suddenly turn more flier-friendly", *Wall Street Journal*, December 30, 1994, pp. A4.
26 "Jet Airways: high flier", *India Business Intelligence*, April 1997.
27 "Market development: Jet Airways", *Air Transport World*, February 1, 2001, **28**(2).
28 "Jet Airways launches mail order shopping", *The Hindu Business Line*, May 11, 2001.
29 "Minis and curves", *The Week*, May 16, 2004.

30 http://www.jetairways.com/Cultures/en-US/About+Us/Awards/.

31 "Jet Airways tops in domestic circuit", *The Hindu Business Line*, August 2004.

32 "Jet Airways, fly by wire", *Business World*, November 2004.

33 "Jet Airways, on a wing and a prayer", *Business World*, September 2003.

34 "Jet Airways lists on NSE", http://www.ndtv.com, accessed 4 May 2005.

35 Part of the case is based on author interview with Giordano's management.

CHAPTER 9

10 STEPS TO BUILD AN ASIAN BRAND

Vision without action is a daydream. Action without vision is a nightmare.   Japanese proverb

The orientation of brand management has gone through substantial changes over the past few decades, and has evolved as a more integrated and visible part of overall corporate strategy. The evolution of the brand equity concept during the 1990s, the development of advanced financial brand valuation methods and their adoption by advisors and their clients, and the emergence of better brand tracking tools have all facilitated the elevation of the branding discipline beyond middle management and into the boardroom.

Asian boardrooms generally lag behind this trend and tend to manage brand marketing from a bottom-up instead of a top-down perspective. There are a couple of reasons for this. As marketing and brand decisions traditionally have been managed in mid-level marketing departments in most Asian companies, a large emphasis has been placed on tactical marketing activities as opposed to strategic branding approaches led by corporate management. Branding has been widely perceived as advertising and promotions.

But several indications show rapid progress in the right direction for a number of Asian companies, where branding as a strategic tool has become more recognized and accepted within their boardrooms. This is also driven by the increasing attention on branding and its value-driving capability among stakeholders, media and opinion makers across Asia. Strategic branding and its implications for Asian companies and governments is a much debated topic, with coverage from the media and a number of conferences and seminars across the region. Asian companies may have great intentions and aspirations to move up the value chain through branding to capture the financial and competitive benefits described in the previous chapters. But to achieve these objectives successfully, Asian companies must follow a comprehensive brand strategy framework, supported by a systematic process throughout the organization. The successful implementation of these processes will help Asian boardrooms to achieve sustainable revenue and cash flow streams for the future.

The brand vision, objectives and multiple marketing activities must be closely aligned with the corporate strategy. They must blend together, as they serve the same purpose – driving profitability and shareholder value. Branding is the sum of all the parts and elements involved, so getting the strategic balance right between the brand, the corporate vision and the entire organization is crucial. The boardroom must ensure that the brand delivers successfully and seamlessly on every customer touch point, so that it supports the overall strategic intention. This is easier said than done. It requires a systematic and dedicated framework to succeed and it takes a considerable period of time to get it right.

There are 10 crucial steps to follow to build a successful branding strategy and manage its implementation (Table 9.1). The steps enable the Asian boardroom to focus its attention on the required areas, and serve as check-points which can be tailored to the individual company's specific needs and requirements. Hence the steps need not be followed strictly and in the same sequence. As branding is an iterative process, it has to strike a balance between several objectives, tradeoffs, resource constraints and many other factors involved throughout the organization. These steps are meant as a useful guide for Asian branding projects – irrespective of scale, scope and time horizon.

TABLE 9.1 **10 steps to build a successful Asian brand**
1. The CEO needs to lead the brand strategy work
2. Build your own model as not every model suits all
3. Involve your stakeholders including the customers
4. Advance the corporate vision
5. Exploit new technology
6. Empower people to become brand ambassadors
7. Create the right delivery system
8. Communicate!
9. Measure the brand performance
10. Adjust regularly – be your own change agent

Source: VentureRepublic

1. The CEO needs to lead the brand strategy work

The Asian business landscape requires a different path for Asian companies and their boardrooms to be successful. Companies need to achieve a fine balance between low-cost production (competitiveness), constant innovation (differentiation) and enhanced customer satisfaction (value capture through branding).

Brands are not just, if ever, built from traditional advertising and promotions, but rather by using a comprehensive range of corporate-wide activities delivered by people throughout the organization. Therefore, the crucial balance between brand promise and brand delivery has implications for all company functions and it becomes a managerial responsibility reaching far beyond marketing and communications departments.

Therefore, branding can no longer be delegated to the mid-level marketing function in the typical Asian organization. Instead, the Asian boardrooms and the CEO must take charge of the brand strategy, lead the brand development, manage its implementation and be fully involved in performance tracking and benchmarking.

The marketing and communications departments do not have managerial authority over other company functions. The following three examples illustrate this clearly:

1. If the service level of the frontline staff of an airline slides, according to surveys, it could quickly harm the brand promise. But the marketing department will find it difficult to exercise authority to implement any necessary actions. They will only be able to influence the process. The internal political complications could be significant and the crucial time to action may be relatively slow.

2. The success of any brand depends on the company culture and the right type of people working in the company. Service businesses are dependant on this, for example. Marketing people would find it hard to set guidelines and influence the specific type of future talent to be recruited by HR.

3. The brand might have to enhance its visual appeal or innovate to maintain its relevance and stay competitive. The marketing departments would find it difficult to influence and exercise authority over the objectives and development plans in the R&D department.

The above examples are of boardroom and corporate management responsibilities and carry ultimate weight when led by the CEO. Therefore, branding should be represented in the boardroom by a person responsible for branding so that he/she is able to participate equally with corporate executives like the CEO and CFO. The CEO and the CFO have until now been the typical inseparable, influential and strongly coordinated twins running the company.

Philips, the Dutch conglomerate, appointed a chief marketing officer (CMO) in January 2003.[1] This example illustrates an emerging trend in Western boardrooms where the marketing function is increasingly represented along with the CEO and CFO to provide a better representation for marketing and branding. Even the chief brand officer is an emerging title illustrating the same trend.

Think about the following example of marketing's role within the organization. When Asian companies disclose financial results and forecasts for the future to analysts and media, the spokespersons are usually the CEO and even more often the CFO. But what are the drivers of the future revenues? As mentioned in the beginning, one of the three key drivers for Asian companies going ahead is the ability to capture value by closely linking it to customer satisfaction and the price premium the brand is able to command. The CFO is rarely a savvy marketer and lacks a detailed knowledge of or any in-depth experience in branding. Instead, a senior and strategic marketing person, the CMO, would be most appropriate and capable to address that crucial aspect of the corporation's future objectives and how it helps to drive profitability and financial value. This highlights the need to train marketing staff or hire external marketing talent to ensure branding skill sets and experiences are sufficient on a strategic level.

Naturally, there is a limit to the direct involvement and supervision of the CEO in managing the marketing and branding activities. To ensure his/her continuous involvement in branding despite his/her other responsibilities, the CEO must be backed by a strong brand management team of senior contributors, who can facilitate the continuous development and integration of the brand strategy. The CMO can serve as the crucial (and often missing) link in the Asian boardroom, enabling corporate management to design and control the brand strategy directly, and allocate the required resources to implement the strategies successfully.

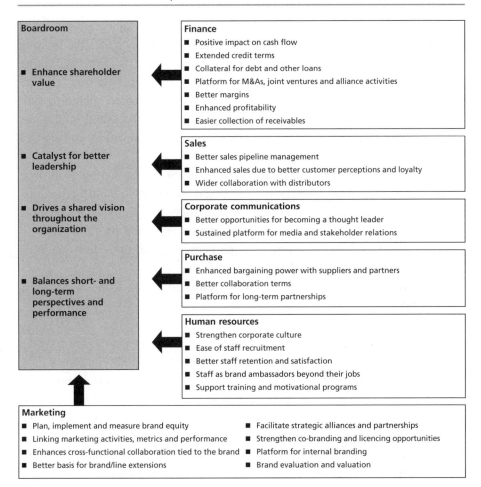

Boardroom

- Enhance shareholder value
- Catalyst for better leadership
- Drives a shared vision throughout the organization
- Balances short- and long-term perspectives and performance

Finance
- Positive impact on cash flow
- Extended credit terms
- Collateral for debt and other loans
- Platform for M&As, joint ventures and alliance activities
- Better margins
- Enhanced profitability
- Easier collection of receivables

Sales
- Better sales pipeline management
- Enhanced sales due to better customer perceptions and loyalty
- Wider collaboration with distributors

Corporate communications
- Better opportunities for becoming a thought leader
- Sustained platform for media and stakeholder relations

Purchase
- Enhanced bargaining power with suppliers and partners
- Better collaboration terms
- Platform for long-term partnerships

Human resources
- Strengthen corporate culture
- Ease of staff recruitment
- Better staff retention and satisfaction
- Staff as brand ambassadors beyond their jobs
- Support training and motivational programs

Marketing
- Plan, implement and measure brand equity
- Linking marketing activities, metrics and performance
- Enhances cross-functional collaboration tied to the brand
- Better basis for brand/line extensions
- Facilitate strategic alliances and partnerships
- Strengthen co-branding and licencing opportunities
- Platform for internal branding
- Brand evaluation and valuation

Figure 9.1 The brand boardroom model
Source: VentureRepublic

As shown in the brand boardroom model (Figure 9.1), all the different line functions of an organization not only contribute to branding but also benefit from it. The model shows the value that different departments within a company derive from strong brand management. For example, the finance department reports better margins due to strong brand recognition and brand equity, and the HR department gets better talent applying as they will want to work for a well-known brand. Therefore, brand strategies must be led by boardrooms to ensure that the whole company, with its many line functions, works in tandem toward a stronger brand.

The company can also gain significant advantages by creating a brand board chaired by the CEO and led by the CMO. This creates the missing link between the boardroom (corporate management) and the marketing function (implementation of brand strategy). The key people from all relevant departments should be represented on the brand board, including staff from the marketing department. This ensures that the brand strategy is commonly shared and understood throughout the organization, and enables everyone to take ownership of it.

This proposed reorganization is beneficial for the marketing profession in Asia as a whole and will help Asian brand marketers to build a reputation for being financially responsible. Shareholders and analysts are pushing companies and boardrooms to deliver on revenue and profit objectives. Therefore the CEO must ensure that marketing expenditures deliver a satisfactory return and help to drive the bottom line.

According to Nirmalya Kumar, a professor at the London Business School:

> To improve value to a company, marketers must engage the CEO and the top leadership in meeting the two market challenges that all companies face: enhancing customer loyalty and reducing downward pressures on prices. To meet this, companies are looking for growth-related initiatives like expanding to new and growing channels of distribution, selling solutions instead of products, and pursuing radical rather than incremental innovation. Marketing executives have the skills to lead such initiatives if they are willing to take the leadership role and be more cross-functional in their thinking. None of these initiatives can be successfully implemented by the marketing function alone.[2]

Elevating the Asian brand marketer to the boardroom creates a new trio consisting of the CEO, CFO and CMO, which encompasses the corporate strategy as well as the brand strategy. It is not a question of titles (it could be marketing director, vice-president or the like) but rather the dedication from shareholders and owners to make the brand strategy an integrated part of enhancing and accelerating cash flows and financial value throughout the organization.

2. Build your own model as not every model suits all

All companies have their own sets of business values and a unique way of doing things, influenced by the company heritage and culture. There are many brand models available and more are being developed every year. Even the best and most comprehensive brand strategy model has to be tailored to these specific company needs and requirements. Often, only a few but important adjustments are needed to align these models with other similar business models and strategies of the company to create a simplified framework and toolbox for branding. It must be remembered that as branding is the face of a business strategy, these two aspects must go hand in hand for the company to become successful.

Corporate management should set clear and quantifiable objectives for the brand portfolio – and stick to them. Brand building is a long, drawn out process. Therefore, companies need to take a long-term view and not be discouraged by unrealistic expectations of achieving results in the short term. Brand metrics are important tools to measure performance and benchmark against several indicators.

The company must determine the brand identity, strategy and implementation plan, and make sure it is aligned with the corporate strategy. The entire process is important in itself, as it forces the corporate management team to discuss and agree on crucial issues related to the brand and its implications for the company. For example, if enhanced service aspects or new innovation capabilities are believed to be future drivers of the brand, it has implications for several functions and managers throughout the organization and the way service and innovation initiatives are implemented and managed.

Branding requires the right and adequate organizational and financial resources, so the corporate management team needs to ensure that brand promise and brand delivery are closely aligned. This involves a thorough examination of the entire operational system of the organization and how well it is equipped to deliver on the brand promise that is communicated to the market. A comprehensive customer touch point program plays a crucial role in managing and measuring the entire process throughout the company.

3. Involve your stakeholders including the customers

Who knows more about a company than the customers, the employees and many other stakeholders? This is common sense, but many companies forget these simple and easily accessible sources of valuable information as useful background information for creating and managing powerful brands.

It is important not to underestimate the value of market research. The company should get an external and unbiased view of the competitive landscape, including the current brand image among stakeholders, the brand positioning and critical directions for the brand identity and strategy in the future. However, it is also important to add its own observations, cultural understanding and intuition to achieve a well-balanced platform for decisions. For example, it can be difficult to get respondents in research situations to talk openly about their aspirations or imagine things they want in the future. A simple rule is to use 5 percent of the brand marketing budget on market research to establish a platform for strategy development.

Research can comprise retail visits to gain an understanding of a local market and its customers. It is important to have a constant pulse on market trends and watch competitors' actions in the marketplace. Lindsay Owen-Jones, chairman of L'Oreal, tries to visit a major market every month to get a better understanding of what the company's target customers are buying and wearing. It also means visiting other types of retail outlets and not just L'Oreal's typical stores. These visits have an important effect internally: they send the message to the global organization that the CEO himself does what he expects the entire company to do, namely listen to the customers.[3]

4. Advance the corporate vision

The branding strategy is an excellent reason and channel for advancing the corporate vision throughout the company. It allows the management to involve, educate and align everyone around the corporate objectives, corporate values and future strategy of the company. It provides a guiding star and leads everyone in the same direction. Internal efforts contribute at least 50 percent to making a corporate branding strategy successful, and it serves as a platform for communicating the corporate vision internally as well as externally. By involving all the internal stakeholders, corporate management not only ensures a total buy-in for its branding initiatives, but can also use the entire exercise to motivate its employees and rejuvenate the corporate culture.

A classic example is that of Nike. Nike's entire corporate and hence its brand philosophy is centered and leveraged around its "Just do it" tag line. To extend its corporate vision, a number of Nike's senior executives hold the additional title of "corporate storyteller". They ensure that stories around the brand, its heritage and philosophy are circulated and shared internally. This helps to align the corporate culture with corporate strategies.[4]

RedBull: the energy drink

RedBull is one of the few brands that has created a whole new category – the energy drink. It has led this category since its inception almost 20 years ago. It commands a 49 percent market share worldwide and US$2 billion in total revenues.[5] From a humble start with unconventional marketing tactics, RedBull has become one of the most popular drinks in the world after the cola giants. RedBull has its origins in Thailand, where it was known as Krating Daeng, which means "red water buffalo". RedBull was founded in 1987 when Dietrich Mateschitz, a marketing executive at Unilever and P&G, introduced the energy drink in Europe. He modified the ingredients of the drink to suit Western tastes and this created a new "energy drink" category in itself.

One of the main reasons for RedBull's success has been its unconventional marketing communications, ranging from creating "buzz", word-of-mouth publicity to sponsoring extreme sports. The communications have been in line with the overall brand personality of being a cool, hip, rebellious brand. The initial ban on RedBull entering the German, French and other key European markets due to the drink's ingredients also added to the mystique of the brand.

RedBull's initial channel was through opinion leaders in its target segments of students, hip and high-end bars and athletes in extreme sports. By seeding in the product through these groups, RedBull created a positive buzz for its brand. RedBull followed it up by sponsoring team events and extreme sports to build up its personality rather than using celebrities. From windsurfing, hangliding, sponsoring a Formula One team to its own flying team, community and music-based events, RedBull sponsors almost 500 athletes around the world. In 2004 alone, it spent around US$600 million or 30 percent of its revenues on marketing and other supporting events. Coca-Cola on the other hand spent a mere 9 percent of its revenue on marketing.[6]

Despite its origins in Asia, RedBull is headquartered in Austria, and has grown into a brand that spans continents. RedBull serves as a classic example of how a long-term vision and strong branding initiatives can turn an ordinary drink into a widely popular brand across the world. It also highlights how Asian companies need to develop such a vision and take up opportunities like this to bring out strong brands.

Many successful Asian companies are constantly driving organizational change as a managerial instrument to keep up with the dynamic environment and thereby allocate resources where needed. Branding has the ability to help drive change internally. Datacraft, an independent IT services and solutions company in Asia Pacific, rejuvenated its brand identity in 2004 as an integral part of an internal change management process. The company aimed at being positioned as a solutions partner rather than a pure technol-

ogy provider. Led by corporate management, the brand rejuvenation helped
the entire organization to focus on the future business strategy and served as
a compelling event for changing mindsets internally. In other words, the
brand rejuvenation was an important channel for the CEO to communicate
the new corporate vision and its directions.[7]

5. Exploit new technology

Modern technology must play an integral part of the branding strategy and
it helps the organization in developing, managing and measuring the activities of the brand. Furthermore, technology helps to gain effectiveness and
improve the competitive edge of the corporation.

A well-designed and constantly updated intranet is a must in today's
working environment which has become increasingly virtual, with employees working from home, from other locations and traveling across the
globe. An extranet can facilitate seamless integration with strategic partners, suppliers and customers. It can help to avoid time-consuming paper
work and manual handling of many issues.

A company website is a crucial channel for any modern corporation,
regardless of industry and size. Many Asian companies still underestimate
the power of the internet as a communication channel to build their brands.
If a corporation does not have a strategy for and is not accessible on the
internet, it does not exist! People expect companies to be present on the
internet. The more professionally and interactively the website is structured and managed, the better the brand perception among the increasingly
internet-savvy customers. It provides an excellent platform for micro-
marketing as it can be used as a targeted communication channel with
customers and other stakeholders.

A rapidly increasing communication channel like blogs is becoming an
extremely important way for customers and other stakeholders to express
positive as well as negative ideas and views. Blogs allow company executives to monitor feedback and reactions from customers in real time. It also
provides a conduit for inviting customers to share their experiences with the
brand, but at the same time it serves as a channel for customer complaints,
which must be tracked accordingly and responded to.

In general, word-of-mouth marketing, involving all stakeholders including the staff, can be extremely valuable and have great impact on the overall
image of the company and its brand portfolio.[8] Word-of-mouth marketing is

sometimes referred to as "buzz".[9] A case in point is marketing leader Procter & Gamble which in 2001 set up a unit called Tremor. The unit has enlisted 280,000 teenagers between the ages of 13 and 19 to help spread the word about products in environments and communities which are traditionally hard to reach for marketers.[10]

Customer relationship management (CRM) solutions can be a powerful tool for Asian companies to align the brand with distribution, customers and other stakeholders. It gives companies a well-structured system through which they can monitor and manage the entire spectrum of customer inter-action. CRM also enables companies to build strong databases which can be used in multiple ways to enhance customer experiences across all cross-functional touch points. Many companies have faced challenges in imple-menting the CRM strategy successfully, including organizational resistance and lack of ownership. The key to success is to get the relevant departments involved and implement the right systems and processes through ongoing training and adjustments, so that motivation and accountability become the drivers of the project.[11]

Enterprise resource planning (ERP) systems also facilitate a better way of performing many of the crucial functions within a company. By ensuring that the latest technologies are effectively used, companies can be better geared to support the overall branding initiatives internally and externally. The integration of modern technology enhances efficiencies, reduces costs and releases resources that could be redirected to customers.

6. Empower people to become brand ambassadors

One of the most important assets in a corporation is its human resources. They interact every day with colleagues, customers, suppliers, competitors, industry experts and many others. But staff members also interact with an impressive number of people totally unconnected with the corporation, in the form of family members, friends, former colleagues and many others. Hence they serve as the most important brand ambassadors of the company as their attitudes and behaviors will significantly impact perceptions.

The most effective way to turn employees into brand ambassadors is to train everyone adequately in the brand strategy (including vision, values and personality and so on) and make sure that everyone fully understands exactly what the corporation aims at becoming in the minds of its customers and stakeholders.

In 2003, HSBC invested US$750 per employee on training, equal to almost four days of training for each employee on average. The company has more than 1,100 global training staff and operates regional training centers including many other learning activities.[12]

Brands like Nike and Apple are known for their comprehensive company-wide efforts in attracting, developing and retaining talent. They are aware of the risks inherent in having new talent joining and potentially contributing to their unique and strong company cultures. New applicants have to meet several current staff members who assess how the applicants will fit into the company culture. So, a lot of effort is put into the recruiting processes to make sure that the new talent fit into their company cultures which are strongly aligned around their brands. Their dedication to HR is an important part of their success.

Companies aspiring to build strong brands must also review how their talent recruiting and training systems are supporting their brands. This is particularly critical with a larger company. WPP is an example of a company where human resource management is an integral part of corporate management. The company is one of the world's leading communications services groups, which controls several of the largest advertising and communications agency networks. The entire group employs 64,000 people in 103 countries, and services many of the Fortune Global 500 companies. In 2002, WPP hired a chief talent officer to put talent at the heart of the company's strategy together with the CEO.[13]

There are three guidelines which can be used as checkpoints:

1. Does the entire organization understand the key brand strategy? The values?

2. Has everyone been given training and guidelines on how to support and live the brand?

3. Is everyone given feedback on how their behaviors and attitudes fit with the brand strategy?

Internal branding is best achieved by getting buy-in from all the employees. The company should treat its employees the same way it treats its customers and use this as a benchmark. A classic example is how Starbucks gives stock options even to its temporary workers. The logic is – if Starbucks wants to be seen as a third place (apart from work and home) for its customers – then it should make its employees feel that way as well. This way, the organization should earn the loyalty and buy-in from its entire staff into living the brand. Howard Schultz, chairman of Starbucks, said: "If we want to exceed the trust of our customers, then we first have to build trust with our people. Brand has to start with the culture and naturally extend to our customers".[14]

Another example from Asia is Shangri-La Hotels and Resorts, which has realized the importance of internal branding and practices it religiously throughout the entire organization to enhance the overall brand experience (see box).

Internal branding – making the organization live the brand

Shangri-La Hotels and Resorts' Shangri-La Care[15] is a good example of how a leading Asian hospitality brand practices branding within the organization by aligning its staff and management with the overall brand strategy. Shangri-La's stated mission is to delight its customers each and every time. To delight the customers, it has to ensure that its staff offer top-notch service and are consistent across the group's 44 hotels to protect the brand image. With this intention, in 1996 Shangri-La Hotels launched Shangri-La Care, an integrated training program to train the managers and staff of its hotels.

The training program is divided into three modules called Shangri-La Care, Delighting Customers and Recover to gain loyalty. The aim is to train staff in improving service delivery. It includes training on how to live the corporate values, how to offer a memorable experience to customers by personalizing services and how to retain and recover loyalty from customers when some uncontrollable mistakes happen.

Corporate management has made it mandatory to allocate a separate budget for the training and regularly ensures that the training programs are being conducted. By concentrating on branding inside the organization, Shangri-La has been able to project a consistent brand image in all its hotels, from Hong Kong to Australia. Also, with every staff member acting as a brand ambassador, it has been able to deliver its brand promises consistently.

---

7. Create the right delivery system

A brand is the face of a successful business strategy and it promises what all stakeholders can expect from the corporation. The brand will only add value when these expectations are consistently met. Therefore, the delivery of the right products and services as promised is crucial for companies, as promise without delivery is worthless. Think of the cradle-to-grave concept of a lifelong customer and the value he/she will provide in such a time span. Companies should ensure that customers are handled with great care, according to internal specifications and outside expectations. The moment of truth is when the corporate brand promise is delivered well – and the ideal situation for the brand will be to exceed customer expectations.

Singapore Airlines has a rigid, detailed and in-depth description of all customer touch points within the corporation, and resources are spent on making sure it actually does happen every time to every customer. All Singapore Airlines' employees, regardless of title and geographical location, spend a significant amount of work days every year being trained. The case study on Giordano in Chapter 8 illustrated how service was practiced throughout the organization with a structured training program.

One of the challenges for companies in general, and for diversified or expanding companies in particular, is to put in place a systematic structure to deal with the many challenges. To ensure consistency in delivering brand promises, companies should establish some benchmarks and guidelines. These should guide all the different functions within the company. The guidelines just provide the blueprint; the important aspect is to drive these initiatives to their logical conclusion. By implementing and managing the customer touch point model discussed in Chapter 6, companies can ensure that both internal and external stakeholders are adequately aligned in the overall process.

The ever-changing market trends and customer mindsets make the brand management process an ongoing process. The process should act as a loop by constantly taking in inputs from the market and customers and evolving the branding processes.

The company also needs to decide on the structure of the marketing organization, and whether it should have a centralized or decentralized structure. An example of a central marketing organization is the case of Samsung which aimed at building a premium brand positioning. The company wanted the brand to be managed in a unified manner with a longer term horizon. Jong-Yong Yun, CEO of Samsung Electronics, explained:

> Prior to Samsung's decision to manage the brand image through a central organization, many of the marketing activities were localized to the region. What we found was dilution of the brand and a misconception of the corporate identity.[16]

8. Communicate!

According to a report from Accenture, 70 percent of marketing executives have difficulty capturing the attention of customers due to noise and clutter in the marketplace.[17] Gone are the days when a good product would sell itself in the marketplace. With the ever-increasing number of products, proliferation of brands and overcommunication in the markets, creating the right perception has become equally as important as the product itself, if not more so.

Bill Bernbach, founding partner of advertising agency DDB Worldwide, was clear on brand impact: "Nobody counts the number of ads you run, they just remember the impression you make."[18] Asian companies must realize that communications is not just about creative advertisements. Instead, it is a more comprehensive exercise, encompassing the entire mix of communication channels, with the sole goal of connecting with customers at both the functional and emotional level.

Throughout the 1980s and 90s, the Hong Kong Shanghai Banking Corporation grew rapidly through organic growth and acquisitions. In 1999, the company decided to use HSBC as the brand name and international symbol. The rebranding exercise involved 19 different banking brands in 79 countries. Consumer research showed that while customers appreciate the strength of a global organization, they still value the personal and local touch.[19] Therefore, HSBC developed a unique positioning around "The world's local bank", with tailored advertising to different markets and cultures which has been successful in differentiating the brand. For example, in January 2004, HSBC kicked off the rebranding of the newly acquired Mexican bank GF Bital with a free live concert with pop singer Luis Miguel in Mexico City for 10,000 people. On another occasion, HSBC gained attention by offering free taxi rides in a cab decorated with the bank's red and white logo to any passenger with a HSBC bank card.[20]

Companies should ensure that through their integrated marketing communications, the brand is brought to life and made to resonate with its customers. All the brand messages should be consistent, clear and relevant to the target audiences and easy to comprehend.

More often than not, companies are focused on buying advertising campaigns. Instead they should buy marketing effect that will add brand value. By focusing on value creation, companies can establish long-term relationships with the right communications partners like ad agencies, PR and media agencies and so on. These partners should be made strategic partners with the brand and held responsible for their results.

HSBC's adaptation to local cultures
Courtesy HSBC Ltd. Photography by Richard Pullar

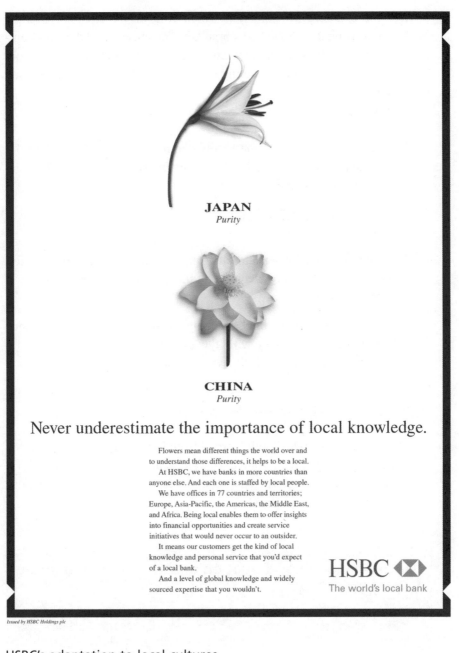

HSBC's adaptation to local cultures
Courtesy HSBC Ltd. Photography by Richard Pullar

Take for example McDonald's, which follows an effective triangle model comprising the McDonald's brand, its franchisees and the communication agencies. All three partners are closely involved in all aspects from business review, marketing planning to implementation of communication plans and tactics.

The following are guidelines to effective communications:

1. Explore multiple ways of marketing communications like public relations, interactive online advertising, event sponsorships and others instead of just mass media advertising

2. Involve the society gate keepers and opinion makers in the communication process

3. Never let the ad agencies and other parties decide the communication strategy – this should be decided by the company but in consultation with the agencies

4. As strong brands reflect the happenings in society, maintain a balance between being consistent with the message and being relevant by adopting the latest trends and ways to communicate

5. Adopt an integrated marketing communications approach by fully using all the available channels to effectively communicate.

BritishIndia, a lifestyle clothing brand from Malaysia, serves as a classic example of tapping into a compelling story about the colonial past. It conveys the brand through selective communication and other visual identities in its retail stores (see box).

BritishIndia – brand built on a distinct brand identity and personality[21]

Originally from Malaysia, BritishIndia has carved out a niche for itself in the lifestyle clothing segment of the market. With daring foresight, Pat Liew, the brand's founder and CEO and a veteran in the Malaysian retail industry, set about building a brand name across Asian countries. In the 10 years since its inception, BritishIndia has built a strong chain of 49 stores in Southeast Asia, Australia and the Middle East.

BritishIndia's signature store front
Courtesy BritishIndia

BritishIndia is a classic example of how a start-up company became a strong brand within a short span of 10 years by practicing classic brand management. The brand owes its success to its distinct brand identity and personality that have been created and communicated consistently.

BritishIndia started the branding strategy with its name. By naming the brand BritishIndia, the goal was to evoke nostalgic memories of the British Raj era, the colonial feel and to call upon the rich heritage that the British Empire left behind. This was in line with the initial strategy to differentiate itself in the marketplace. To sustain this differentiation, the company had to come up with a strong identity. It created an exciting blend between the British heritage and its timeless elegance and a distinct personality that would be relevant to the current customer base.

BritishIndia has optimally used its retail outlets to communicate its personality and positioning by creating an exciting atmosphere. It has created visual treats in terms of decor, music, lighting, and the material used. This has enabled the brand to extend this identity not only to the main brand but also to its many brand extensions. A case in point is a new line of clothing that the brand has come up with, Wh. This new brand is a different concept from BritishIndia and based on a distinct personality of fun, savvy, value-priced clothes for the whole family. This brand brings a fun environment to a normally boring segment of the market dominated by department stores.

This strategy of creating a strong brand identity and personality has been so successful that the brand has a following of loyal customers. Another clear advantage of building a brand on identity and personality has been the ease with which BritishIndia has been able to position itself as a lifestyle brand, a level above a mere clothing brand. This positioning has in turn helped the company to venture into different lines, such as gardening accessories, home furnishing and even cafés (planned for the future).

BritishIndia's unique store layout and design
Courtesy BritishIndia

In less than 10 years, BritishIndia has attracted and charmed both locals and foreigners alike. Holistic living, natural fabrics suited to the tropical climate and superior quality are some of the core values of BritishIndia that are imbued in all its merchandise.

In line with continuous innovation, the brand has introduced a unique lifestyle concept store, from clothes to home furnishings, making it a new, one-stop shopping experience for BritishIndia customers. This is one of the steps BritishIndia is taking toward satisfying tomorrow's consumers today.

Another signature of the brand is the first yoga collection, launched four years ago into the Asian market. This collection is a personal interest of CEO Pat Liew, who adopted the philosophy and practice of yoga to improve her physical and mental well-being. After many months of research and experimenting, the yoga collection was launched with extremely comfortable and easy-to-wear garments that could be used for yoga, or other activities.

Unlike the usual way of leveraging the Asian tradition as done by many Asian brands, BritishIndia has been successful in evoking nostalgic memories of a bygone era through the colonial decor of its easternized Western designs, and backing it up with a high-quality product with a sophisticated, elegant and timeless appeal. It is indeed a commendable task for an Asian company to establish such a strong brand in a category which has world-renowned names as competitors.

9. Measure the brand performance

An organization must deliver shareholder value and be accountable. The same applies for brands. How much value does it provide to the corporation and how instrumental is the brand in ensuring profitability and competitiveness? These are some of the questions which need to be answered and which corporate management will automatically seek as part of a constant commitment to run the strategy successfully.

As shown in Chapter 6, brand equity consists of various tailor-made metrics (including the brand value in financial terms), and these need to be tracked regularly. A brand scorecard can help with an overview of the brand equity and the progression of brand metrics as the strategy is implemented. Also, the company should have the right combination of qualitative and quantitative research tools to measure the brand equity.

For example, one important marketing metric is the lifetime value of a customer which indicates how much revenue a company can expect from a customer. Research has estimated that a BMW customer is worth an estimated US$143,500 and a Coca-Cola customer is worth US$1,200.[22]

Customer satisfaction is another important metric related to lifetime value which Starbucks faced as a dilemma caused by the success of the brand. Customers experienced long waiting times for service, thus reducing their overall satisfaction with the brand. An analysis found that unsatisfied customers stuck with Starbucks for just one year, made 47 visits and spent US$200, whereas highly satisfied Starbucks' customers patronized the brand for more than eight years, made 86 visits per year and spent more than US$3,000 during the period. The results provided by improving customer satisfaction were so convincing that Starbucks decided to spend US$40 million to add staff in order to reduce waiting times.[23] Market research had also shown that 75 percent of customers valued friendly, fast and convenient service. But only 54 percent of customers were being served in less than three minutes. This figure increased to 85 percent when new staff joined and the company introduced the Starbucks Card to speed up payment. Customer satisfaction also increased 20 percent.[24]

These examples illustrate the need for marketing decisions being elevated to the boardroom for two reasons. The marketing metrics convey a powerful message to the CEO about the ability of branding to drive profitability, and also because a decision of that caliber would not have happened within the limited scope of the marketing department. Marketers need to become more cross-functional and work in teams within the organization.

To elevate the discipline of branding to boardroom level, companies must prove the financial implications of branding investments and their contribution to overall company growth. Currently, there are many measures used by companies which put a value on the brand and also track the return from branding initiatives. Over the long run, companies should adopt a method of tracking brand returns based on certain company and industry-specific parameters instead of merely adopting some proprietary tool, as discussed in Chapter 6.

A recent report from consulting company Accenture noted that 68 percent of marketing executives have difficulty measuring the ROI of marketing programs and that metrics are department-focused rather than integrated around customers.[25] This has been the main problem of marketing executives – their inability to show tangible returns from marketing and branding investments. But, by adopting one of the measures detailed in Chapter 6, this problem can be effectively tackled.

Ultimately, the CEO and corporate management should be remunerated based on the brand's strength, its performance measured by metrics such as market share, product quality and customer satisfaction ultimately contributing to shareholder value.[26] Only if business leaders are held accountable for their actions will they take the reins and dedicate efforts to build strong brands. This issue relates to investor confidence and corporate governance which is only slowly being adopted in Asian boardrooms. It is particularly the trend among listed companies and companies owned by financial shareholders who increasingly scrutinize Asian boardrooms for strategies leading to better shareholder value.[27]

10. Adjust regularly – be your own change agent

The business landscape is changing almost every day in every industry. Hence the corporation needs to evaluate and possibly adjust its branding strategy on a regular basis. Obviously, a strong and resonating brand should stay relevant, differentiated and consistent over time, so the crucial function is to maintain a balance between all the parameters. The basic parts of the branding strategy, like vision, identity, personality and values, should not be changed too often, as they are the basic components. Instead, the changes are rather small and involve the thousands of daily interactions and behaviors throughout the organization, which corporations employ as part of their brand marketing efforts.

A key factor for corporate management is to make sure that complacency does not take root in the organization and affect the goal setting. Strong brands are those which are driven forward by leaders who never get tired of raising their own bars. They become their own change agents – and champions for building great brands.

Building any successful brand is dependent on the buy-in from company shareholders, who must in the end allocate the necessary resources needed for branding as well as evaluate the ROI. This raises questions about the type of non-executive directors and their knowledge of and beliefs in branding as a strategic discipline. Most executives in Asian boardrooms are elevated from technical, operational or financial career tracks, and hardly any from the brand and marketing tracks. Asian shareholders and companies can benefit significantly from having one or two non-executive directors on the board with brand knowledge, tools and international experience as a balance to the traditional technical and financial overrepresentation. The discussions held among non-executive directors about brand strategy and its resource needs versus profitability and performance will become more qualified and nuanced with details.

Branding is potentially a strong tool for realigning a corporate strategy and ensuring that the corporation, regardless of industry and size, is leveraging the untapped internal and external resources. A strong CEO and a dedicated management team are always seeking to raise their own bars and be change agents for their corporations, backed by a strong corporate branding strategy. Moreover, these teams also act as active brand mentors by instilling the same commitment toward brand building throughout the company.

A well-drafted and professionally managed branding strategy and implementation plan can become a significant part of the Asian boardroom set of tasks in the future. It can help to drive profitability and shareholder value, aligning the interests of stakeholders, the management and the company.

Notes

1   "Can Andrea Ragnetti make Philips cool?", *The Economist*, 10 June, 2004.
2   Quote from *The Strategic Role of Marketing*, Harvard Business School Working Knowledge, 31 May 2004.
3   Richard Tomlinson, "The 2004 Global 500 – L'Oreal's CEO on Managing Globally", *Fortune*, 7 December, 2004.
4   "Selling the brands inside", Colin Mitchell, January 2002, *Harvard Business Review*.
5   "The soda with buzz", Kerry A. Dolan, *Forbes*, 28 March, 2005.

6   Kerry A. Dolan, *Forbes*, 28 March, 2005, ibid.
7   Author interview with CEO Bill Padfield, Datacraft.
8   For more insights on word-of-mouth marketing, check the Word Of Mouth Marketing Association on http://www.womma.org.
9   For more on buzz, see: "The buzz on buzz", Renee Dye, *Harvard Business Review*, **78**(6), November/December 2000.
10 http://www.forbes.com/forbes/2004/0202/084_print.html.
11 "Organizing for CRM", Anupam Agarwal, David P. Harding and Jeffrey R. Schumacher, *McKinsey Quarterly*, (3), 2004.
12 http://www.hsbc.com.
13 Talent spotter, *Human Resources*, May 2003.
14 *Business Week*, 6 August, 2001.
15 Shangri-La Hotels and Resorts at http://www.shangri-la.com/aboutus/care/en/index.aspx.
16 CEO's on Managing Globally, *Fortune*.
17 "Survey on Global 1000 companies", Accenture, 2003.
18 DDB Needham booklet.
19 "Asia's Top Brands", *Media Magazine*, 27 June, 2003.
20 "Cult brands", *Business Week* online, 2 August, 2004.
21 Author interview with the company management.
22 "Connecting marketing metrics to financial consequences", Knowledge@Wharton, November 17, 2004.
23 Knowledge@Wharton, November 17, 2004, ibid.
24 "Bringing customers into the boardroom", Gail J. McGovern, David Court, John A. Quelch and Blair Crawford, *Harvard Business Review*, November 2004.
25 "Survey on global 1000 companies", Accenture, 2003.
26 "A new era in corporate governance", Robert F. Felton, *McKinsey Quarterly*, (2), 2004.
27 "Asia's governance challenge", Dominic Barton, Paul Coombes and Simon Chiu-Yin Wong, *McKinsey Quarterly*, (2), 2004.

CHAPTER 10

ASIAN BRANDS TOWARD 2020 – A NEW CONFIDENCE IN THE BOARDROOM

Imitation can be commercial suicide.

Bill Bernbach, founder, DDB Worldwide

Implications for successful brand strategies in an Asian context

The business landscape in Asia will change rapidly in the coming years, and the opportunities for Asian companies to benefit from international branding will be larger than ever before. The growing emphasis on international branding will move up the boardroom agenda and branding will become one of the most prominent drivers of value in Asia Pacific in the next two decades. Branding is being discussed almost daily in the Asian media and at numerous conferences and seminars.

As this book has illustrated time and again, branding is a boardroom agenda. The branding process cannot reach its logical conclusion unless the chairman and the CEO buy into it and back it up with the required resources. But merely having the branding knowledge will not suffice. Leaders need to have a holistic vision and an in-depth understanding of the discipline, as well as being excellent business leaders and brand marketers with a truly international edge.

Asian boardrooms have traditionally been the playing fields for technology and finance professionals, and most directors either have technology, operations or finance backgrounds. In the future, these capabilities alone will not be sufficient for sustained growth and enhanced shareholder value. With branding taking center stage, it is crucial that the boardroom represents brand capabilities and experiences to ensure that brand guardianship is practiced at the highest level. This can be accomplished in two ways.

Firstly, the education and training of boardroom directors can bring them up to a common understanding of the discipline, its opportunities and challenges. Secondly, the company can elevate people with strong marketing and branding backgrounds to the board. Ideally, companies can combine the above two ways to achieve optimum results.

Asian brands can indeed challenge the global players, but it requires a new mindset, resources and capabilities. Asian boardrooms and their brands face new opportunities, as the following points illustrate.

Challenges for aspiring Asian brands

Low cost becoming a commodity

Low cost, once the competitive advantage for a select few Asian companies, is now something that companies around the world are able to achieve. It has become the entry ticket into most markets these days. In other words, low cost has become a commodity. Given this change in market dynamics, Asian companies need to find alternative sources of sustainable competitive advantage. Adopting a more brand-oriented thinking and building strong brands would be a desirable way for Asian companies to increase growth opportunities and margins.

The opening Chinese economy

Much has been said about the tremendous opportunities that the opening Chinese economy offers, most importantly China's entry into the WTO and the Chinese government's policy to allow foreign investment in sectors hitherto controlled by the state. But it also brings with it an equally tough set of challenges. As branding is still a fairly new and evolving concept in China, there will be a number of companies that will still compete on price alone and try to undercut the value players. With this kind of market structure, in the short term, brand-oriented companies will find it an uphill task to compete against them on price, on one hand, and maintain their focus on branding, on the other.

A case in point is Coca-Cola's pricing strategy in China to gain a wider distribution. To compete against the many copycats, Coca-Cola is selling Coke at 1Rmb (US$0.12). Although the brand might achieve wider distribution in distant and less accessible areas, it will be at the cost of risking its brand equity. Colgate is another example that testifies to the above point. A survey conducted in China showed a 30–50 percent price difference between premium and mass market brands in China, so Colgate has been forced to slash its price to gain acceptance in the market while maintaining its core identity of cavity protection. In the future, many brands in various sectors will face this challenge.[1]

The Asian trading mindset

Even today, the majority of Asian companies still function with a trading mindset, where short-term sales and investments in tangible capital assets are predominant. A study carried out by McKinsey shows that tangible assets are becoming less relevant in Asia's battle for global success. It shows that the biggest value creators of Asia have a 1:1 sales to asset ratio as against a 1:4 sales to asset ratio for an average Asian company.[2] Going ahead, Asian boardrooms need to realize the importance of intangible assets and invest in them. Asian boardrooms will have to accept and support consistent investment in brand building, the results of which will take a few years to accrue.

Dominance of large, diversified conglomerates

Brand building costs a considerable amount of money. Global brands have been able to reap scale economies by combining their branding expenses across their many related business units. Asia, however, is still dominated by large conglomerates that have diversified interests in many B2C as well as B2B companies. This hinders Asian companies from reaping any scale economies in their branding investments.

A McKinsey study shows that 90 percent of Asia's value creators derive more than 80 percent of their revenues by focusing their businesses in one industry sector. Moreover, these companies focus on intangibles, like fostering human capital, exploiting network effects and creating synergies based on brands and reputation, rather than investing in physical assets.[3] Additionally, interests in diversified areas pose a great challenge, as creating and managing a consistent brand personality is much more difficult.

The Reliance group of India is a typical example of such a diversified conglomerate, with businesses in petrochemicals, financial advisory, telecommunications, and oil explorations. Although the Reliance brand is doing very well in the Indian market, it needs to focus on a more directed corporate branding approach. To brand different businesses across a wide array of sectors will prove to be a resource drainer in the longer run. Small and medium-sized firms that aspire to build strong brands but have resource constraints, will find it especially difficult to carry out successful branding if their businesses are highly diversified.

Asia's excess capacity

China and India together are attracting the entire world with their rapidly expanding economies with large growth potentials, and their large populations. With an ever-increasing assault by global brands as well as home-grown companies, the market is facing an overcapacity of products. For example, in China alone, there is an estimated 30 percent overcapacity in many industry sectors.[4] A direct implication of this would be immense pressure on companies to turn over their stock regularly. This would in turn lead to a dumping of these products in the market, which could lead to tough price wars and price dumpings. In such a situation, it would be difficult for companies to sustain the branding investments and cling on to the value proposition.

Intellectual property and trademark protection

Apart from countries like Singapore, Hong Kong, South Korea and Japan, countries in Asia are not known for their strong IP laws. With innovation, technological advancements and branding becoming the center of business activity, the existence and implementation of strong IP laws becomes crucial.

With even local Chinese home-grown brands like Li Ning suffer the counterfeit burn (they have three full-time employees to track counterfeiters), there is additional pressure on governments in Asian countries to enforce stringent IP laws and implement effective enforcement measures to ensure the smooth transition of Asia's potential succession to a higher position in the value chain.

Lenovo Group, China's biggest computer manufacturer, achieved much publicity and recognition when it bought IBM's PC division in 2004. Part of the deal was the right to use the IBM Think brand for another five years. Prior to this, and like many of its Asian peers, Lenovo had learned the hard way that protection of trademarks is an important step to becoming successful when expanding internationally. Legend, as the company was called then, had already been trademarked by others in several countries.[5] That led the company to overhaul its marketing, change the brand name and reduce its 40 sub-brands. In April 2004, the company renamed itself Lenovo Group. The new name had the advantage of starting with "L" and also being connected to the Chinese name "Lianxiang". It also passed tests in different languages, had availability of website addresses and was easy to pronounce and spell.[6] But most of all, Lenovo passed trademark procedures in most countries.

The global brand landscape will change significantly

Emergence of a large Asian value segment

Despite Asia's emergence into the value economy, a considerable percentage of Asia's population still lives in poverty, with little education and inferior infrastructure and support systems. Prahalad and Lieberthal refer to this as the bottom of the pyramid.[7] This segment still lacks the purchasing power to go for global premium brands and affordability is the most important decision criteria. For example, Hindustan Lever, Unilever's Indian subsidiary, introduced shampoo sachets at low prices that addressed the needs of this segment and proved quite successful. In a nutshell, this huge value segment represents an enormous untapped potential. Global brands need to adapt their offerings and plan appropriate brand extensions to suit this huge market segment.

Emergence of complex brand systems

With more and more global brands entering the Asian market and Asian brands expanding internationally, there will be a lot of alliances and joint ventures between Asian and global brands. This presents the difficulty of managing a complex portfolio of brands. The dilemma for global brands will be to strike a balance between standardized offerings and customizing locally. The dilemma for Asian brands will be to maintain their own brand despite tying up with a bigger global partner.

Brands need to build resonating stories (myths)

With the tremendous proliferation of brands in the global market, brands need to find innovative and forceful ways of conveying their value proposition. They need to excite customers by creating lasting associations and stories that resonate with them. As Douglas Holt says in his book *How Brands Become Icons*, it will be crucial for companies to weave their brands into the social fabric and make them a part of the community to ensure enduring success.[8] Tapping into popular culture and society are two main drivers of successful branding.

Fiji Water is a brand that has grown based on a powerful story (myth) related to the mystique of an island situated far away from its target market. By weaving the story into customers' daily lives, it has been able to maintain excitement around the brand (see box).

Fiji Water: The exotic water brand

Fiji Water is one of the newer examples which testify that competent branding can elevate even the simplest commodity to celebrity status. In a category dominated by France's Evian, Coca Cola's Dasani and Pepsi Co's Aquafina, Fiji Water has come to occupy third place within a short span of eight years and has grown its sales by more than 61 percent in 2004 as against a 23 percent loss of its French rival Evian. By following non-traditional methods of marketing, a distinct positioning, and a high-end pricing of US$5.90 as against Dasani's US$2.99 and Aquafina's US$2.49, Fiji Water has been able to establish strong brand equity among the top-tier market segments including celebrities, Hollywood stars and the best restaurants of New York and California.[9]

Fiji's background

Fiji Water, the company that owns the Fiji Water brand, was founded in 1988 in Basalt, Colorado by David Gilmour, a businessman with interests in hotels, real estate and gold mining. The Fiji Water brand came into life in the early 1990s when Gilmour secured a 99-year deal with the Fijian government to tap the aquifer discovered by government contracted geologists and market the water under the Fiji Water brand name.[10] Fiji Water has made extensive use of product placements in leading Hollywood movies, high-profile events and exclusive restaurants to include the brand in the elite community.

Branding philosophy

As many in the bottled water category have commented, all water tastes the same. This means branding in this category is not product-focused, but story-focused. The company which tells a better story and backs it up with credible facts, thereby creating an exciting myth, wins the day. Fiji Water seems to have understood this underlying truth extremely well. The Fiji Water brand is built on three pillars: creating an exciting myth, precision marketing (including personal relationships and product placements) and a controlled distribution strategy.

As the physical attributes of the product cannot be differentiated in themselves, Fiji Water has resorted to creating a powerful story around the product. Fiji is a 332-island nation in the South Pacific, far from the US market and customers. This physical inaccessibility has enabled Fiji Water to create the story of this water being extracted from a virgin ecosystem far from acid rain, herbicides, pesticides and other pollutants, having for years been filtered naturally through layers of silica, basalt and sandstone, as communicated through its packaging. This story provided customers with something unique to sit up and take notice of. The story was backed by the credible fact that Fiji is an unexploited land full of tropical forest surrounded by coral reefs, unpolluted by the modern world's necessary evils and protected by nature as it were. This created a strong myth about the brand among customers, which in turn built the brand.

The myth creation was backed by precision brand marketing. Fiji Water did not resort to the usual mass media advertising for its product launch. It formulated a two-pronged strategy:

1 Building personal relationships with the chefs of leading restaurants, resorts and spas to promote the buy-in of the brand

2 Placing the product in leading Hollywood movies and other high-profile events to attract attention and create buzz.

Gilmour used his contacts in the hotel industry to pitch his product to the top-end hotels, resorts and restaurants. By coming out with an award-winning slippery silver bottle design, Fiji water has been able to replace Evian in many of the top-end restaurants.[11]

Fiji Water has resorted to product placement as a major channel of promotion and brand building. By hiring Creative Entertainment Services, a Hollywood marketing consulting firm, Fiji has been able to fit Fiji Water bottles into the scripts of many major Hollywood movies. These exposures to the brand, when combined with the exciting mythical story, have made the brand noticeable. Fiji Water has also sponsored many local events such as golf tournaments, sailing regattas, and musical events.[12]

Another important aspect of Fiji Water's branding philosophy has been its controlled distribution strategy. In line with its positioning as a high-end product, Fiji Water has ensured that it is available at the best hotels, resorts and spas used by the leading stars, and managed to get chefs' recommendations. As is generally known, the bottled water category is notorious for its difficulty in making money. "What we offer distributors as well as retailers is the opportunity to make profits in a category that they have become used to not making any money in. Bottled water can be very difficult to make money in if you're selling a commodity product" says Edward Slade, President and COO of Fiji Water.

With its unique positioning and pricing strategies, Fiji Water has been able to make money and help its distributors to make money. Although Fiji Water's bottles were off the shelves due to its initial inability to keep up with the huge demand, this has added to its feel of exclusivity. This controlled distribution has helped Fiji Water to be at the right places at the right time, thereby helping in brand building.[13]

Future challenges

In the bottled water category, Evian pioneered the idea of elevating a commodity to a brand status. Looking back, Evian did the things that Fiji Water is doing now. Fiji Water has until now been quite successful with its marketing, story telling and distribution strategies.

The biggest challenge for Fiji Water in the future will be to sustain this level of interest in its brand. The problem of basing the brand heavily on such a myth is that it does not create any barriers for any new entrants to come up with another, equally exciting, myth. Given the low level of involvement of customers in selecting water, customers would be willing to try out newer and more exciting brands as and when they come up. In this regard, Fiji Water should focus on formulating a strong customer loyalty and retention drive in the light of impending competition.

Although Fiji Water has managed to be included in a Forbes list of things "worth every penny", it will require more than a strong story to carry it through in the future.[14]

Branding in the Asian boardroom

Have a CMO on the corporate board

Brand management is a dynamic and continuous process. It requires consistent investment and support to be a successful process. Having a chief marketing officer on the board, squarely in charge of marketing and branding at the board level, would ensure continuous management support to keep the brand management process going. As has been illustrated by

Singapore Airlines, branding is beyond the CEO. Singapore Airlines has stuck to its brand strategy despite having a couple of CEOs during its life span. Moreover, it would help corporate management to understand the significance of branding, and would also help in tracking the financial implications of brand management.

Match corporate strategy to branding strategy

Asian companies have traditionally handled branding as a tactical function along with other functions. In the future, this needs to change and companies need to realize the strategic significance of branding. In line with this, branding should be aligned to the overall corporate strategy and formulated and managed at the board level. This would give CEOs a powerful instrument to enhance shareholder value.

Strategic shift from sales orientation to brand orientation

The biggest challenge for Asian boardrooms would be the shift in mindset from sales orientation to brand orientation; a change from short- to long-term value creation. Corporate management needs to understand that branding is a long-term activity, the results of which might not be immediate. The board, led by the CEO, should create an atmosphere where emphasis is more on long-term and sustaining competitive advantage. Despite its intangibility, corporate management should be oriented to understand the implications of building a strong brand and its effect on the business.

Contribution to brand growth a part of performance appraisal

Asian companies can build strong brands only when they are well implemented internally. A major onus is on management to create a culture inside the company that proves conducive for everyone to live the brand. Companies should enforce and motivate everyone to contribute to the brand's growth. This should become one of the most important measures for performance appraisal. This needs a commitment from corporate management. By installing such measures, companies would be able to reap the full benefits of brand management, as brand strategy objectives are aligned with staff interests.

Build a strong talent base

In the coming decade, Asia will see a war of talent, where all the major companies will strive to pick up the best talent in the market, as this directly translates into better business success. In the future, the best talent in Asia will become increasingly choosy about the fit between their expectations, personality and the corporate culture. One of the better ways for Asian companies to attract and retain the talent is with an impeccable corporate reputation, an open corporate environment and strong brand names with which people would be proud to be associated.

Cost advantage is meant for investment – not short-term profit making

Invest in channel management

In two of the largest Asian markets, India and China, the key to business success is still good distribution. Given the huge size of these two countries, it becomes all the more important for global brands to reach every nook and cranny of the market. As personal relationships and trust are still the chief factors driving the channel partners, any brand planning to have operations in Asia needs to spend a lot of resources in cementing these relationships. Moreover, these widespread channels act as multiple touch points for the brand. Companies must ensure that all these touch points are managed properly in order to deliver consistently on all brand promises.

Reverse the Asian innovation deficit

Recently, Asia has thrived primarily by adapting Western technologies to local markets. But in the future, this needs to change if Asia wants to accelerate away from the low cost OEM trap and thus innovation becomes the key factor to drive better margins. Asian companies need to invest substantially more in R&D and come up with new and proprietary technologies to survive among the impending competition. Huawei Technologies, the telecom equipment company from China, spends more than 10 percent of its revenues on R&D, while Samsung spends more than 8 percent of its revenue on R&D. They serve as examples of Asian companies which focus strongly on innovation.[15]

Invest in strategic acquisitions

This is one of the three strategies mentioned in Chapter 6 for Asian companies to acquire brands to leapfrog into other markets. Asian companies should consider investing their profits in identifying compatible brands and acquiring them, should the need arise to enter different markets, different product categories or different business lines. The future is not about acquiring manufacturing plants and other tangible assets.

Can the West maintain its branding edge?

Western brands in Asia need to customize their offerings

Brands are about personality, about relevance, and about resonating with customers. Therefore, Western brands entering Asia should be ready to adopt a two-pronged strategy. On one hand, they should be responsive to the unique needs and preferences of customers in the different Asian markets. On the other, they should retain certain standardized features like attractive packaging, the overall identity and so on.

Western brands need to be more culturally sensitive

Despite the globalized world, each region in Asia has its own culture, heritage, beliefs and value systems. Any global brand that aspires to be successful in Asia needs to be sensitive to these subtleties, both internally with respect to its employees and also externally with respect to the markets and customers. This has been the entry ticket for many Western brands in China and India. McDonald's is a classic example of how a global brand has customized its offering and also built a personality that reflects the local values and belief systems, as discussed in Chapter 3.

Keep the heritage or adjust?

When Giorgio Armani opened its retail store in Beijing in 2001, the company installed a large red-lacquer door in line with traditional Chinese design and architecture. But the Chinese did not like it and it was replaced. In contrast, Vivienne Tam, a Hong Kong-born designer based in New York, kept the same items she used outside China featuring Asian design elements and kept labeling her clothing as "Made in China" in a new Shanghai retail store, despite opposition from the local staff. Vivienne Tam said she looks forward to the day "when Chinese people have enough self-confidence to support their own luxury brands and stop buying stuff just because it comes from somewhere else".[16] There are around 10–13 million Chinese luxury goods customers – mostly entrepreneurs and young professionals working for multinational firms – so luxury brands are keen to get their brand strategies right.[17]

Western brands need to collaborate with Asian brands to gain a foothold

In this fast-paced world, time is money. Moreover, the many Asian countries give rise to a complex set of cultural sensitivities. With this combination, it would be much easier for global brands to gain a firm foothold in hitherto uncharted territories by collaborating with local players who better understand the local market, customers and competitors. In China, for example, the Shanghai Volkswagen Automotive Company was formed as a result of collaboration between Shanghai Automotive Industry Corp. and Volkswagen. In India, the collaboration between Japan's Kawasaki and India's Bajaj to form the highly successful Kawasaki Bajaj is another typical example.

Western brands need to become part of the Asian community

As discussed earlier, companies need to ensure that they weave their brands into the social fabric and become part of the community. For Western brands this means that they have to respond to local tastes, spend on building local relationships, and react to social needs. More importantly, Western brands need to be proactive toward corporate social responsibility (CSR) which will grow significantly in importance throughout Asia in the coming years.

For Western brands that seek to establish a strong foothold in Asian markets, CSR will act as a powerful channel as it will showcase the brand's concern toward the society that the brand operates in.

Conclusion

All the factors discussed in this chapter provide a blueprint of the Asian landscape by 2020. They also serve as useful guidelines for both Asian and Western companies planning to grow in Asia. This chapter has explored in detail the importance of branding in Asia in the future and also the challenges that Asia faces in adopting a long-term branding perspective in the corporate world to drive shareholder value. Moreover, Asian companies must understand that overcoming the barriers to branding with all its implications is indeed possible.

The following case study on Banyan Tree Hotels and Resorts is a testament to this fact. It describes Banyan Tree's brand journey and how Banyan Tree has evolved into a widely recognized and well-managed international brand with a large potential. This case can inspire other Asian companies to tread the branding path with renewed rigor.

Banyan Tree – branded paradise

From an early start in 1992, Banyan Tree Hotels and Resorts has grown into one of Asia's most successful hospitality brands with numerous international awards and accolades from publications like the prestigious Condé Nast *Traveller* and others. Banyan Tree is one of the youngest chains of upmarket and privately owned luxury boutique hotels and resorts. By successfully blending its environmental concern with the unique Asian traditions and heritage and the concept of individual luxury villas offering an intimate experience, Banyan Tree has emerged as one of the leaders in the hospitality industry.

The brand portfolio managed by Banyan Tree
Courtesy Banyan Tree Hotels and Resorts

Branding has been part of the strategy from the start, and was born out of a necessity to differentiate a traditional overseas Chinese family business. Banyan Tree wanted to escape being overrun by cheaper competitors from Indonesia and China, on the one hand, and to take the focus away from tough pricing, on the other.[18] These have been the typical challenges for many Asian businesses trying to compete in the new environment and building competitive advantages. It proved to be a successful way of breaking away from an Asian commodity business and changed the focus onto higher value-added revenues. The brand is led by a centralized team headed by corporate management and its promise, illustrated in the tagline "Sanctuary for the senses", is delivered throughout the organization as part of a dedicated business strategy centered around branding.

The Banyan Tree company manages 15 hotel resorts, 35 spas and two golf courses in 12 countries, with the headquarters based in Singapore. The company is a good example of the importance of corporate management's involvement in investing, building and driving the brand and all the related branding activities.

Background

The majority of Banyan Tree is owned by Singapore-based Ho Kwon Ping, who named the brand after a place in Hong Kong where he and his wife spent idyllic days when he was a reporter and editor for an Asian magazine. He returned to Singapore after his father fell ill. As the eldest son, he had to take on the responsibility of the family business and run it. After a while, Ho Kwon Ping was looking for a new idea to take his father's family-run business, the Wah Chang Group, ahead and away from the traditional revenue streams into different areas, spanning property to manufacturing.

In 1994, the couple opened the first Banyan Tree resort in Phuket, Thailand, with some investors and Ho Kwon Ping's brother as the architect. There it began the trademark pool villa concept, which was an innovation at that time and became one of the signatures of the brand.[19] Today, the private pool villa concept has proliferated to other resort groups and is used as a benchmark in the hospitality industry.

Brand building

Given the inevitable turmoil in the volatile hospitality industry, Ho Kwon Ping was convinced from the beginning that a strong focus on branding would give Banyan Tree a sustainable competitive advantage. This was proved right as Banyan Tree withstood the Asian financial crisis of 1997/98, the events of September 11 and the Iraq War. During the SARS outbreak in Asia in 2003, the company still emerged profitable by achieving average occupancy rates of 65–67 percent.[20]

The company has based its brand on the two main beliefs of the organization. Banyan Tree resorts would become a "romantic escape for couples" and Banyan Tree would be an environmentally sensitive and socially responsible organization. These underlying themes have driven all the branding activities of Banyan Tree.

Branding started from the locations of the Banyan Tree resorts and has been consistent through the designs, the facilities offered, and the ambience created in each of the resorts. In line with the "romantic escape for couples" theme, Banyan Tree has placed a strong emphasis on the locations as a key element of the brand identity. The company has chosen exotic locations with exclusive access to sun-bathed beaches, an exciting environment and a good transportation infrastructure to connect the resorts to the main destination highlights.

The ocean view from one of Banyan Tree's villas in the Maldives
Courtesy Banyan Tree Hotels and Resorts

The resorts offer a unique experience for visitors by providing them with a luxury holiday complete with self-indulgent and pampering experiences like the Banyan Tree spas which offer traditional treatments and fresh ingredients. The company operates a training academy in Phuket where all spa therapists must go through the compulsory 400 hours of training, which is above the industry standard.

Banyan Tree believes in the value of the local heritage of a destination, so guests can find a Banyan Tree gallery which exhibits and sells indigenous artifacts and handicrafts in every resort.[21] This enables guests to extend the brand experience a little longer by taking home some products relating to the place where they have had memorable experiences. The company constantly ensures that everything is in sync with the brand theme of romance, intimacy and rejuvenation.

Concern for the nature and environment surrounding the resorts has been a trademark of Banyan Tree. Many environmentalists appreciate its efforts to nurture and protect the surroundings of its resorts. True to its belief that environmentally sustainable and socially responsible tourism is compatible with making profits, Banyan Tree has established the Green Imperative Fund to extend financial assistance to environmental conservation and community projects. It has also taken a conscious decision to minimize damage to the natural environment when building new resorts. The company built villas around trees and boulders rather than cutting or excavating them. The company also engages in numerous projects such as the sea turtle protection program and has built health clinics, schools and a temple for the communities they are located in.

These actions have endeared Banyan Tree to the public and the media which often features the brand and its resorts. It has also taken a keen interest in providing schooling to children in Phuket and sources most of the materials required for its artifacts in the Banyan Tree gallery from the Asian cottage industries.

When the Asian tsunami struck in December 2004, none of the properties were badly damaged during the disaster. As part of its continual efforts to provide assistance to the local community, Banyan Tree decided to focus on medium- and long-term relief efforts aimed at rebuilding shattered lives. To address these concerns, the company set up the Tsunami Recovery Fund working with the local authorities to determine the community needs. The staff contributed 5 percent of their salaries to the recovery fund run by the company. Additionally, guests at the resorts could donate US$2 per room per night, which Banyan Tree matched.[22] With these funds, the company purchased boats for fishermen and building materials for use in the construction of houses and schools.

Banyan Tree has been successful in creating a strong personality around these core values. Delivering all that it promises and leading by example in social causes, Banyan Tree has built a brand with minimal advertising and other traditional brand building methods.

The result is that the brand is able to command between US$400 and US$700 a night on average. The Banyan Tree in the Seychelles offers the presidential suite at US$3,600 a night – the resort is built on a plot of land previously owned by the actor Peter Sellers and former Beatles' guitarist George Harrison.[23]

Brand communication

Banyan Tree initially used advertising to build awareness in the market, but the advertising budget was soon cut to save costs. In fact, the overall marketing budget of Banyan Tree has been 7 percent of the total revenue, with 60 percent allocated for trade and 40 percent allocated for consumer promotions.[24] From then on, the entire brand communication strategy has been based on third-party endorsements, word of mouth and public relations.

With its very first resort in Phuket, Banyan Tree won the coveted Ecotourism award for the total environmental regeneration of Bang Tao Bay. This made the entire hospitality industry take notice of the new entrant, as the UN had previously declared the site impossible to rehabilitate.

This was followed by a string of awards for the best beach resort, world's best spa resort, and many others, from such reputed magazines and organizations as Condé Nast Travellers UK, TTG awards, World Travel awards and many others.[25] This generates a lot of awareness and curiosity in the industry. Banyan Tree also uses public relations as an important brand building strategy, and the company invites editors and writers of prestigious travel and leisure magazines to visit the resorts. Banyan Tree makes sure that high-quality photo shoots are ready for use by the media, which ensures that the resorts are portrayed in line with the brand promise.

Editorial coverage combined with word-of-mouth recommendations from customers and co-branding activities with strategic partners have served as the major channels for brand communications. The media coverage has helped to build the brand's international awareness and credibility.

Expanding the brand portfolio

The strong belief in branding by Banyan Tree's corporate management has started to pay off, and the Banyan Tree brand equity has enabled new revenue streams for the organization. It has enabled Banyan Tree to come out with a brand extension in the form of Angsana Resorts (launched in 2000), targeted toward young families and at different price points – typically 20–30 percent lower than Banyan Tree resorts themselves. Today, Angsana operates resorts in Indonesia, Australia, India and the Maldives, with more to come. It also operates stand-alone Angsana Spas in almost 20 locations including cities. With the backing of the Banyan Tree brand and its strong recognition in the leisure industry, Angsana has been well received in the markets it has entered so far, with occupancy rates around 65 percent.

The latest line extension has been Colours of Angsana, a sister chain of resorts under the Angsana brand, which opened in 2003. The hotels are launched in more remote areas of the world, including UNESCO's World Heritage sites. The hotels are located in off-the-beaten track destinations like Laos, Sri Lanka and China.

Leveraging its strong brand equity, Banyan Tree spun off the Banyan Tree Spas, the Angsana Spas and the Banyan Tree Galleries as separate revenue generation units (the Spa and Gallery were started simultaneously with the resort in Phuket in 1994). The brand extension for Spa and Gallery grew further and the company now manages 14 Banyan Tree Spas in 14 Oberoi Hotels under the name of "Oberoi Spa by Banyan Tree". The brand extension of Banyan Tree Gallery called "The Museum Shop by Banyan Tree" is aimed at preserving Asian culture and heritage, and operates four shops in Singapore within the museums.

Serene ocean view at Banyan Tree's Seychelles resort
Courtesy Banyan Tree Hotels and Resorts

These measures not only allow Banyan Tree to increase its awareness in new markets and gain international momentum, but also create a strong platform for a portfolio of sub-brands that can be a source of long-term revenue generation.

The future strategy of the Banyan Tree company is described as "to string a necklace of resorts around the world. It's not about being everywhere, but having a presence in chosen places. It is not about quantity but building quality jewels that form a chain", according to Executive Chairman Ho Kwon Ping.[26] The company plans to expand the brand to Europe and North America and create a truly global brand. New destinations include Morocco and Greece, and the company is planning to spend between US$250 million and US$300 million to develop projects in Mexico opening in 2006/2007. Banyan Tree also has plans for China, which is expected to be a huge growth market due to booming domestic travel patterns and rising new affluent consumer groups seeking status and luxury experiences as well as the enormous inbound tourism market.

The company has full ownership of its resorts in Asia, but part of the strategy outside Asia is to establish partnerships and joint ventures with local partners. Banyan Tree will typically hold a smaller equity stake, do all in-house design and decoration, and manage the property in the following years. This ensures good alignment between brand promise and brand delivery, and is an effective way of staying in control of the brand despite the involvement of foreign partners. This is not always an easy task, as the management's decision-making power runs the risk of being diluted, thereby affecting crucial decisions related to the brand.

The international strategy is also part of having more diverse revenue streams from separate regions and markets of the world. The leisure industry is volatile and Banyan Tree is hedging against unexpected events and cyclical economies by having hotel resorts in different locations.

Future challenges

Distinctively Asian versus developing a global image
With plans of expanding beyond Asia, Banyan Tree faces the typical dilemma of any Asian brand to find a balance between being distinctively Asian and developing a more globally oriented image. Although the entire brand is based on the unique Asian touch and cultural heritage, Banyan Tree has to evaluate its relevance and sustainability carefully as it enters new territories.

It can localize its offerings to better suit the local tastes and environments, but Banyan Tree should be sensible about the extent of localization. If Banyan Tree were to keep localizing its offerings, especially in Western markets, it might ultimately affect its core brand identity and drain it of its main differentiating factor – the unique Asian heritage.

Consequences of brand extensions
The company's brand portfolio has increased, and comprises different business lines, target groups and price segments. This is a challenge which goes to the very foundation of the company – management of the brand and allocation of resources. Although Angsana has a lower price point and is targeted primarily toward family guests, these resorts still have much of the typical Banyan Tree feel. The challenge is to balance two distinct brands and differentiate them

without diluting the leading brand Banyan Tree in particular. With the ongoing company expansion, there will be a resource allocation tradeoff sometime in the future.

The centralized marketing and branding team is overseeing resorts in different parts of the world, so successful management of the brand portfolio will be extremely challenging and requires stringent procedures and decisions for each of the brands in order to stay in touch with market dynamics.

Keep innovating and avoid copycats
The market is crowded with many entrants running similar branded resorts in the upper end. Particularly in Asia Pacific, where Banyan Tree has its stronghold and traditional base, new entrants are facing only small barriers of entry other than huge capital requirements and availability of good locations – something Asia is not short of. A new entrant can always try to copy the "romance-intimacy-rejuvenation" theme and replicate the serene locations with beautiful villas, providing them at lower prices to gain foothold in the market.

Therefore, Banyan Tree needs to keep innovating and exceeding customer expectations which require substantial resources, management focus, and control of the brand portfolio to stay relevant and competitive.

Factors contributing to Banyan Tree's brand success

- A well-managed balance between brand promise and brand delivery

- A visionary, guiding and supporting corporate management team involved directly in overall brand decisions

- Centralized brand management function at senior level

- Constant innovation – right from coining the original concept of individual villas, the superior feel and quality of service to the unique, traditional spa treatments

- Making use of unconventional methods of brand communications

- Being a socially responsible and environmentally sensitive organization

- By combining the Asian culture and heritage with world-class service and luxury, Banyan Tree has been able to build a brand that has appealed to people across countries in Asia and beyond, and successfully capitalized on the pan-Asian sentiment.

Notes

1 "Research: Marketing to China", 7 February 2005, *Brand Strategy*.
2 "Winning Asian strategies", Tobias C. Hoschka and John Livingston, *McKinsey Quarterly* 2002 (1).
3 Tobias C. Hoschka and John Livingston, *McKinsey Quarterly* 2002 (1), ibid.
4 "China's power brands", Dexter Roberts, Frederick Balfour, Bruce Einhorn and Michael Arndt, 8 November 2004, *Business Week*.
5 "Taking it Haier", Kerry A. Dolan, *Forbes Global*, 13 May, 2002.
6 "How Legend became Lenovo", Evan Ramstad, *Far Eastern Economic Review*, 8 April 2004.
7 "End of corporate imperialism", C. K. Prahalad and Kenneth Lieberthal, *Harvard Business Review*, August 2003.
8 *How Brands Become Icons*, Douglas B. Holt, Harvard Business School Press, 2004.
9 "Bottled water brand uses celebrity exposure to ring up sales", Candice Choi, *Daily News*, Los Angeles, Knight Ridder/Tribune Business News, 1 September 2004.
10 "Fiji brand gains on Evian as bottled water hip to sip – closely held U.S. firm proves the world's simplest drink still can be touted as trendy", Betsy McKay and Cynthia H. Cho, *Asian Wall Street Journal*, 17 August 2004.
11 "Fiji the new hotbed of cool water", Susan Reimer, *Baltimore Sun*, 4 November 2004.
12 Betsy McKay and Cynthia H. Cho, *Asian Wall Street Journal*, 17 August 2004, op. cit.
13 "Island water flows on luxury and prestige (Fiji natural artesian water)", 1 September 2000, *Beverage Industry*, 70, ISSN: 0148-6187, 91(9).
14 Susan Reimer, *Baltimore Sun*, 4 November 2004, op. cit.
15 Samsung Electronics – As good as it gets? *The Economist*, 15 January 2005.
16 "Luxury brands are rushing into China's red-hot market", Clay Chandler, *Fortune*, 26 July, 2004.
17 "Business: luxury's new empire; conspicuous consumption in China", *The Economist*, Volume 371, 19 June, 2004.
18 "From a little Banyan grows a big brand", *Far Eastern Economic Review*, November 2003.
19 *Far Eastern Economic Review*, November 2003, ibid.
20 "Banyan Tree branching out", Ming Wu, www.brandchannel.com, November 2003.
21 "Paradise promised", *Straits Times*, November 20, 2003.
22 *Straits Times*, "Public listing no longer Banyan Tree's top priority", 10 January, 2005.
23 *SilverKris*, Singapore Airlines' in-flight magazine.
24 *Banyan Tree Resorts and Hotels: Building an International Brand from an Asian Base*, INSEAD, Singapore, 2003.
25 http://www.banyantree.com/accolades/index.htm.
26 "Tree's company", *SilverKris*, Singapore Airlines' in-flight magazine, January 2005.

CHAPTER 11

CONCLUSION

Without action, the world would still be an idea.

Georges Doriot, founder, INSEAD

It is quite clear that this is going to be Asia's century. The opening of China, the rise of India and the resurgence of the Asian tigers make Asia the most vibrant business playground in the world. There is a slow but steady shift in the Asian business mindset. Gone are the days when low cost and manufacturing prowess alone served as competitive advantages for Asian companies. Asian corporations are realizing the importance of moving up the value chain. One of the main ways to achieve this is to create strong brands. This will not only serve as the main competitive advantage for these companies, but also enhance shareholder value in the medium and long term. As has been argued throughout the book, this is easier said than done, given the dominant Asian business mindset of trading and sales.

A substantial part of shareholder value in successful companies derives from their ability to successfully manage and leverage their most important intangible assets: their brands' equity. In turn, Asian companies will have to realize that branding must be led by the boardroom and corporate management. It is too important to be left to the marketing function alone. Brand management is a dynamic and continuous process which requires attention and involvement from senior leadership. This requires the marketing function to be presented at boardroom and corporate management level.

Contrary to common perceptions in Asia, branding is much more than advertising and marketing communications alone. Nice company logos or modern design identities are not key ingredients for branding – only a tactical face to it. Instead, successful branding is strategic, involves all functions and aspects of a company and must be deeply embedded throughout the entire organization and aligned around multiple touch points. This ensures a successful balance between brand promise and brand delivery. In the future, this requires the Asian marketing function to become more cross-functional, to manage and measure their results through several marketing metrics, and work in teams to play an important part of brand building.

As more and more global and local companies enter the market in all possible categories, there will be intense competition and overcapacity in the marketplace. This will exert immense pressure on companies to resort to price wars to capture the market on a short-term basis. But Asian board-rooms need to take a strategic look and find a balance between short- and long-term financial performance. Corporations need to look beyond quar-terly results, monthly sales figures and factory turnovers. This will be highly valued by shareholders and financial markets, as we have shown. Financial resources spent on brand management must be treated as an investment rather than an expense. Boardrooms need to invest in sustain-able intangible assets through branding strategies to survive, sustain and grow in the market.

As more Asian countries open their doors to global companies and attract foreign investment, building strong brands becomes not only an important strategy but also a matter of survival for many Asian companies. In the changing market dynamics, being a domestic market leader does not guar-antee long-term success, as global players entering domestic markets can easily challenge local players with their business might. A McKinsey study shows that the top ten Asian value creators derive more than 50 percent of their revenues on average from outside their home markets. A case in point is India's software giant Wipro Technologies, which derives more than 80 percent of its revenues from non-Indian customers.[1]

Many global brands have established strong relations with local partners, invested heavily to build robust distribution networks, worked in tandem with the local authorities to establish a good working rapport and recruited local people to gain the crucial local "Asian" knowledge. As this levels the ground for local and global brands in terms of local market and customer knowledge, Asian companies will increasingly come under pressure to defend their traditional comparative advantage. This again stresses the need for local Asian companies to invest in building resonating brands with compelling stories if they are to compete with global brands and survive in the marketplace.

Asian brands like Singapore Airlines, Banyan Tree Hotels and Resorts, HSBC, Samsung and Shiseido have demonstrated that it is possible for Asian companies to build brands on a par with those of Western countries. They have also proved the fact that a strong brand will enable companies to survive difficult times and maintain their financial robustness. Despite the Asian financial crisis, the 9/11 disaster and SARS (severe acute respiratory syndrome) threat, Singapore Airlines, for example, has been as financially strong as ever. It has been one of the few airlines in the world to be operating profitably and steadily through all the above crises. The main reason for this has been the strong contribution of the brand and the excellent brand management and guardianship its boardroom and corporate management has followed.

This book has provided in-depth discussions and recommendations for companies to build strong brands and be ready for the next round of competition. It has highlighted the importance of building successful brands as an effective way to capture higher financial value and emphasized the importance of corporate management's involvement and commitment in making this happen. A branding drive in Asia is finally emerging and will change the global landscape in the next few decades, if taken seriously by boardrooms and managed properly throughout the entire organization.

As the management professor Peter Drucker once said: "Whenever you see a successful business, someone once made a courageous decision." Asian cultures have always valued the long-term aspects in almost any aspect of life. Let this unique strength influence Asian branding efforts in the years to come. Now it is up to Asian boardrooms to take courageous decisions. Good luck in the future!

Note

1   "Winning Asian strategies", Tobias C. Hoschka and John Livingston, *McKinsey Quarterly* 2002 (1).

FUTURE CHAPTERS

Although the final chapter of this book is entitled Conclusion, it is in fact the beginning of branding in Asia. Throughout its 11 chapters, *Asian Brand Strategy* has guided you through the Asian branding journey. Asia is a fast evolving landscape of markets, each one with different growth dynamics, business practices and belief systems and whilst this book provides a snapshot of some, there is still more to cover, and continual updating is required.

As industry leaders, business managers, advertising specialists, brand consultants, students of marketing and branding and readers interested in this area, you doubtless have many ideas on the various aspects of branding on which you would like further insight and additional, ongoing research. This is the perfect platform for you to share those ideas with the author of *Asian Brand Strategy*. Your ideas and interests will help to channel research on topics that are relevant to you and your businesses. Based on your ideas and relevant topics, additional free electronic chapters in PDF format will be written and distributed after the publication of *Asian Brand Strategy*.

To be part of this initiative and to get the free chapters as they are released, sign up with your email address or download them from:

www.asianbrandstrategy.com

Be among the first to receive these additional chapters when they are launched and keep yourself updated on *Asian Brand Strategy* as the landscape changes.

INTERBRAND BRAND VALUATION

1. Market segmentation

Brand influences customer choice. The influence of a brand differs by market. The first step in the brand valuation process is to divide the market/s in which the brand is sold into mutually exclusive and materially relevant segments. Such segmentations enable us to determine the variances in the brand's economic value across specific customer profiles.

This knowledge has broad strategic application in building and measuring customer relationships.

2. Financial analysis

Because we define brand value as the net present value of the expected future earnings of the brand, accurate forecasting of these earnings is crucial. The brand creates customer demand that translates into revenue for the underlying business.

This is assessed in terms of purchase price, volume and frequency. To forecast the future sales and revenues generated, we perform a detailed review of the brand's equities, industry and customer trends, as well as historic financial performance across each segment. Once we have established Branded Revenues, we deduct all associated operating costs to derive earnings before interest and tax (EBIT).

We also deduct the appropriate taxes and a charge for the capital employed to operate the underlying business. The leaves the Intangible Earnings, that is, the earnings that can be attributed to the intangible assets of the business.

3. Role of branding

We assess the proportion of Intangible Earnings that can be attributed to the brand in each market segment. This is calculated by firstly identifying the various drivers of demand for the branded business, then determining the degree to which each driver is directly influenced by the brand.

The Role of Branding assessment is based on market research, client workshops, interviews and our own expertise. If necessary, we can create a specific market research program to provide the required data.

The Role of Branding represents the percentage of Intangible Earnings that is generated by the brand. Brand Earnings are derived by multiplying the Role of Branding by Intangible Earnings.

4. Brand strength

A detailed assessment of the brand's strength profile is undertaken to determine the likelihood that the brand's forecast earnings will be realized. This comprises extensive competitive benchmarking, and a structured evaluation of the brand market, stability, leadership position, growth trend, support, geographic footprint and legal protectability.

For each segment we then apply industry and brand equity metrics to determine a risk premium for the brand. The overall Brand Discount Rate is derived by adding a brand risk premium to the risk free rate, represented by the yield on government bonds. The Brand Discount Rate is applied to the Brand Earnings forecast, to derive the net present value of the Brand Earnings. The stronger the brand, the lower the discount rate, and vice versa.

5. Brand value calculation

Brand Value is the net present value (NPV) of the forecast Brand Earnings, discounted by the Brand Discount Rate. The NPV calculation comprises both the forecast period and the period beyond, reflecting the ability of brands to continue generating future earnings.

This calculation is also used in a wide variety of Brand Value Modeling situations, such as:

■ Predicting the effect on marketing and investment strategies

■ Determining and assessing communications budgets

■ Calculating the return on brand investment

■ Assessing opportunities in new or underexploited markets

■ Tracking brand value management.

Courtesy Interbrand Australia Ltd

JOURNALS, PERIODICALS, NEWSPAPERS AND PRESS AGENCIES

Advances in Consumer Research
Journal of Academy of Marketing
  Sciences
Journal of Advertising Research
Journal of Consumer Behavior
Journal of Consumer Psychology
Journal of Consumer Research
Harvard Business Review
INSEAD
Journal of International Business Studies
Journal of Japanese Studies
Journal of Marketing
Journal of Marketing Management
Journal of Marketing Research
Journal of Portfolio Management
Journal of Strategic Marketing
The McKinsey Quarterly

Adweek
Advertising Age
Asia Inc
AsiaWeek
Brand Strategy
Brandweek
Business Week
Campaign
Financial Times
Forbes
Forbes Global
Fortune
Marketing
Media Magazine

Media Asia
The Economist
Time Asia
Time US edition

Air Transport World
Asian Wall Street Journal
Bangkok Post
Business Times
Business World
China Daily
Far Eastern Economic Review
India Business Intelligence
International Herald Tribune
Japan Today
Los Angeles Daily News
New Sunday Times
South China Morning Post
The Baltimore Sun
The Economic Times
The Hindu Business Line
The Japan Times
The Korea Economic Daily
The Korea Times
The Nation (Thailand)
The Saigon Times Daily
The Straits Times
The Sunday Times
The Taipei Times
The Vietnam Investment Review
Wall Street Journal

BIBLIOGRAPHY

Aaker, A. David, *Building Strong Brands*, Free Press, 1996

Aaker, L. Jennifer, Dimensions of brand personality, *Journal of Marketing Research*, **34**, 1997, 347–56

Abate, A. James, Grant, L., and Stewart III, G. Bennett, The EVA style of investing, *Journal of Portfolio Management*, Summer 2004

Agarwal, Anupam, Harding, P. David, and Schumacher, R. Jeffery, Organizing for CRM, *McKinsey Quarterly*, (3), 2004

Aitchison, Jim, *How Asia Advertises: The Most Successful Campaigns in Asia-Pacific and the Marketing Strategies Behind Them*, John Wiley & Sons Asia, 2002

Ambler, Tim, Market metrics: What should we tell the shareholders?, *Balance Sheet*, Bradford, **10**(1), p. 47, 2002

Ambler, Tim, *Marketing and the Bottom Line*, 2nd edn, FT Prentice Hall, 2003

Appadurai, Arjun, *Modernity at Large: Cultural Dimensions of Modernity*. University of Minnesota Press 1996

Ashekenazi, Michael, and Clammer, John, (eds) *Consumption and Material Culture in Contemporary Japan*, Columbia University Press, 1999

Balfour, Frederick, Matlack, Carol, Barrett, Amy, and Capell, Kerry, Fakes! The global counterfeit business is out of control, targeting everything from computer chips to life-saving machines, *Business Week*, February 7, 2005

Barnet, Kim and Yue Sai Kan: *The face of modern China*, brandchannel.com, April 1, 2002

Barth, E. Mary, Clement, B. Michael, Foster, George, and Kaszkik, Ron, Brand values and capital market valuations, *Review of Accounting Studies*, **3**, 1998

Barton, Dominic, Coombes, Paul, and Wong, Simon Chiu-Yin, Asia's governance challenge, *McKinsey Quarterly*, (2), 2004

Beech, Hannah, From heroes to brands, *Time Asia*, May 31, 2004

Bijoor, Harish, Branding the Government of India, http://www.indiainfoline.com/nevi/bran.html

Brealey, A. Richard and Meyers, C. Stewart, *Principles of Corporate Finance*, 5th edn, McGraw Hill, 1996

Chadha, Radha (forthcoming), *Luxury Brands in Asia*, Columbia University Press

Chandler, Clay, Luxury brands are rushing into China's red-hot market, *Fortune*, July 26, 2004

Chang, Leslie, China firm faces sneaker rivals on home court, *Asian Wall Street Journal*, June 23, 2004

Choi, Candice, Bottled water brand uses celebrity exposure to ring up sales, *Daily News*, Los Angeles, Knight Ridder/Tribune Business News, September 1, 2004

Chua, Amy (2003) *World on Fire*. Doubleday

Cialdini, B. Robert, *Influence: Science and Practice*. Allyn & Bacon. 4th edn 2001

Cunningham, Scott M., The major dimensions of perceived risk, in Donald F. Cox (ed.) *Risk Taking and Information Handling in Consumer Behavior*, Harvard University Press, pp. 82–108, 1967

Davis, Ian, How to escape short-term trap, *McKinsey Quarterly*, April 2005

Dawar, Niraj, and Frost, Tony, Competing with giants: survival strategies for emerging market companies, *Harvard Business Review*, March–April 1999, 119–29

Devan, Janamitra, Millan, Anna Kristina, and Shirke, Pranav, Balancing short and long-term performance, *McKinsey Quarterly*, (1), 2005

Dolan, A. Kerry, The soda with buzz, *Forbes*, March 28, 2005

Dolan, A. Kerry, Taking it Haier, *Forbes Global*, May 13, 2002

Doyle, Peter, Value-based marketing, *Journal of Strategic Marketing*, **8**, 2000

Dye, Renee, The buzz on buzz, *Harvard Business Review*, **78**(6), 2000

Elkin, Tobi, and Snyder, Beth, Samsung's DigitAll tag takes a democratic turn, *Advertising Age*, **70**(10), p. 77, 2005

Erdogan, Zafer B., Celebrity Endorsement: A Literature Review, *Journal of Marketing Management*, 1999, **15**, pp. 291–314

Enright, M. J. (1998) Regional clusters and firm strategy, in Chandler, A. D., Hagström, P. and Sölvell, Ö. (eds) *The Dynamic Firm*, Oxford: Oxford University Press, pp. 315–42

Felton, F. Robert, A new era in corporate governance, *McKinsey Quarterly*, (2), 2004

Fong, Mei, The little people: personal avatars are big business in Korea; can they make it big in other countries? *Wall Street Journal* (Eastern edition), March 22, 2004

Fong, Tanya, Singapore on world map of extreme sports, *Straits Times*, August 27, 2004

Forney, Mathew, Daren Fonda, and Gough, Neil, How Nike figured out China, *Time* US Edition, October 25, 2004

Fraser, Lynn, and Omniston, Aileen, *Understanding Financial Statements*, 5th edn, Upper Saddle River, NJ, Prentice Hall

Friedman, Hershey, and Friedman, Linda, Endorser effectiveness by product type, *Journal of Advertising Research*, October 5, 1979

Gardyne, Tom Bruce, Will a celebrity bond with your brand? *Director*, September, 2004

Geertz, C., *Local Knowledge: Further Essays in Interpretive Anthropology*. New York: Basic Books, 1983, p. 59

Ghosal, Sumantra, and Butler, Charlotte, *Hindustan Lever Limited: Levers for Change*, INSEAD case study, 2001

Giddens, A., (1991) *The Consequences of Modernity*. Stanford, CA: Stanford University Press, p. 54

Ging, D., and Feng, Y., (eds), Chinese: golden sayings of Chinese thinkers over 5,000 years, Beijing: 1994, *Sinolingua*, p. 55

Gordon, Alastair, *How consumers identify good brands*, AC Nielsen paper

Grahame, R. Dowling, and Staelin, Richard, (1994), A model of perceived risk and intended risk-handling activity, *Journal of Consumer Research*, (21), pp. 119–34

Gurhan-Canli, Zeynep and Durairaj Maheswaran, Cultural variations in country of origin effects, *Journal of Marketing Research*, 2000, **37**(3), 309–17

Hamlin, Michael Alan, Celebrity branding, *TeamAsia*, September 20, 2004

Han, C. Min, Country image: halo or summary construct? *Journal of Marketing Research*, 1989, **26**, May, pp. 222–9

Hesseldahl, Arik, Garmin signs NBA's Yao as pitchman, *Forbes*, April 13, 2004

Hofstede, G., *Culture's Consequences: International Differences in Work-related Values*, Beverly Hills: Sage, 1980

Hofstede, Geert, 1991. *Cultures and organizations: Software of the Mind*. Maidenhead: McGraw-Hill.

Hing, Lee Kam, and Ping, Lee Poh, Malaysian Chinese business: who survived the crisis?, *Kyoto Review of Southeast Asia*, Review Essay, October 2003, p. 7

Holt, Douglas, *Brands and Branding*, Class discussion note, Harvard Business School, 2003

Holt Douglas, *How Brands Become Icons*, Harvard Business School Press, 2004

Holt, Douglas, Quelch, John, and Taylor E., How global brands compete, *Harvard Business Review*, 2004, **82**(9), 68–75

Hoschka, C. Tobias, and Livingston, John, Winning Asian strategies, *McKinsey Quarterly* (1) 2002

Huang, Patricia, Pouring it on, *Forbes*, March 28, 2005

Hwee, Chua Chei, Banyan Tree Resorts and Hotels: Building an International Brand from an Asian Base, in Clifford Geertz (ed.) *Local Knowledge: Further Essays in Interpretive Anthropology*. New York: Basic Books, 1983, p. 59

Iwabuchi, Koichi, *Recentering Globalization: Popular Culture and Japanese Transnationalism*. Durham, NC: Duke University Press 2002

Iwabuchi, Koichi, *Feeling Asian Modernities: Transnational Consumption of Japanese TV Dramas*, Hong Kong University Press 1992

Jackson Hole, *Wyoming's Amangani Resort: Aman America*, www.travelandleisure.com, February 1999

James, Victoria, How Korea became cool, *New Statesman*, March 7, 2005

Jong, Lee Tee, Korean wave lifts the economy, *Sunday Times*, May 1, 2005

Jordan, Miriam, India's skies, filled with competition, suddenly turn more flier-friendly, *Wall Street Journal*, December 30, 1994

Kafka, Peter, Celebrity by the share, *Forbes*, March 21, 2000

Kahle, L. R., and Homer, P. M., Physical attractiveness of celebrity endorser: a social adaptation perspective, *Journal of Consumer Research*, 1985, 11 March, pp. 954–61

Kamen, Joseph M. Azhari, Abdul C. and Kragh, Judith R., What a spokesman does for a sponsor, *Journal of Advertising Research*, 1975, **15**, pp. 17–24

Kan, Wendy, Welcome back to paradise, *Time Asia*, April 2001

Karsanbhai, Patel, A clean sweep, June 2002, seen at http://www.indiaprofile.com/people/karsanbhaipatel.htm

Keller, L. Kevin, *Strategic Brand Management*, 2nd edn, Prentice Hall 2003

Kerin, A. Roger and Sethuraman, R., Exploring the brand value–shareholder value nexus for consumer goods companies, *Journal of Academy of Marketing Sciences*, **26**, 1998

Klein, Jill G., Ettenson, Richard and Morris, D. Marlene, The animosity model of foreign product purchase: An empirical test in the People's Republic of China, *Journal of Marketing*, 1998 **62**(1), 89–100

Kumar, Nirmalya, *Marketing as Strategy*, Harvard Business School Press, 2004

Lowry, Tom, How big is Yao Ming?, *Business Week*, October 25, 2004

Lowry, Tom, and Roberts, Dexter, Wow! Yao! *Business Week*, October 25, 2004

Luce, Edward, Rural India humbles Vajpayee, *Financial Times*, May 14, 2004

Luo, Michael, Yao Ming boosts ethnic pride, *Times Union*, Albany, New York. February 9, 2003

Madden, J. Thomas, Fehle, Frank, and Fournier, M. Susan, Brands matter: an empirical demonstration of the creation of shareholder value through branding, *Journal of the Academy of Marketing Science*, 2005, forthcoming.

Markus, H., and Kitayama, S., (1991), Culture and the self: implications for cognition, emotion and motivation, *Psychological Review*, 1998, pp. 224–53

Marn, V. Michael, Roegner, V. Eric, and Zawada, C. Craig, The power of pricing, *McKinsey Quarterly*, (1), 2003

Mazzarella W., *Shoveling Smoke: Advertising and Globalization in Contemporary India*. Durham, NC: Duke University Press 2003

McGovern, J. Gail, Court, David, Quelch, John, and Crawford, Blair, Bringing customers into the boardroom, *Harvard Business Review*, November 2004

McCracken, Grant, Who is the celebrity endorser? Cultural foundations of the endorsement process, *Journal of Consumer Research*, 1989, **16**, pp. 310–21

McGray, Douglas, Japan's gross national cool, *Foreign Policy*, May–June 2002, pp. 45–54

McKay, Betsy and Cho, H. Cynthia, Fiji brand gains on Evian as bottled water hip to sip – closely held U.S. firm proves the world's simplest drink still can be touted as trendy, *Asian Wall Street Journal*, August 17, 2004

Mitchell, Colin, Selling the brands inside, *Harvard Business Review*, January 2002

Murakami, Yasusuke (1984), *Ie* society as a pattern of civilization. An introduction by Kozo Yamamura, *Journal of Japanese Studies*, **10**(2): 281–363

Normandy, Madden, Brand origin not major factor for most Asians, **74**(14), p. 33, *Advertising Age*, 2003

Normandy, Madden, Study: Chinese youth aren't patriotic purchasers; Most favor global brands such as Coke and Nike over local rivals, *Advertising Age*, 6, **75**(1), 2004

Parks L. and Kumar S. (eds), *Planet TV: A Global Television Reader*. New York University Press, 2003, pp. 341–59

Park, Seah, Coming to a theater near you?; South Korean movie exports mark shift away from manufacturing, *Wall Street Journal* (Eastern edition), October 3, 2003, p. A.10

Pilling, David, When Chinese desire transcends politics, *Financial Times*, April 1, 2004

Prahalad, C. K. and Lieberthal, Kenneth, The end of corporate imperialism, *Harvard Business Review*, August 2003

Prahalad, C. K. and Hammond, A., Serving the world's poor, profitably, *Harvard Business Review*, 2002

Prahalad, C. K. *The Fortune at the Bottom of the Pyramid*. Wharton School Publishing, 2004

Probert, Jocelyn and Schütte, Hellmut, (1999), *De Beers: Diamonds are for Asia*, INSEAD Euro-Asia Centre, Case 599-011-1, p.12

Ramstad, Evan, How legend became Lenovo, *Far Eastern Economic Review*, April 8, 2004

Reimer, Susan, Fiji, the new hotbed of cool water, *Baltimore Sun*, November 4, 2004

Richardson, Michael, Disappearance of Jim Thompson: the silk magnate mystery/30 year puzzle, *International Herald Tribune*, March 26, 1997

Roberts, Dexter, Balfour, Frederick, Einhorn, Bruce, and Arndt, Michael, China's power brands, *Business Week*, November 8, 2004

Rugman, Alan, *Regional Multinationals: MNEs and Global Strategic Management*, Cambridge University Press, 2005

Rugman, Alan, and Verbeke, Alain, (2004), A perspective on regional and global strategies of multinational enterprises, *Journal of International Business Studies*, **35**(1), (2004), 3–18

Russell, W. Belk, Third world consumer culture, in E. Kumçu and A. Fuat Firat (eds), *Research in Marketing*, supplement 4, JAI Press, Greenwich, CT, 1988

Sanghvi, Vir, *The Big Idea: Hubris at the Hustings*, http://www.freeindiamedia.com, accessed February 18, 2005

Schütte, Hellmut, and Ciarlante, Deanna, *Consumer Behaviour in Asia*, Macmillan Business – now Palgrave Macmillan, 1998

Seely, John, and Hagel III, John, Innovation blowback: disruptive management practices from Asia, *McKinsey Quarterly*, (1), 2005

Seth, Suhel, *Taking the Shine off India*, www.india-seminar.com, accessed February 17, 2005

Shameen, Assif, Can Samsung keep roaring?, *Asia Inc*, June 1, 2004

Sim, Glenys, STB woos weekend visitors for fun breaks, *Straits Times*, October 21, 2004

Speck, Paul Surgi, Schumann, David W., and Thompson, Craig, Celebrity endorsements – scripts, schema and roles: theoretical framework and preliminary tests, *Advances in Consumer Research*, 1988, **15**, pp. 69–76

Srivastava, K. Rajendra, Shervani, A. Tasadduq, and Fahey, Liam, Market-based assets and shareholder value: A framework for analysis, *Journal of Marketing*, January 1998

Srivastava, K. Rajendra and Reibstein, J. David, Metrics for linking marketing to financial performance, working paper, October 19, 2004

Steenkamp, Jan-Benedict E., Batra, Rajeev, V. and Ramaswamy, Dana Alden, How perceived brand globalness creates brand value, *Journal of International Business Studies*, **34**(1), 53–65, 2003

Suman, A., *Political Advertising: The India Shining Campaign*, ICFAI Center for Management Research, 2004

Sung-jin, Kim, Hallyu boosts Korea's GDP by 0.2%, *Korea Times*, May 3, 2005

Sung-hoon, Bang, Samsung eyes third position in US patents race, *The Chosun Ilbo*, January 17, 2005

Tan, Jessica, I'll have that Snoopy please, *Straits Times,* Monday, October 4, 1999

Tripp, Carolyn, Jensen, D. Thomas, and Carlson, Les, The effect of multiple product endorsements by celebrities on consumers' attitudes and intentions, *Journal of Consumer Research*, 1994, **30**, pp. 535–47

Tse, D., (1996) Understanding Chinese people as consumers: past findings and future propositions, in M. H. Bond (ed.) *The Handbook of Chinese Psychology*, Hong Kong: Oxford University Press.

Tversky, A. and Kahneman, D. (1973), Availability: a heuristic for judging frequency and probability, *Cognitive Psychology*, **5**, pp. 207–32

Tversky, A. and Kahneman, D. (1974), Judgment under certainty: heuristics and biases, *Science*, **112**, pp. 1124–30

United Nations Population Division (1999), *The World at Six Billion*

Wang Gungwu, *China and the Chineseeng* (2004)

Wangreporter, Annie, Gimbela, Barney and Dahong, Zhang, Holding up half the sky, Five Chinese women: Some are smart, rich, and running the show; others just want a piece of the booming economy, *Fortune*, October 4, 2004

Wee, C. J. W.-L. (2004), Staging the Asian modern: cultural fragments, the Singaporean eunuch, and the Asian Lear, *Critical Inquiry*, **30**(4), p. 781

Weidenbaum, Murray, *Greater China: The Next Economic Superpower?*, St. Louis: Washington University Center for the Study of American Business, Contemporary Issues, Series 57, February 1993, pp. 2–3

White, Amy, Li-Ning taps into patriotic fervour, *Media Asia*, August 13, 2004

Williamson, Peter, *Winning In Asia,* Harvard Business Press, 2004

Williamson, Peter, and Wilson, Keeley, *CP Group: From Seeds to Kitchen of the World*, INSEAD Euro-Asia Centre, Singapore, 2003

Wong, Kelvin, Star cruises rebounding from Tsunami blip, *Straits Times*, January 31, 2005

Worm, V., (1997), *Vikings and Mandarins*. Copenhagen: Munksgaard International Publishers, pp. 116–17

Wu, Ming, *Banyan Tree branching out*, www.brandchannel.com, November 2003

Xiaoming, Hao, and Teh, Leng Leng, (2004), The impact of Japanese popular culture on the Singaporean youth, *Keio Communication Review*, (26), pp. 17–36

Yeong, Nicole, Boost for tourism, investing in Asia, *Asia Inc*, August 2004

Yeong, Nicole, Investing in Malaysia: boost for tourism, *Asia Inc*, August 1, 2004

Yong, Jeremy Au, Zen versus iPod, *Straits Times*, November 28, 2004

INDEX

Page numbers in *italic* refer to case studies